HOW TO BE

Y

P

st

*Everything You
Need to Know
to Act like a PR Pro*

HOW TO BE Your Own Publicist

Jessica Hatchigan

McGraw-Hill

Chicago   New York   San Francisco   Lisbon   London   Madrid   Mexico City
Milan   New Delhi   San Juan   Seoul   Singapore   Sydney   Toronto

49320567

3-26-03

Library of Congress Cataloging-in-Publication Data

Hatchigan, Jessica.
  How to be your own publicist : everything you need to know to act like a PR
pro / Jessica Hatchigan.
        p.   cm.
    Includes index.
    ISBN 0-07-138332-8
    1. Publicity.   I. Title.

    HM1226 .H38   2002
    659—dc21   2002025489

McGraw-Hill

A Division of The McGraw·Hill Companies

1 2 3 4 5 6 7 8 9 0   AGM/AGM   1 0 9 8 7 6 5 4 3 2

ISBN 0-07-138332-8

This book was set in Sabon
Printed and bound by Quebecor Martinsburg

Cover design by Amy Yu Ng
Back-cover photograph by Michelle Branum
Interior design by Rattray Design

McGraw-Hill books are available at special quantity discounts to use as premiums and
sales promotions, or for use in corporate training programs. For more information, please
write to the Director of Special Sales, Professional Publishing, McGraw-Hill, Two Penn
Plaza, New York, NY 10121-2298. Or contact your local bookstore.

This book is printed on acid-free paper.

Contents

Part II

Tools of the Publicity Trade

Part III

How to Get Continuous Great Publicity

Acknowledgments

To my parents, Albert and Helena, with love and appreciation.

To my husband, Frank, and to my children, Jenny and Jim—three never-ending sources of encouragement, humor, enlightenment, and love.

To my sister, Chris, whose sense of humor and fun is pure sunshine, and whose wit and insight make conversation an art and a cup of tea a learning experience.

To my Superagent, Pamela Harty of the Knight Agency, and to her sister, Deidre Knight. I couldn't ask for a better agent or for two nicer literary associates.

To my outstanding editor, Danielle Egan-Miller, whose expertise and insight have been invaluable, and whose guidance has been appreciated. And to Susan Moore, editorial team leader, who has ably shepherded this book through the production process.

To my professional colleagues: Anne Doyle, Beryl Goldsweig, Jon Harmon, Terry Herron, John Jelinek, Mary Sharon Joseph, Becky Kirk, Sharon McMurray, Nick Sharkey, Frank Sopata, and Joy Wolfe, who are outstanding professionals and friends—thanks for the memories.

To Jim and Anne Bright, Andy and Lin Cummins, John and Susan Ochs, Mike and Heidi Parris, and Tim and Vicki Yost—PR aces, good buds, and patient and unfailing sources of great advice, both book- and life-related.

To the following people who generously took time out of their busy schedules to answer questions and provide information for this book: Judy Anderson, Joan Brewer, Patrick Combs, Cherylanne DeVita, Mike Dillon, Sue Doerfler, Brian Donnelly, Jeff Fitzsimmons, Eileen Fox, Joyce Greenbaum, Katherine Hutt, Donna

Maria Coles Johnson, Lisa Kanarek, Kent and Darcie Krueger, Mark A. Le Doux, Terri Lonier, Susan O'Neil, Jill Sabulis, Tobias Salgado, Mike Sante, Norman Scarborough, Nancy Shepherdson, Ken Skier, Mike Stoll, and Leslie Wilder—to each and everyone of you, my deepest appreciation.

And, last but not least, to my Sheltie, Angel, for her loyal and warm (and fuzzy) friendship.

Introduction

You can't buy publicity.

People know that reporters in newspapers and on TV and the radio strive to "tell it like it is." They don't get paid by special interest groups to bend the facts any which way.

That's exactly why publicity is so effective.

If your business needs a boost, publicity can give it a shot in the arm like nothing else can. A positive word or two about your enterprise in the media can pull customers to you and make you feel pretty darned good to boot.

This is a publicity book for the rest of us. I say that confidently because I know I am probably the opposite of what anyone thinks of when they think publicist. I'm pretty low-key and soft-spoken. Recently, when my husband and I were touring Europe, a new acquaintance traveling with us—I'll call her Virginia—said, upon finding out my professional inclinations: "You? A publicist?" in a disbelieving tone. (Mentally, I spluttered, "But, but—it's true. I've coordinated local, national, and even international events—all with outstanding results—*honest*." But a moment later, I got my bearings and chuckled instead. I understood.)

No, Virginia, you don't have to be Don King or Colonel Parker to succeed at the publicity game. All you have to do is learn what news is—recognize what's newsworthy about you or your business—and then convey it to the news media in the way they expect it to be conveyed. It isn't rocket science. I was lucky enough to have great mentors—some of the best publicity pros around—show me the ropes.

In the pages that follow, I'll take you step by step through the basics of publicity (the way I learned it as a newbie to the process). To tell you the truth, I wish I'd had this book when I started my career as a publicist. There's nothing like having a book that spells it all out clearly and makes you realize, "Hey, I think I can do this."

Does everyone have the makings of a great publicist? Well, I think you know the answer to that. Of course not. You do have to be quick on your feet and a little creative, and you have to have an ability to write and speak clearly and logically. But if you're reading this book and considering taking on your own publicity, I'll bet you are closer to fitting the bill than not.

Why don't you give it a shot? I'd love to read about you and your business in the papers, see you on TV, or get a letter or E-mail detailing your super media successes.

You? A publicist?

Hey, if I could do it, you can too.

Let's go for it!

## Part I

How Publicity Works—and How to Make It Work for You

1

Don't Make "the Million Dollar Mistake"

The Basics of Publicity

"The two words *information* and *communication* are often used interchangeably, but they signify quite different things. Information is giving out. Communication is getting through."

–Sidney J. Harris

As a businessperson, you produce a product or service and you have particular customers or clients in mind for that product or service—people who for one reason or another would find what you offer a perfect solution to a problem or a just-right way to fulfill a need. These people make up your target market.

Business success results when you convince enough of the people in your target market to purchase your product or service. It should be simple. You've found a need. You want to fill it. And isn't that the old formula for business success?

So why isn't business better?

The reason is that, as many businesspeople have found out, the old find-a-need-and-fill-it formula is more complicated than it appears at first blush. In fact, seasoned businesspeople know that the *real* formula for business success is: find a need and fill it—and then make sure enough people in your target market hear about what you have to offer—and that they keep hearing about it.

3

Your service may be great. Your product may be wonderful. But if enough people don't know about it, sales volumes will be low. In worst cases, doors will close, windows will be whited out, and a forlorn and empty property will sport a "for lease" sign.

Let's repeat that formula for business success: find a need and fill it—and then make sure enough people in your target market hear about what you have to offer—and that they keep hearing about it.

That's where publicity comes in. Publicity means getting noticed by your public through exposure in print and broadcast media, including newspapers, magazines, TV and radio talk shows and programs, online publications and discussion groups, and websites. Publicity can mean the difference between a successful, thriving business and one that struggles or fails. As a businessperson, your goal should be to get an ongoing stream of positive stories about your business into media outlets that your potential customers and clients read, view, and value.

This is the most effective and believable way to deliver sales information. Publicity of this kind generates credibility that advertising can't match—credibility that wins consumers' minds and hearts—and produces sales. One publicity "hit" (media mention) in a key trade publication or a program geared to your target customers' or clients' interests can do much more to boost your business than expensive paid advertising ever could.

Major corporations know this. Even though they have advertising budgets in the multimillion dollar range, they pay huge sums to public relations (PR) companies and maintain stables of high-priced in-house publicists to ensure a stream of positive publicity. They know publicity packs a wallop that advertising can't match.

The good news is, publicity is free. No media outlet worth a particle of salt ever charges a business for running a story. To do so is a violation of media ethics. Reporters who plant stories for pay get fired. That means that all media people want from you is a darned good story. Skilled publicists learn to provide them with just that.

And you don't have to be a huge company like Microsoft or Coca-Cola or General Motors to get ink or airtime for your product or service—nor do you have to have the kind of publicity budgets that Fortune 500 companies command to succeed at the publicity game. Even the high-priced PR talents employed by the Fortune 500 can't beg, borrow, or steal their way into the pages of *USA Today* or your local city daily. They have to earn their way in. They do that by offering media people stories that have news value. Small businesses can do this too—and they can do it on a shoestring budget.

Learning how to recognize—and then produce—stories that have news value is a skill. But, like learning a sport or a new computer program, it's a skill you can acquire with a little effort and persistence.

So, Just What Is (and Isn't) Publicity?

Traditionally publicity has meant mention of your business in the media (newspapers, radio, TV, the Web, etc.). This book treats "publicity" in a wider sense to include a variety of communications that can effectively influence the media to run stories that reach the people in your target market and draw them to do business with you.

Often publicity can be achieved in the traditional (direct) way—via a news release, say, that results in a mention in the *Wall Street Journal*, *USA Today*, or the local weekly paper or a spot on a local or national TV news program. At other times, publicity can result from an indirect approach—holding a workshop or giving a speech to an audience at an event to which key reporters have been invited, sending a catalog that showcases innovations in your business to media people who report on your area of manufacturing or service, displaying a product at a trade show attended by media you've targeted, or participating in or hosting an online discussion board that reporters regularly check out.

Publicity Versus Advertising

What about advertising? What's the difference between publicity and advertising?

Advertising is information about a business, product, or service that you pay to have published or announced. That means you control the information in an ad. That's why advertising is a lot less effective than publicity. Because people know that businesses pay for (and control content of) spots in a newspaper or on a TV program, they don't believe advertising.

Say you're a plumbing supplies manufacturer and you've developed a nifty new sealant that's ten times more effective than anything currently on the market. You place a half-page ad in a national plumbing trade publication. The ad will cost you hundreds of dollars. It might generate sales, and it might not. Readers will won-

Bonus Points
Martha Stewart's Publicity Breakthrough (It Was a Good Thing)

Perhaps one of the most spectacular publicity successes is Martha Stewart, who started a catering business out of the basement of her farmhouse in 1976 and sold specialty foods and supplies for entertaining from a retail store in Westport, Connecticut. Ten years later, her business was worth a million dollars. Today, Stewart is worth millions, and her name has become a brand that represents stylish living.

Stewart recognized the importance of establishing herself as an expert early on. She wrote articles for the *New York Times* and for *House Beautiful* magazine and, in 1982, published her first book, *Entertaining*. She credits the book, which became a bestseller, as the major turning point in her career.

Not all of us, of course, can write like Martha Stewart or break into print in the *New York Times*. But it doesn't take too much effort to establish ourselves with local media as experts or to get published on a smaller, local scale, even if it means hiring a professional writer who can polish our work (as Stewart herself did to produce *Entertaining*).

People don't think of Stewart primarily as an author. She's a television personality/author/brand name on household products. That's because her writing efforts were only part of her overall business-building efforts—valuable publicity for what's become a highly recognizable American brand.

der if this new product is all the ad claims it is—or whether what they're reading is a lot of hype. A half-page story in the same publication, however, written by a reporter whom readers know and trust—a story that enthusiastically informs readers that your new sealant is the best thing since the dawn of indoor plumbing—will boost your business like nothing else can.

Think about how you react to sales brochures or ads for new products and services. You're skeptical, aren't you? But if a reporter from a respected newspaper or magazine praises a company's new product or service, you're much more likely to consider a purchase.

And advertising is expensive—costing up to hundreds of thousands of dollars for a spot in a major national media outlet. You can achieve publicity, on the other hand, at low cost or virtually no cost. In some cases, a phone call, fax, or letter might be all that's needed to produce a story on the evening news or a feature article in a major daily newspaper.

Can you successfully build a business on the strength of publicity alone? Yes, a number of businesses have spent very little on advertising. And some very successful businesses proudly boast that they never advertise.

Is Publicity the Same as Marketing?

Both publicity and marketing aim to convey the benefits of your product or service to your target market and increase sales. However, marketing is the overall effort you make to sell your product or service, including what to call what you sell, how to price and distribute it, and what efforts you make to persuade potential clients and customers that they need or want your product or service. Publicity is narrower than that. It focuses on the work you do to achieve media mentions that promote your product or service.

Publicity is part of the larger marketing umbrella.

Is Publicity the Same as PR?

Public relations, or PR, includes all of the things you do to create strong and positive public opinion, goodwill, and loyalty for your company and its products and services. You create good PR when, for example, your company buys equipment for the local softball team, donates money to an area soup kitchen, publishes free pamphlets that provide valuable non-sales-oriented information, holds a walkathon to raise funds for charity, or forms a team of volunteers to paint the home of a disabled citizen.

Publicity can amplify your company's PR efforts by getting the word out about these good deeds—for example, through press releases sent to the media.

Publicity and Buzz

"What's the buzz?" has become another way of saying, "What's the latest news?" Buzz is word of mouth that spreads about your business, products, and/or services through informal networks. Certain groups of people in each target market tend to be trend spotters and trendsetters. When these trend leaders adopt a fashion or begin to use a product or service, word (buzz) gets around, and others follow. Recently, some marketers have tried to control and influence buzz by identifying the particular trend leaders in their target markets and getting them to use the product or service they're trying to promote.

Where does publicity fit in vis-à-vis buzz? If your publicity efforts are creative, unique, and memorable, chances are people will talk about them—thereby creating buzz. Publicity, marketing, and advertising can all help jump-start buzz.

Where Spin Fits In

The word *spin* is generally used to describe the process of trying to influence the news media to present your business in a positive light.

Facts are often open to interpretation. Businesspeople quite naturally want the media to make a positive interpretation of facts about their businesses. If negative information about your business comes out, media people expect you to try to recast (spin) the facts in a more positive light. They expect you to try and reframe the information and present positive interpretations or bring to light background information that softens or ameliorates negative facts. Media people, of course, also use a skeptical filter to sift through the information thus offered. And they're naturally wary of people who try too hard to influence them to write an unrealistically positive story where one isn't merited.

The word *spin*, by the way, has a mildly "put down" flavor. To call a publicist a "spin doctor" is like calling a surgeon a "sawbones"—it can be affectionate or insulting, depending on the context.

While newspeople expect businesspeople to try to spin the news so that it's positive, there are rules and caveats to the spin game. If you badly misrepresent the facts or lie outright, you've gone past spinning—and heaven help you. The media do not forgive or forget. Blow your credibility with media people and it's almost impossible to regain.

That's why the best way to spin the news is to take a proactive long-term approach—to position yourself as a resource to the media, to be available when they need your help on a story, and to be scrupulously honest and fair. Media people will consider you a good (honest and accurate) source of information, and good and kindly inclined press for your business will flow from that.

Publicity and Stunts

A stunt is a staged event designed to generate news. Stunts have—or should have—an element of drama, humor, suspense, or cleverness about them. Mention "stunt"

Bonus Points
SitStay.com: Publicity Goes to the Dogs

Kent and Darcie Krueger started SitStay.com (sitstay.com), which sells top-quality dog supplies, as a hobby in a spare room of their home in 1996.

The Kruegers take pains to be flexible and responsive with the media.

"We've had local TV news crews call and ask if they could come out to the store to do some filming," says Darcie Krueger. "Of course, we always say yes. We'd be on TV that same night. That's happened three times.

"Recently, a reporter from *Inc.* called wanting to do a story. We agreed to let her come stay with us for a few days."

From the start, the Kruegers were regular participants of online discussion boards. They say they "use and post to the boards information about a number of things like running online stores, customer service, creating websites, problems with particular software or hardware, market trends, and current events."

A *New York Times* reporter who was also a member of one of the discussion boards read some of the Kruegers' posts, contacted them, and ran a story on the couple accompanied by a photo on the front page of the *Times* business section. "That particular article brought us inquiries from investors as well as lots of new customers," Darcie Krueger says.

Their business rapidly expanded from its original spare-room-of-the-house location. The Kruegers quit their day jobs in 1997 and moved their business to a warehouse and offices in August 1999.

to a media person or a publicist and you will get a wide range of reactions. Some wrinkle their nose at the word—probably remembering badly done stunts. Others consider a stunt to be simply another way to say "special event."

If there is a problem with stunts, it's that media people are wary of them. And that's because so many are poorly done. When they're well done, however, they can be quite effective.

Back when Marilyn Monroe was a struggling starlet, a publicist at 20th Century Fox had the studio wardrobe department create a dress made from a potato sack. A photo of Marilyn in the potato sack dress, along with a caption noting that she "even looked good in a potato sack," was published in newspapers across the nation. Publicist Jim Moran once got national media attention for General Electric by going to Alaska and selling a refrigerator to an Eskimo. Both of these stunts would be considered corny today and would get little media attention.

However, the Chrysler Corporation, now DaimlerChrysler, reaped a bonanza of publicity not too long ago by lowering a new-model automobile from the ceiling of Detroit's Cobo Center during the city's annual auto show. In the staid world of automotive news press conferences, the brash product introduction was a welcome gimmick that sparked a lot of favorable press.

And the curators of George Washington's Mount Vernon home recently boosted tourism there by reenacting George Washington's last moments and funeral on the bicentennial of his death. They re-created the death scene in Washington's bedroom and held a service to which only family members were invited (and to which *USA Today* was given exclusive coverage rights). The funeral reenactment was the culmination of a yearlong effort in which the curators and their PR agency convinced more than fifty thousand civic and military groups across the nation to observe the bicentennial at some point during the year. The result? The highest attendance figures for Mount Vernon in twenty-plus years.

Stunts, however, can and do backfire. Perhaps the most embarrassing example in recent years is that of the Internet security company that ran a contest during a London computer security conference offering fifty thousand dollars to hackers who could break into a Web server protected by the company's intrusion protection security product. The contest was supposed to run throughout the week of the exhibition but was stopped short when a group of hackers broke into the target server to claim the prize.

In other words, like nitroglycerine, stunts are volatile and unpredictable—and must be handled with care.

Benefits of Publicity

Why should businesses make the effort to pursue publicity?

Because publicity helps businesses to succeed.

Speaking about his own product (movies), one of Hollywood's most respected studio chiefs recently said, "There's chaos out there—an overload of information. It's like a fog where everything seems fuzzy and indistinct. Our job is to make our product cut through that fog—like a searchlight."

That's exactly what publicity does for your business. It creates a "searchlight" that focuses a laser beam on the particular benefits of your product or service in a way that attracts customers.

Publicity gets the word out about your business, distinguishes you from the competition, and positions you as the "quality provider." It increases positive public awareness about what you do, make, or provide. It educates your potential customers and clients about the value of what you do, make, or provide and creates a desire and demand for your products and services. It pulls customers to your business, makes those you approach more receptive, and boosts your other marketing efforts. It can increase your personal credibility and turn you into "the expert" (via TV and radio appearances and mentions in magazines, newspapers, and E-'zines). It also can boost your confidence and add to your prestige. In short, publicity can be an entrepreneur's best friend.

The rewards of entrepreneurship include personal freedom, financial independence, and inner satisfaction. How much are those worth to you? A million dollars? Ten million? More? Successful entrepreneurs enjoy these rewards throughout their lifetimes. Once you "get" how publicity works—and how to make it work for your business—you can apply what you've learned and use the knowledge to generate media coverage that can be a life-sustaining force for your entrepreneurial dreams.

Bottom Line: Publicity Builds Your Business like Nothing Else Can

Here are some examples of the results publicity can achieve for businesses:

- After ABC TV displayed pumpkins carved to look like the announcers on *Monday Night Football* during one of its programs, sales (until then lackluster) of the Pumpkin Masters carving kits used to carve the pumpkins took off. The company now sells more than two million kits each year.
- *New York Times* writer Peter Lewis featured a large-type word processor from the SkiSoft Publishing Corporation in a syndicated column read in twelve of the nation's largest cities. Orders for the new word processor, which makes it possible for the visually impaired to use a word processing program, poured in from across the country.
- Cherylanne DeVita, founder of Devita International, a company that produces a line of creams and lotions made from natural ingredients,

sent a press release about her products to *Spa Resorts* magazine. When the magazine featured an article on the products, DeVita got a call from Sharon Stone's office requesting some of the products for a charity event. The call led to contacts with, and endorsements from, music and film industry celebrities.

Take Charge of Your Publicity Fate

Entrepreneurs like Martha Stewart, Kent and Darcie Krueger, and Deborah Rhein (see the three "Bonus Points" in this chapter) have all enjoyed admirable success. One thing they share in common is that they didn't leave their publicity fates to chance. Each made a methodical, sustained effort to get word out to their target markets about what they had to offer. The results speak for themselves.

The "Right (Publicity) Stuff"—Do You Have It?

If publicity is so effective, why isn't everyone going after it? The answer is: because most people don't know how. The ability to generate news coverage for your business is a skill you must learn and master.

Can you do it? Should you make the effort? The answer to both of these questions is, of course, yes.

First, and most important, you need to grasp one essential fact: publicity isn't rocket science. In fact, once you understand the basics, the process of getting your story in the news is fairly simple.

Second, realize that publicity will provide the credibility that is crucial to your business success.

Third, take action. Do you feel psychological roadblocks about "tooting your own horn"? Learn to overcome them, and get your show (literally) on the road.

Fourth, don't let limited resources block your publicity dreams. Use the resources you have at hand—the family car, the telephone, and the willingness to make those calls.

Fifth, don't leave getting publicity to chance. Formulate a clear and exciting message about the benefits your product or service has to offer. Then make sure you get that message out. Communicate what you have to offer and do it with passion. Excitement is contagious. You can spark reporters' enthusiasm for your product or service by conveying your own sense of exuberance about it.

In the chapters that follow we'll be learning to do all of these things.

Bonus Points
A Methodical Approach Can Have Exciting Results

Entrepreneur Deborah Rhein, owner of D. L. Rhein, makes picture frames and other home decor accessories. She introduces herself to editors she meets at trade shows and compiles a list of all the publications she thinks might run articles about her business. When she develops a new product, she sends press kits to the editors whose publications are the best fit. She keeps her business in magazine editors' consciousness by sending them seasonal-themed postcards on which she sometimes jots personal notes every month or two. She follows fashion trends and designs products that reflect those trends. (Reporters and editors are keen to keep their readers updated on new trends.) The result? Her products have been featured hundreds of times in trade journals and magazines and in mainstream publications as well.

The One Basic Trick to Getting Publicity

Success at the publicity process requires many things. It requires you to tap into your creativity. It requires you to invest some "sweat equity." It requires persistence. And it requires that you learn how to build relationships with the media and others. But one thing it doesn't require is a stratospheric IQ. The chapters that follow will show you that giving your business a major boost through the use of publicity is really very simple. They will show you easy ways to master the basics—targeting your audience, approaching the media, packaging your information, and leveraging your successes.

The one basic "trick" to getting publicity is this: learn to recognize what makes news—and what media people will deem newsworthy about your business. Everything else you do to achieve positive publicity for your business builds on that knack.

You can begin today to train yourself to develop the "nose for news" that is essential if you want to be a successful publicity hound. Start reading newspapers and watching news programs with a publicist's eye. Analyze each story about a new product or service or company event, and try to think through (a) how this story came to the media's attention, (b) what's newsworthy about this story, and (c) if there are any elements to the story you can pull out and adapt to create a newsworthy story about your own business.

Don't Make "the Million Dollar Mistake"

Orator and Temple University founder, Russell H. Conwell—as famous in the nineteenth century as our top celebrities and politicians are today—earned an estimated eight million dollars (a stunning amount in his day—and not too shabby in our own!) from a speech called "Acres of Diamonds." "Acres" was also made into a book. It's been in print since it was first issued in 1915. The speech, which Conwell gave more than six thousand times until his death in 1925, outlined his formula for success.

In "Acres," Conwell told the story of Ali Hafed, the owner of a farm in Africa, who heard that his country was full of rich diamond mines. Wanting to become rich and famous, Ali Hafed decided to leave his farm and to go search for diamonds. He sold his property, left his family with neighbors, and set out to find diamonds. He wandered about for many years but never found the precious gems he longed for. Finally, broke and broken, he threw himself into the ocean and drowned.

Meanwhile, back at Ali Hafed's farm—the farm he had sold to go look for diamonds—the new owner had a visitor come to dinner. The visitor admired a big rock on the fireplace mantle and asked the new owner where he'd found it. The new owner replied that he'd found it in his backyard. In fact, he said, he'd found a lot of rocks just like it all over his land. Every time he tilled the soil, he said, he found many similar rocks, although they were of a lesser size.

The visitor, a mineral expert, informed the farmer that the object sitting on the mantle was a diamond. It didn't look like a diamond, he explained, because it was in its raw, uncut state. The farmer and his guest went out together and confirmed that the farmland—Ali Hafed's farmland—was rich with diamonds.

The point of this story is that Ali Hafed wasted his life seeking what he already had—in his own backyard. Wealth and fame—acres of diamonds—were right beneath his feet. His downfall was that he didn't recognize it, and he didn't recognize it because his diamonds were scattered around in their raw form. His property—the property he had despised and abandoned—was the site of the Golconda diamond mine—the source of the immense Kohinoor diamond, now one of Britain's crown jewels. Ali Hafed made "the million dollar mistake."

What does the story of Ali Hafed have to do with publicity? Simply this—as a businessperson, you are sitting on "acres of diamonds" too. You don't have to look enviously at your competitor's "greener pastures" and regard your own publicity opportunities the same way Ali Hafed looked at his diamonds—like lumps of useless rock. Recognize that there are diamonds hidden beneath your "rocks" too—news stories about your product or service that simply need to be detected and polished.

Publicity works. Learn how to work it—and it'll work for you.

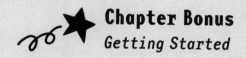

Chapter Bonus
Getting Started

1. Look at every news story about a business similar to yours that you read, hear, or see over the next few days and weeks. Ask yourself: What did the business owner do to earn a spot in the news? How might this story have come to the media's attention?

2. What magazines, newspapers, newsletters, E-'zines, radio shows, and so on do the people who need your product or service (your target audience) read, listen to, or view? (The list you produce as an answer is your target media list.)

3. Can you expand your target media list? (An Internet search engine or a visit to the research room of your local library—where you can look through a directory of media outlets—can expand your list dramatically.)

4. Select a few shows and/or publications from your target media list. Watch/read them with an analytical eye. Do you find any patterns in the business news stories they run? Do you notice some of your target media are more likely to run certain types of stories?

5. What kind of publicity would do the most for your business? What one step can you take today to start achieving that kind of publicity?

2 Ground Rules That Help You Soar

Straight Talk on "Spin"

"Advertising you pay for, publicity you pray for."

—Publicist's motto

The ground rules of publicity are those simple, basic—and crucial—tidbits of information that media people assume you know if you present yourself as a spokesperson (i.e., publicist) for your business.

What are these bits of information?

Well, let's peek into the mind of a businessperson or PR pro who is well regarded by the media and who is consistently successful in landing media coverage for his or her business. What are the insights you, as a publicity newbie, might not share?

Get Ready! . . . Key Insights to Absorb

Here are some of them:

• **Key Insight #1:** The biggest misconception about publicity is that it's a matter of luck—that certain business owners just happen to be in the right place at the right time to catch the attention of a reporter on the prowl for a story, or that they accidentally create businesses that appeal to the media.

Yes, some businesses do get lucky. However, these are the exceptions—not the rule. More often, businesses get media attention because their owners have planned it that way. They've taken the time and trouble to make their businesses newsworthy (more on that in Chapter 3).

• **Key Insight #2:** Another common misconception is that businesspeople who get publicity (e.g., TV, radio, newspaper, E-'zine coverage) are important or prominent folk who happen to know reporters and news producers and so can use their relationships with the media to generate ink or airtime.

The truth is that businesspeople who get publicity *might* be important or prominent, as well as influential, but that's not what gets them media attention. Even small-business owners can take the time to develop relationships with media people. They can initiate a series of courteous professional contacts that puts them—and keeps them—on the radar of any given media contact, thereby increasing their chances that they will come to mind—and be contacted—the next time the media person is working on a story that involves their business or area of expertise. (See the chapters that follow for guidelines and rules of etiquette on how to initiate and maintain contacts with the media.)

• **Key Insight #3:** A third misconception is the false belief that businesspeople who get publicity do so because they also buy advertising from a given media outlet. This is *not* the way things work.

Take Journalism 101, and the first thing you'll learn is that one of the commandments of journalistic integrity is as follows: the advertising department and editorial department of any self-respecting media outlet must never coordinate efforts.

Yes, we all know that in the Real World commandments can get broken. A small minority of media outlets may indeed be more likely to write stories about businesses that pay for advertising that supports their operations. But make no bones about it: this *is* a breach of journalistic ethics. That's why even media outlets that indulge in this type of behavior show their partiality by simply being "more alert" to newsworthy events that happen to feature their advertisers—or more likely to give a nod to stories that have borderline news value.

When all is said and done, any story a media person runs must be able to pass one simple criteria: it must be newsworthy. This means that nonadvertisers with newsworthy stories should have no problem getting coverage. Fortunately, the media outlets that have lost their integrity are few and far between.

Get Set! . . . Ground Rules to Grasp

If luck, influence, and money are not the keys to publicity success, what are? Well, here are the ground rules:

- **Ground Rule #1:** To be successful at the publicity game, you must learn to identify what's newsworthy about your business, or, if there is little that is newsworthy about your business, you must take action to change that.
- **Ground Rule #2:** You must take action to bring what's newsworthy about your business to the attention of the media.
- **Ground Rule #3:** You must not leave publicity to chance. You can—and should—plan for and create publicity for your business.
- **Ground Rule #4:** Always remember that no business is entitled to publicity. However, if you give the news media what they want—newsworthy story ideas—you will get what *you* want—publicity. The law of reciprocity is definitely at work in the publicity arena.
- **Ground Rule #5:** Successful publicists must take a long-term and ongoing approach to getting publicity. Ongoing positive publicity is much more effective as a business builder than a single brief mention in the media.
- **Ground Rule #6:** To get the maximum effect from your publicity efforts, you must think strategically about how to build news value into your business.
- **Ground Rule #7:** You enhance your chances of getting publicity by developing professional contacts with media people. Do this by presenting yourself as a resource. (If you follow the unwritten rules for dealing with media people, they will welcome your contacting them. See Chapter 6 on how to establish yourself as a media "source.")
- **Ground Rule #8:** You must always remember that publicity is as much an art as a science. Results and outcomes are not always predictable. Sometimes you seem to have all the right ingredients and to do all the right things—but results are disappointing. To succeed, you need an ability to objectively figure out things gone wrong and things gone right—and then regroup and persist.
- **Ground Rule #9:** You must recycle your publicity successes. Success builds on success in the publicity game. Keep the momentum going.

Go! . . . Adopt the Publicity Mind-Set

The previous ground rules require action, confidence, and persistence. And that brings us to the real underpinnings of publicity success—something known as "the publicity mind-set." What's the publicity mind-set? It's a mental perspective that's expressed in a specific set of personal characteristics. With the right mind-set, a publicist will succeed at the publicity game.

Do you have the right publicity mind-set? You do if the following characteristics describe you:

articulate You're able to describe your business and your products/services clearly, even (and especially) to people who know very little about what you do.

enthusiastic You're passionate about what you do and it comes through. When you talk about your business, you're able to spark interest in your audience—whether it's one person or hundreds.

action-oriented You know "if it has to be, it's up to me." You don't wait for good luck to come your way. You think of ways to create opportunity.

positive, upbeat, and willing to take risks You're realistic, but you're also open to possibilities. You know no one can guarantee what a news release or a special event or any other publicity effort will bring. You hedge your bets by doing your homework, and you count on the saying, "The smarter I work, the luckier I get."

authentic You operate from an authentic core. Your values are solid and it shows in the way you run your business/publicity campaign.

able to be objective and tough-minded You recognize what's working and what isn't. You take action to fix what needs fixing. You bounce back from failures and setbacks. When disappointed, you simply get to work on the next project. As the ad slogan goes, "You haven't got time for the pain."

The abilities and traits of successful publicists also happen to be the abilities and traits of successful entrepreneurs. It's no surprise, when you think about it, that business success and the ability to successfully garner publicity go hand in hand.

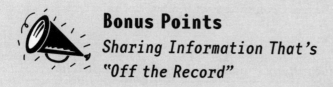

Bonus Points
Sharing Information That's "Off the Record"

Be aware that any information you provide to a reporter is fair game as grist for the mill. Media people have an ethical obligation to collect facts and then report them to the public. So don't share any potentially embarrassing information. And don't say anything you don't want to see in print (e.g., "Sure, we use the lowest-cost components, and our product may not be totally reliable, but it's as good as some of our competitors' low-end models . . .").

If you feel you need to share information with a reporter that you don't want to see in print, protocol dictates that you must ask the reporter, "Can I tell you something 'off the record?'" The reporter must then tell you if he or she agrees to keep what you are going to tell him or her confidential. If he or she does not agree, keep the information you don't want to see publicized to yourself.

Know also that reporters' memories are not always perfect. This means that a reporter may honestly forget that a piece of information you provided is meant to be off the record. As far as sensitive information is concerned, remember what a wise man once said about keeping secrets: "Even a fish wouldn't get in trouble if he kept his mouth shut."

But what if you're lacking in one or more of these abilities or traits? What do you do?

The only nonnegotiable trait is the need to be authentic. All the rest—assuming you have the desire—can be acquired, developed, or learned. Other business-people have transformed and reinvented themselves on the journey to success. What others have done, you can do too.

Bumps in the Road? Here Are the Roadblocks You'll Have to Overcome

Although you will greatly boost your chances of success by adopting a publicity mind-set, you may still face roadblocks in the form of limiting beliefs. There are a number of psychological roadblocks that can make you reluctant to seek publicity. Here are some of the more common ones—along with the reasons why you should ignore them:

Limiting Belief: *I don't think my product or service is unique enough.*

Reality: *No two snowflakes are created alike.* No two businesses are either. Even if your product is as ordinary as paper clips, you can find something newsworthy about them. Are they paper clips made with aluminum recycled from local pop cans? Is your company celebrating its tenth anniversary—and your one billionth paper clip? Do you run a contest at local schools in which kids create art that features paper clips? Do you donate a dollar to charity for every one hundred boxes of paper clips a business customer buys? Or does your business sell paper clips to celebrities—or supply them to local charities for free? You get the idea.

Limiting Belief: *I don't have any contacts in the media.*

Reality: *You don't need any.* Yes, contacts are helpful. But perhaps the best reason for having friends in the news business is that they will point out to you what is and isn't newsworthy about your business. (This book will do the same.) No bona fide reporter or producer runs a story about anybody's business for friendship's sake. The story has to have a news angle.

Limiting Belief: *I'm not the publicist type.*

Reality: *There is no publicist type.* What's your image of a publicist? Is it of a wild-haired Don King or an over-the-top Colonel Tom Parker? Someone loud and brash? Just as many successful publicists are low-key and soft-spoken.

Reporters and editors aren't impressed by blustery, forceful personalities. They respond best to publicists who understand what they're looking for and give it to them—and that's news. Period.

The Grandpappy of All Publicity Roadblocks: "Modesty Forbids . . ."

"What a show-off!"
"Nobody wants to hear it!"
"Stop bragging."

These phrases are floating around in your head somewhere. All of us heard them as we grew up. Part of our socialization process was learning *not* to "toot our own horns."

Let's go back to those schoolyard days for a moment. Who were the "braggarts" we found irritating? They were the kids who made "it's-all-about-me" statements ("*I* got all As on my report card." "*My* dad's bigger than *your* dad." "Guess who just asked *me* to the prom?").

As long as we're visiting that long-ago schoolyard, take a moment to remember the messages you welcomed, or at least wanted to hear. They were the "grapevine" news flashes like: "I heard we're getting a new math teacher next month. She's a lot nicer than Mrs. Scowler." "If you save forty of those bubblegum cards, you can get a free Frisbee." "Trash your Barney T-shirt. Barney isn't cool anymore."

The news we welcomed told us something we needed to know or that was helpful or of interest to us in some way. Likewise, good publicity offers media people information that's interesting or useful *to their radio and TV listeners and viewers*, and *to their newspaper and magazine readers*.

Here are four ways to break down the mental roadblocks to publicity:

1. **Ask yourself, "What's the worst that could happen?"** Now exaggerate it. Is it possible, for instance, that an editor or reporter—or the whole newsroom— will find your release laughable? Do you think producers will get angry at you for calling, tell you off, or even hang up on you? Or, maybe they'll make it obvious they find your ideas boring?

All of those things are in the realm of possibility.

The question to ask yourself is: Am I willing to endure a moment or two of possible discomfort or embarrassment in order to build my business? Of course you are. And the fact is, few reporters will be that rude. Most of the people you deal with will be polite and businesslike at best, a bit harried or preoccupied at worst.

2. **Remember to bring something to the party.** What fascinating, new, and/or useful information can you provide to the media (that just happens to mention your business)? If you have something of value to offer, you'll be welcome at the party.

Remember that newspeople need expert sources of information. They can't be experts at everything, and they know it. Position yourself as an expert who is graciously lending his or her expertise to them. You will build a solid relationship with media people that way.

3. **Think long-term.** Be prepared to help even if your assistance doesn't result in a mention of your business every time. As leading business consultant Brian Tracy says, "There is a principle of reciprocity in business that is extremely powerful. It is simply this: if you do something nice for someone else, they will feel obligated to do something nice for you."

4. **Visualize success.** One of the best definitions of faith anyone ever made is that "faith is the substance of things unseen." Substance is something real—something you can touch, taste, smell, hear, and feel. Unseen, in this instance, means not yet real. Faith, in other words, is believing so strongly in something that isn't as yet a reality that you can, as the saying goes, "just about taste it."

Close your eyes right now and give "substance" to your publicity success. Use all five senses—feel the crinkly newspaper featuring articles about your business, feel the hot lights of the TV studio where you are being interviewed by your local talk show host, hear the small talk of the radio host as he chats with you during a commercial break—you get the idea.

Repeat this exercise often. You'll find it encourages you and sparks creative ideas you wouldn't have come up with otherwise.

Why Honesty Is the *Only* Policy

In a recent article in the *Los Angeles Times*, staff writer David Shaw notes that Hollywood studio chiefs Mike Ovitz and Joe Roth have excellent relationships with the media. The reason? The studio chiefs established themselves with reporters as open, honest, and reliable sources of information early in their careers. Shaw suggests that the good press Ovitz and Shaw received throughout much of their careers was the result.

"There's little that a reporter likes more," Shaw writes, "than a source who returns calls and answers questions truthfully and on the record. No matter how objective and evenhanded a reporter tries to be, such people are bound to fare well in the long run."

Ovitz and Shaw were careful to be completely honest with the media. Did that mean they revealed everything they knew? No. Reporters understand that certain subjects—products in the development stage or mergers in the making, for instance—can be off-limits or something you can't talk about at the moment. They never, however, understand dishonesty.

One stereotype of publicists and PR people is that they make a practice of stretching the truth. But any publicist who values his or her career will be squeaky-

Bonus Points
Why Media People "Keep Their Guard Up"

If you're anything like me, you like to feel that you're on a friendly footing with people you regularly interact with in business. You may, therefore, find yourself puzzled by the coolness and aloofness that some media people project.

It's useful to always keep in mind that media people pride themselves on being objective. They aim to report the news without partiality. They despise fellow media people who throw "puffball" or "softball" questions at people they interview. They also wisely recognize that it will be harder for them to throw tough questions at you in the future once they've entered into a backslapping friendship with you.

For that reason, good reporters often have their guard up against being too friendly with their sources. They don't want relationships to develop in a way that affects their news judgment—their decisions about what is and isn't a story, what the facts are, and how they are going to report on them. That's the reason why almost all newspapers and magazines have policies against their reporters accepting gifts from companies or people they write about. All of this is designed to ensure objectivity. For that reason, don't send reporters gifts. Limit yourself to sending a card during the holiday season, but don't go beyond that.

The aloof media person is signaling to you that he or she is "on duty" and that you are "on the record," which—when you think about it—is a courteous and professional thing to do.

By the way, there are some media people who can be disarmingly friendly and warm to the people they interview. The interviewees let down their guard and then are surprised and distressed to see, hear, or read bits of information they shared in what they supposed was confidence to their newfound "friend."

clean with reporters and producers—no matter what the temptation. Get caught in a lie and you've shot your credibility with a reporter. For good. And word gets around.

What kind of credibility do you want? Try for the kind that Alabama football coach Bear Bryant had. One Southern businessman who had frequent business dealings with Bryant said this about him: "If Bear tells me it's raining, I don't look out to see. I go get an umbrella."

"If the Truth Isn't Tellable, Fix It So It Is."

John E. Powers, a nineteenth-century advertising pioneer, had some timeless advice about how to be effective in advertising. It applies to publicity as well. He said it was necessary to stick to the truth and added, "If the truth isn't tellable, fix it so it is. That is about all there is to it." He had it right. In dealing with the media, always think beyond the present story, because the goal of publicity isn't to get one story in a newspaper or one mention on a talk show. The goal of publicity is a continuous stream of positive mentions. To achieve that, honesty isn't the best policy. It's the only policy.

In these days of rapid, nonstop change, the enduring things still matter—in fact, they matter the most. Character certainly matters. So does integrity. It can be faked for a time—but not for very long. To succeed at publicity, you need to be straight-arrow honest—always.

So Who *Really* Controls the Media?

There are, of course, some interesting conspiracy theories out there. A number of suspense novelists and screenwriters have made a good living crafting tales of powerful cliques and sinister "hidden forces" that control the government and the press. I love a good yarn as well as the next person, but I also know that if a businessperson is successful at getting publicity, it's not because he or she is in cahoots with hidden conspirators.

Three things control what news most media outlets report on: journalistic integrity, market forces, and a media outlet's editorial mission.

Let's look at each of these.

Integrity

Joseph Pulitzer, who initiated the renowned journalism awards that bear his name, once said, "The highest mission of the press is to render public service." Our Founding Fathers meant for the media to play an important role in influencing public policy and in acting as a watchdog for public interests. That's why they instituted freedom of the press. Media people are free to report the news—the truth about what's happening in their communities—as they find it out. They're not only free to do so, they have an obligation to their publics—the people who watch, read, or hear their news reports—to actively ferret out the news. "News" here means significant events that have just happened or are about to happen and important and/or interesting new trends that are developing.

Media people must report the facts about these events and trends as accurately and objectively as possible, and they must also make an effort not to allow any personal biases or prejudices affect the way each story is reported. That's journalistic integrity.

Here's an illustration of how committed media people are to this kind of integrity: after the September 11 attacks on New York and Washington, DC, some news anchors, like many Americans, began wearing U.S. flag pins on their lapels during news broadcasts. ABC news banned the practice. And renowned NBC anchor Tom Brokaw defended the ABC ban. Speaking to a group of journalism students at Northwestern University, Brokaw said wearing the pin was a sign of solidarity with the government and "that is not our role [as journalists]." A journalist's role, he said, includes asking questions and examining issues that will lead to some improvement of the country.

Of course, many newspapers and magazines and other media outlets do have biases. Some clearly have an agenda—environmental, liberal, conservative, and so on. But even publications that have strong political agendas will attempt to report news stories as objectively as they can manage to do—given their particular slants—and to reserve their strongest opinions for the editorial pages, which traditionally allow for the expression of beliefs as opposed to facts.

Market Forces

In addition to journalistic integrity, market forces also affect the way the news is reported. We can see this in the way television news has changed in the past couple of decades. Take a look at any television news program today and you'll see quick-paced visuals, distilled-to-the-essence reporting, and plenty of sound bites (one- or two-sentence comments from people featured in the news that forcefully and/or emotionally provide facts and viewpoints). These are meant to hold the shorter-than-ever attention spans of viewers increasingly distracted by eighty-plus cable TV channels, the lures of the Internet, and the explosion of special interest print media.

It's important, by the way, for you to notice how the particular media that serve your target audience respond to market pressures in the way they present and filter the news. This will help you to understand how best to package the information you present about your business as you approach these media outlets.

Editorial Mission

Of course, there's one additional filter that determines what news a particular media outlet will report—its editorial mission. This will vary from one media outlet to another.

The editorial mission of a major city daily is to report the news that develops in the city and its suburbs and national news as it affects the city and its suburbs. The editorial mission of CBS's *60 Minutes* is to present news that examines important and controversial issues facing the country.

Trade publications and magazines and newsletters that cater to professionals have a narrower focus. The mission of *Produce Merchandising*, for example, is to provide retail produce executives and managers with information that keeps them abreast of trends related to produce and helps them increase sales. The mission of *Managers Report*, a national trade journal for condominium and home owner association managers, is to help them function more effectively. The editorial mission of *Contract Professional* magazine is to keep computer consultants up-to-date on the latest trends and developments affecting the computer consulting field.

That's why you don't want to try to pitch a story about a new product that helps produce managers track shipments more efficiently to *60 Minutes* while *Produce Merchandising* might be exactly where you'll find interest—and reach your target market. And a small company that has begun manufacturing innovative roofing tiles might easily find a home for the story in publications like *Managers Report*, with its audience of condominium and home owners association managers, or in newsletters and magazines that cater to building and construction firms.

Each media outlet's editorial policy is designed to appeal to a specific segment of the public, its targeted audience. Taking all these factors into account, who can we say really controls the media? If you think about it, the correct answer is "Joe and Jane Q. Public."

Reporters, editors, and producers aren't interested in providing free publicity to businesspeople. Their loyalties are to their target audiences. In the media's eyes, no one is entitled to coverage, and that's why you should never approach the media with any sense of entitlement. You have to earn publicity by presenting materials that media people know will be of interest to their target audiences.

Bonus Points
Four Things You Should Never Say to Media People

There are four things you should *never* say to a media person.

1. **"No comment."** You don't want to be quoted using this phrase. It's gotten a bad connotation as something that shady characters say to the media. It sounds as if you've got something to hide. If there really is something you can't talk about, say things like, "I can't talk about that at the moment," or, "I have nothing to report at the moment," or, "I'm not at liberty to discuss that at the moment." If asked about a decision your company isn't ready to announce yet, you can say something like, "Any talk of a decision is premature." If a reporter presses you for a comment, simply stay calm and composed and repeat yourself politely.

2. **"We really need some publicity."** This is unprofessional and a sure way to create a bad impression. Journalists are trained to be objective and to ferret out news—and nothing else. If you really want publicity, learn to "crack the news code"—figure out what journalists consider news, and give it to them.

3. **"How much would it cost for you to do a story about my business?"** Offering to pay a journalist to run a story is probably the biggest insult you can throw at a newsperson. It hits at the heart of journalistic integrity. We are talking major insult here. If you're lucky, the media person in question will recognize you are simply terribly naive and unaware of the way things work. If he or she doesn't recognize this, be prepared for sparks to fly.

4. **"Will you let me review/check the article you're writing before it's published?"** No self-respecting media person would dream of letting someone providing information to him or her control the way the information provided gets used. This means you should not ask to see an article before it's run. **Exception:** If you are providing highly technical information, some journalists may ask you to review an excerpt or two for accuracy.

Few of us like high-pressure salespeople. That's why the best and most successful salespeople simply present (as enticingly as possible) the information that they know buyers are looking for and will value—but then know how to take "no" for an answer. Skilled salespeople don't look for a quick kill. They are building relationships based on mutual respect. If a contact doesn't result in an immediate sale, they leave the door open for future efforts.

As my friend, top salesperson Karen Priemer, a regional vice president for Arbonne International, says, "sales is merely teaching people how to get what they want." Successful publicists teach media people how to get what they want by providing information for stories. Successful publicists also teach their target audiences how to get what they want—products and services that meet needs and solve problems—by making sure word gets out about what they have to offer.

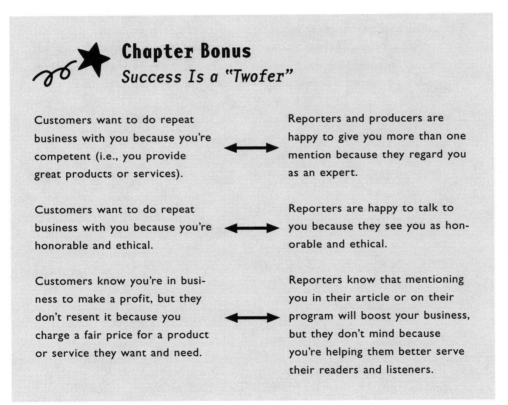

Chapter Bonus
Success Is a "Twofer"

Customers want to do repeat business with you because you're competent (i.e., you provide great products or services).	Reporters and producers are happy to give you more than one mention because they regard you as an expert.
Customers want to do repeat business with you because you're honorable and ethical.	Reporters are happy to talk to you because they see you as honorable and ethical.
Customers know you're in business to make a profit, but they don't resent it because you charge a fair price for a product or service they want and need.	Reporters know that mentioning you in their article or on their program will boost your business, but they don't mind because you're helping them better serve their readers and listeners.

3 Success: It's Born in the USA

What Media People Want

"One small detail, insight, or idea can be the turning point in your career. Never stop looking for it."

—Brian Tracy

To get publicity, all you need to do is give editors, reporters, and producers what they want—news. Successful publicists understand what media people consider news. One definition of news is "information that will interest readers, listeners, or viewers *now*." Have you just launched a new product or service? Has your business just opened—or relocated? Gotten an award? Given an award? Have you renamed your company? Are you offering a new product or service? Expanding the area you service? Has your business earned record profits? Are you donating more to charity this year than last? These events or actions may seem like news to you. But in and of themselves, they may not be enough to earn you a significant amount of publicity. That's because they ring of being run-of-the-mill (i.e., boring).

Spark Publicity by Adding a "Twist"

One of the best ways to generate publicity is to find or create a "twist"—an element of novelty and especially of urgency—that will strike media people as something your target audience will want to hear about now. (Yes, you are allowed to *create* the "twist.")

At times current events provide the twist of a "timely hook." When Vice President Dick Cheney suffered more than one heart attack early in his term, for instance, spokespeople on cardiac health (and their books) came to the forefront. On March 20, 2001, when the core of the Russian space station Mir was about to splash down to Earth in the Pacific Ocean, Taco Bell placed a floating forty-by-forty-foot target in the ocean—with the Taco Bell logo dead center—and offered a free taco to everyone in the United States if the capsule scored a bull's-eye. Because it was timely and humorous, the stunt garnered relatively inexpensive national press attention.

A homeless man dressed as a tree drew national media attention to the plight of the homeless at the Chicago Democratic Convention in 1996 when he followed Mayor Richard Daley, who was fond of planting trees, around and kept asking, "If I were a tree, would you care about me?" The visual quality of the story—which made it a natural for the TV news—combined with the "twist" of the costume, the creativity of the confrontation, and the shrewd choice of locale made the story irresistible to the media. The same homeless man making the same remark without benefit of the costume or the convention locale would have been ignored by the media. There would not have been enough that was new about the story.

Twists can be created by adding features to a product you sell or a service you offer in a way that ties into a current trend. One pillbox manufacturer came up with a discreet blue plastic pill container and garnered an article and photo, and a mention of the website at which it could be purchased, on the front page of *USA Today*'s "Life" section. Why? He marketed it as a container for a medication that at this writing remains controversial—Viagra.

You also can hold an event, sponsor an award or a contest, or run a survey. Lisa Kanarek, founder of HomeOfficeLife.com, a company that provides consultant services to corporations and individuals on all aspects of working from home, ran a contest called "Search for the Most Unusual Home Office." She posted the rules for the contest on her website and contacted other websites to carry information about the contest (with links back to her site). More than fifty sites obliged. "I obtained prizes, handled all of the media, and reaped the rewards of national publicity," Kanarek says.

The Eyes Have It: Make It Visual

One strong visual image can make your story a winner to news photographers and the TV media.

For the October 2000 relaunch of the Microsoft Network and browser software, Microsoft Corporation had skaters dressed as butterflies and wearing the MSN B-Fly logo carry MSN flags and hand out MSN-branded hats and T-shirts and MSN software in sixteen cities in the United States. Operation B-Fly, as it was dubbed, generated print and broadcast coverage in all sixteen cities. It also was featured on the *Today* show and picked up by the AP wire service and the Weather Channel. Following the publicity generated by the event, potential customers initiated more than 900,000 downloads of Microsoft's new browser software.

At a 1993 annual auto show, the then Chrysler Corporation drove its new Grand Cherokee through a plate glass wall for its public introduction at the show. This unusual and innovative way to present a vehicle was the hit of the auto show. The news media gave the "smashing" intro extensive coverage, with the TV media replaying clips numerous times, and the buzz that was created lasted for years.

Recently, a General Motors executive parachuted from the ceiling of an exhibition hall (with the help of a wind machine and a theatrical harness) to the speakers' podium to address a group of college students considering employment with her company. The point that her exhilarating entrance made to the students was that her company was open to new and exciting ideas. Her speech, which might otherwise have been ignored by the news media, made the local TV news programs and earned her company a page and a half (with photo, of course) in the *Automotive News*, the key business magazine for her industry.

So think visually. If your hairstyling salon, for instance, is raising funds for a charity by donating the profits from all haircuts between noon and five on a specified day, let the media know that they can photograph and film your customers getting their hair cut, that your employees will be wearing special T-shirts, and that you'll have signs and balloons hung throughout your shop.

If you're collecting blankets for the homeless, let the media know that you'll have a central collection point—a church hall or the atrium of a local corporation—where the donated blankets will be displayed in huge piles. The news media refer to visuals such as these, which help tell a story, as photo ops or photo opportunities.

If you want TV coverage and photographs to accompany your article make your news "twist" visually appealing. If your twist is that your company is participating in a "hands-on" charitable event—painting homes for the disabled, cooking meals for the homeless, or holding a marathon to help cancer patients, for instance—you have natural draws for the TV media and for photographers (because these events have two elements irresistible to visual media: the story can be told with pictures and the events evoke an emotional response from viewers—and reporters).

Seven Media Pleasers (That Can Help You Publicize Your Business)

You boost your chances of getting publicity significantly the moment you begin to understand and keep in mind what the media wants as you plan for and compose your publicity communications.

So what do media people want? They want to offer their audiences information of value. They want to report breaking news. They want to respond to community concerns. They want to report on trends. And they want to amuse and entertain.

Offer Information of Value

Can you offer your target audience (the people most likely to buy your product or service) something that's unique and of value (that your competitors don't offer)? If so, you might interest the media. Are you a piano teacher? How about offering a free lesson and evaluation session to adults who have always wanted to play? Do you own an art supply store? How about hosting a one-night seminar on "Finding the Artist in You" to explain various kinds of art (clay, watercolor, oil, etc.) available to hobbyists? Do you have a roofing company? How about offering a one-page tip sheet on "How to Know It's Time for a New Roof" or "How to Choose a New Roof"? If you tutor primary school children in math, how about offering a free tip sheet on "Making Math Fun for Your Child"?

Can you draw on your expertise to create information that your target audience will find useful? Numbered lists work particularly well (horse trainers: "Six Proven Ways to Steady a Nervous Horse"; family law attorneys: "Seven Ways to Make Joint Custody Work Smoothly"; health food restaurant owners: "Three Easy-to-Make New Desserts That Can Help You Lose Weight"). Work up an article along these lines and send it in news release format to the media most likely to reach your target audience.

While the horse news release should be sent to publications targeted to horse owners, it's an "evergreen" (it would work any time during the year). The dessert story, however, might find a stronger reception in January when people are trying to drop holiday pounds. The joint custody news release might be best received before any major holiday because holidays are when custody issues most frequently flare up.

Tie Your News into a Trend

Media people (and the audiences they serve) have always been interested in news that ties into current trends. The media loved reporting on the now-legendary pilot Amelia Earhart in the 1920s and 1930s. One reason for her popularity with the press: aviation pioneer Charles Lindbergh had made a historic transatlantic flight just before Earhart came on the scene. Earhart's marketing team capitalized on the excitement Lindbergh generated. They dubbed Earhart "Lady Lindy" and—with an eye to making a profit from the publicity—even arranged for her to endorse her own line of clothing and luggage.

Do you have a new product or service that ties into current news or to a change taking place in our society? Today, for example, more women are rising into executive ranks. Perhaps you own a hair salon "without walls"—the stylists at your establishment visit your clients at work and provide lunchtime or coffee break haircuts for busy women executives—top-quality cuts at lower prices than services rendered at a walk-in salon would cost. If so, it's news.

Each year, more people opt to lease rather than buy vehicles. Perhaps your auto body repair shop saves people who lease vehicles hundreds of dollars by smoothing out dings and dents before a vehicle is turned in. If you write a news release citing the statistics about the number of people who turn in their lease vehicles every month, the typical charges incurred for dings and dents, and how much customers can expect to save when they use your services, the media may well come calling. This will be especially true if you let them know that this is a very visual story. Tell them they are welcome to photograph and videotape your service people using their equipment to smooth out dents and selecting the just-right shade of matchup paint to fill in nicks.

Respond Sensitively to Community Concerns

Responding to community concerns not only generates publicity, it also builds goodwill.

The Winthrop Printing Company in Boston (winprint.com) has donated its services to numerous charities, including printing posters and informational bro-

Bonus Points
Channel It to the Right Person

Once you've decided on your story and written your news release, bring your news to the attention of the person or people in the media who can do you some good. Be sure to send your news release to specific reporters and assignment editors at newspapers and broadcast stations.

Addressing your release to the appropriate party signals that you are familiar with the subject area that a particular media person covers. And, unlike a generic release mailing, it also gives you a better chance to trigger a sense of ownership in the person on the receiving end.

To find the names of the media people who should get your release, do the following:

- Decide on your target media.
- Call the newspapers and TV and radio stations you target and ask for the name and title of the reporter (newspaper) or assignment editor (TV or radio station) to whom you should send your release. E-mail the editors of E-'zines and do the same.

chures to Against the Tide, a swim event to raise funds to fight breast cancer, and donating posters and invitations to the Make-A-Wish Foundation of Greater Boston for its events.

When a heartbreaking series of child kidnappings was in the news in Detroit in the late 1970s (and home video cameras were still expensive luxuries for many middle-income families), one video rental store offered to videotape and finger-print schoolchildren to provide concerned parents with records that would be crucial in emergencies.

After the World Trade Center/Pentagon attacks, Fox News reported that at Galloping Gerties restaurant near Fort Lewis, Washington, owner Rod Mason gave free coffee to all soldiers in uniform and that some apartment complex owners in Manhattan provided lodging the evening of the attacks for people stranded on the island. Food Lion, a supermarket chain located in the Southeastern United States, donated money and also sent two truckloads of snacks and beverages to the American Red Cross to feed volunteers and emergency personnel at the Pentagon and to provide refreshments to those donating blood. LexisNexis, the fee-based legal information service, offered, at no charge, relevant content from its archive of news and legal, legislative, and business information to assist people researching terrorism or requiring other information related to the September 11 attacks.

Following are just a few of the products and services you can donate (and tell the media about) to support a worthy community cause:

- Printing for a brochure, award certificates, tickets to an event, flyers, etc.—free or at a discounted rate
- Use of a meeting room, audiovisual equipment, and so on
- Website design, development, or maintenance

Conduct a Survey

You can "create" timely news by doing research that produces useful information. Make sure it's information your target audience will find especially useful. You can conduct surveys by phone or mail, on your own, or via a firm you hire to run the survey for you.

If you don't have the funds to hire someone or the time to run a survey by phone or mail, there are other ways to collect data. You can hand out survey forms or ask for a show of hands at a gathering of "experts" or people with specialized knowledge. Say you own a shop that specializes in educational toys. Attend a local PTA meeting and quiz parents about the kinds of equipment they think their kids would prefer to use to learn math skills (puzzles, computer games, or flash cards, for example). Then send a press release to your local paper ("Parents Agree: Computer Games Provide Best Boost for Kids' Math Skills").

Increase your chances of getting media attention by tying the news results from your survey to a calendar event. Is it Grandparents' Day? Safe Kids Week? Computer Month? Check *Chase's Calendar of Events* in the reference section of your library to find a holiday tie-in.

Be Creative, Unique, or Unexpected

When Blue Springs, Kansas, entrepreneur Brad Whitt bought the Soft Serv Depot, an independent ice cream shop, he was aware of the stiff competition his shop faced from major ice cream store chains. So he made a number of strategic moves to make his store unique. He bought an ice cream truck fitted with ice cream machines that mix ice cream on location and now can sell ice cream at his town's community festival, employee picnics, and retail store promotions. He can also use the truck to cater children's birthday parties. Whitt also adds ice cream products to the menu, using his own recipes, and creates specialty treats such as the Flying Monkey, which features sliced bananas and hot fudge. In addition, Whitt enhanced the uniqueness of his ice cream shop, which had been designed to look like an old train station, by installing a model-train track so that a miniature train now chugs around the shop as customers enjoy their ice cream.

Some businesses that sell concrete statues, the kind used to decorate gardens, have had trouble competing with large chains that supply building and garden materials. But the Eagle Stone company in Fraser, Michigan, owned by Gino Vettese, has continued to thrive because it offers a wide assortment of unique religious and decorative statuary and stone fountains. The company has the kind of history that reporters love to share. It started when Vettese's father, Alberto, made cement flowerpots and religious statues for his friends and family in his garage. Many of the cement products are unique to Eagle Stone because the molds were made by Alberto Vettese.

Colorado white-water rafters who book trips with Rocky Mountain Adventures are told that the photos of them taken by their tour guide will be flown from the Cache la Poudre River to the photo shop at Rocky Mountain Adventures' Fort Collins outpost for development—not by plane but by Pigeon Express, a carrier pigeon outfitted with a Lycra backpack. It's a twenty-minute trip for the pigeon—faster than a tour guide could go by car. Most customers think the Pigeon Express story is a hoax—until they get back to their starting point and see the developed photos available for purchase. The film is actually delivered by carrier pigeons that trigger electronic sensors as they enter their coop to alert the staff of Rocky Mountain Adventures that another roll has been delivered. Pigeon Express was born because the rafting company needed a way to allow photographers to stay on riverbanks to shoot each batch of rafts and digital cameras and modems were too expensive. Needless to say, Rocky Mountain Adventures and its Pigeon Express have generated significant media interest, including an Associated Press wire story (which was fed to 1,550 newspapers and 5,000 radio and television stations in the United States as well as 8,500 newspaper, radio, and television subscribers in an additional 112 countries).

Be Funny or Whimsical

Reporters and producers are as harried and in need of stress relief as the rest of us are. They love well-done humor. The "well-done" is the hard part.

The Bob Mayberry Ford dealership in Monroe, North Carolina, pulled off a subtle and witty publicity coup when it purchased a 1961 police car like the one driven by the lead characters in the 1960's hit TV show *The Andy Griffith Show* and displayed it in front of the dealership. The vehicle attracts customers and has sparked several mentions in the press.

Ben Cohen and Jerry Greenfield, founders of Ben & Jerry's Ice Cream, launched their business after taking a correspondence course in how to make homemade-style ice cream. Ben and Jerry were outspoken about social responsibility and also injected a lot of whimsy into their business. They paid Vermont artist Woody Jackson five hundred dollars to design the company's trademark cow and a cow billboard and T-shirt. Ice cream flavors were given names like Chubby Hubby, Cherry Garcia, and Chunky Monkey. Today, although it has grown its annual sales to more than $100 million, the company continues to reflect a whimsical image. At the time of this writing, a games section on the Ben & Jerry's website offered an online version of a magnetic kids' game in which you could add hair to the head of a figure—in this case company founder Ben Cohen—or print a Ben & Jerry's cow to cut and fold into three dimensions.

Create a "Hook"

An ordinary fish fry to raise funds for charity would be of only minor interest to the media. A fish fry served by the mayor and other local celebrities might get some serious attention.

When he was selling his first book, self-help expert Anthony Robbins got a lot of media attention by holding "firewalks." He demonstrated that people could successfully employ his techniques for overcoming their own fears by getting them to walk barefoot over smoldering cinders. It was a brilliant "hook" that drew plenty of media attention.

The Zen of Publicity

Zen is a system of philosophy that encourages people to appreciate paradox. Paradox is when two things that seemingly can't coexist *do* coexist. What's the Zen of publicity? It's this: you can't force the media to provide you with publicity, but you must persist in your publicity efforts.

If a news release you thought was a surefire winner falls flat with your target media, you can't give up. Just analyze what might have gone wrong, and, in three

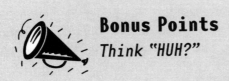

Bonus Points
Think "HUH?"

Hit a reporter over the head with a news release that simply announces you have the "best sandwich shop in the state" or that you've just opened a "brand-new temporary services agency," and the best you can hope for is a one-liner in an announcements column.

Think HUH? (short for "Is it Hip, Unique, or Helpful?"). Then watch what happens if you send out a news release that announces that your soda shop has just installed a special aisle so kids can wheel their scooters in for service (hip). Or that your sandwich shop offers sandwiches (say watercress and eel) found nowhere else in the world (unique). Or that your temp agency has started a program to hire kids from the inner city as summer interns and teach them valuable job skills (helpful).

You've just tripled or quadrupled your chances of getting some ink or airtime.

Joe Kool's sports bar (joekoolslondon.com) in London, Ontario, for instance, has been able to generate press interest with its breezy and irreverent attitude toward its customers. Joe Kool's serves drinks in jelly jars and offers "Soup du Yesterday" on its menu, as well as a tongue-in-cheek TV dinner special served by an employee who will run to a grocery store next door to buy you a frozen dinner of her choosing. Signs on the restaurant walls jauntily proclaim: "We cheat the other guy and pass the savings on to you," "Minutes from all major hospitals," and "At Joe Kool's quality is just a slogan."

Joe Kool's is both hip and unique.

or four weeks, try again from another angle or with a different approach. Keep trying.

Sales expert and world-famous speaker Zig Ziglar tells a great story about a species of tree that grows in Indonesia called the Chinese bamboo. The seeds are planted, then fertilized and watered for five years. During all that time, there is no visible growth. Then, sometime in the fifth year the tree sprouts and—within a six-week period—grows an incredible ninety feet tall. It's a growth spurt so phenomenal that if you stand and watch you can just about see it happening. Zigler uses the story to make the point that diligence and persistence *will* pay off.

James Lofton, wide receiver for the Buffalo Bills, was asked once what tricks he used to achieve success, and he summed them up as follows: "One trick is to work harder than the other guy. The second trick, always hustle. Third trick, study and know what you're doing. Fourth trick, always be prepared. Fifth, never give up." Lofton's tricks—tenacity, taking the time to learn the ropes (then using them), hustle, and hard work—all work in the publicity arena as well.

Eleven Keys to Unlocking Media Doors

To get the results you want from media people, use the following keys:

1. **Establish credibility.** Let them know who you are and what your area of expertise is. Then offer to be a source if they need information in that area. This can be done with a phone call and brief chat. Present your credentials, and be matter-of-fact when you do so. Media people are human beings too. No one likes to do business with braggarts. But don't be too humble either. You need to convey enough about your background to make a convincing case for why you *are* an expert.

> Good morning. Is this Anne Mallory, the food editor? This is Ken Jones. I'm the owner of Bagels-To-Go. I opened Bagels-To-Go here in Boston last year after completing two years of training at the Cordon Bleu with Rene Gallefois, who's considered one of the master bakers of Europe. I teach a baking class at the Pilgrim's Progress Community College, and two of my students have won awards in national bake-offs. I just wanted to let you know I'm available as a resource if you develop any stories that are baking-related.

> Hello, is this the news editor? This is Heather Welch. I'm the owner of Pure Well Water Company. We supply bottled drinking water to homes, offices, and retail establishments. I publish and distribute a quarterly newsletter, *Pure Well Water News*, which provides the latest information related to drinking water. Excerpts from the articles in my newsletter have been reprinted in the *New York Times* and the *Wall Street Journal*. I just wanted to let you know that I'm available as a resource for any stories you develop on water quality.

2. **Get them to see you as a source for breaking news in your industry.** When you send them news releases, make sure your releases provide timely new information. If broad, sweeping changes lie ahead for your industry and you know what's coming before the general public learns, call your press contacts and let

them know. They will appreciate the heads up, even if your business does not feature largely in the change that lies ahead. Media people will value your generosity and, over time, that may well translate into mentions in the press. They are also more likely to review future news releases that relate to your business more carefully. This is because you've demonstrated that you know what they are looking for (breaking news).

3. **Use plain English.** In your contacts with the media—whether via phone, E-mail, or snail mail—show them that you not only "know your stuff" but also can express what you know in down-to-earth language.

4. **Be authentic.** There's an old saying: "What you would seem to be, be really." Publicity is part of your overall business plan, which is designed to offer products and services of value to the public you are in business to serve in a way that (hopefully) reflects your commitment to your set of ethics. If you operate in line with top-notch ethics, over time your business plan and business philosophy and your actions and words (and publicity efforts) will—and should—reflect your commitment to your beliefs and your integrity.

That's another reason you should plan ongoing contacts with the media. Media people may not pick up on the fact that you're an authentic character the first time they deal with you. But over the long haul, it will come through.

5. **Play by the rules.** It's essential to know how reporters think. Respect the media's code of ethics and abide by its sense of protocol and you're halfway to your goals. That means presenting information to the media in traditional formats. (See Chapters 4 and 5 for how-tos.) Yes, if you have the Story of the Century to offer reporters, editors will follow up on it even if you send it on flowered stationery or a brown paper bag. The rest of us need to prepare a professional-looking, solidly written news release. Every news release, press kit, special event brochure, and E-mail you send the media's way should reflect professionalism if you aim for credibility.

6. **Be subtle.** Of course you want to bring your target audience's attention to the products and services you offer. But media people aren't in the business of producing sales for your business. They're in the business of producing news. You must provide them with news that just happens to involve your products and services. Your communications with the media should not be an obvious bid for free advertising.

7. **Follow up—but don't be pushy.** Aim for reporters to see you as the solution to their problems (a source of valuable information)—not as a problem (a pushy or abrasive personality). Courtesy and etiquette go a long way here. If your

phone call or press release prompts a reporter to interview you, then after the interview, give the reporter a follow-up call to make sure he or she got all the information needed. You can then confirm when the article might run and ask what process to follow to obtain copies (if it's an out-of-town publication). If you're interviewed for a TV news program or if you appear on a talk show, ask your contact person for the process to obtain a videotape of your appearance. Most local TV news stations don't videotape their programs for people who've appeared in news segments, but they might know of local companies that provide this service. (It's not difficult to tape your own radio program spots. If you're doing the interviews from your home, you can buy a phone attachment that enables you to tape your phone conversation for around twenty dollars.)

8. **Be patient and professional.** If a media outlet decides not to develop a story from a press release you've sent it, accept the fact politely and professionally and be patient. It's not personal. Publicity is a process—not a one-shot deal. The relationship you establish with a given reporter or editor is as important as any particular article or spot on the evening news. Roll with the publicity punches. Accept a decision to go with a story or to pass on it.

9. **Be a cool cookie.** If they decide to go with your story, don't overdo the jubilance. Think about how you feel when a salesman grins from ear to ear after you sign the bottom line. You begin to wonder, don't you?

10. **Keep up the relationships you develop with media people.** Keep a two-way flow of information going—and not just by sending press releases to reporters. If a story dealing with your area of expertise contains errors, pick up the phone and let the reporter or producer know—in a pleasant and professional way, of course, and keep sending in good ideas for stories—not just about your business, but about your field or industry.

11. **Don't abuse the relationship.** Media people call the shots as far as how often they choose to mention your business in their publications or on the air. That's the way it is—and that's the way it should be. Don't expect a media contact to cover your business every week, or even every month.

A No-Fail Formula for Publicity Success

information of value × timely* hook = publicity success

*"Timely" here means "ties into a trend or into current or developing news."

The Most Vital Ingredient: Your USA (Unique Selling Angle)

Always remember: publicity is not about you or your business. It's about what you or your business can do for others. Media people are interested only in what you or your business can offer the public.

That brings us to the unique selling angle (USA). The USA, also known as the unique selling proposition (USP), is critically important. The USA is the promise you make about your business, product, or service that makes a customer choose you over your competition. Your USA shapes the way people see your business. It's the vital ingredient common to all successful businesses.

What's in It (Your USA) for Your Customer?

The important thing to remember is that the media (and your target audience) are interested in how your USA will benefit them. In his bestselling *Think and Grow Rich*, Napoleon Hill says that the key to success in business is to "Find a need and fill it." Today that might be refined to "Find a need that no one else is filling—or that no one else is filling very well—and fill it in a unique, exciting way."

An effective USA has the following elements:

- It makes your business special.
- It makes you different in a great way from your competitors.
- It triggers your clients and customers to purchase your product or service.

Sears and McDonald's: Two Classic USAs

When Sears and Roebuck ventured into catalog sales in the early part of the last century, it made this promise: "Satisfaction guaranteed or your money back" (a guarantee that was fairly unique in its day). Sears quickly became the top catalog sales company in the country. The Sears and Roebuck guarantee was a USA in its day—one so successful it was widely copied.

When the first McDonald's franchise stores were opened, "fast" food was a new concept. McDonald's USA? Low-cost, great-tasting burgers, fries, and soft drinks—and service much faster than restaurants generally offered before then. Customers didn't have to wait long. McDonald's has spawned scores of competi-

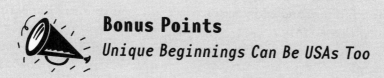

Bonus Points
Unique Beginnings Can Be USAs Too

Californian Steve Demos traveled through India in 1977 and once spent eight weeks meditating. When he returned to the United States, he eventually settled in Boulder, Colorado. There he put a modest toe in the entrepreneurial waters by making tofu in a bucket and delivering it to local stores in a little red wagon. The red wagon delivery story is part of the hippie-ish history of White Wave, now one of the largest manufacturers of soyfoods in the United States. The story is now part of the company's USA—part of what makes it unique to customers.

White Wave launched Silk (the first nationally distributed, refrigerated soy beverage) in 1996. Silk was the only soy milk sold like dairy milk—refrigerated and packaged in dairy milk–style cartons—another USA.

In 2001, White Wave, a privately owned company, had annual sales of more than $85 million and employed more than one hundred people.

The Longaberger Company, which produces unique and collectible handmade baskets, also has a unique history. Entrepreneur Dave Longaberger, who overcame physical disabilities to graduate from high school at age twenty-one, founded the company in 1972 when he sold some baskets on consignment at a general store. Acting on a gut feeling that handmade items would be increasingly in demand, he shocked his family by selling his lucrative restaurant and grocery business to found a basket-weaving company. Unable to get a loan, he persuaded the first weavers he hired to work for almost ten months without pay or benefits. This factory had no rest rooms, was extremely hot in the summer, leaked when it rained, and had no central heat. But hours were flexible, Longaberger inspired trust, and he created an environment in which employees felt appreciated.

Today the Longaberger Company employs more than eight thousand people and has millions of customers. The company's unique history very much figures into the marketing of Longaberger baskets—as does its headquarters building, which is shaped like a huge picnic basket—handles and all.

tors, and the most successful each tweaked the McDonald's formula to come up with its own USA (Arby's low-cost and fast roast beef sandwiches, Taco Bell's low-cost and fast Mexican-style foods, etc.).

Here are other USAs that have become commonplace. Adopt one—or a combination—for your business and add your own "twist," and you may just have a new—and newsworthy—USA.

- lowest prices
- best selection
- always in stock
- near-instant delivery
- highest quality
- lasts longer
- smells/tastes/feels/sounds better
- outstanding service
- cordial service
- one-hour call-back or E-mail response
- one-hour, next-day, etc., service
- extra effort
- more convenient packaging
- best/unconditional guarantee
- best technical support
- around-the-clock service
- "we come to your home" service
- "we deliver to your home/office"
- unique company (history, ownership, mission)
- any combination of the above

Develop a strong fresh twist for your USAs and people will see your business as exciting and interesting—and newsworthy. You'll be seen as a "fresh face" with a new and better way of doing things, and you'll draw the attention of the media. Here are some examples of companies that developed successful USA twists:

- Lifespan Furnishings (lifespanfurnishings.com)—furniture for the elderly and disabled designed to look like regular (as opposed to institutional) furniture
- FragranceNet (fragrancenet.com)—fragrances shipped free on orders of twenty-five dollars or more, and all orders gift-wrapped whether or not they are gifts
- Domino's Pizza (dominos.com)—pizzas delivered within half an hour or the food is free (Domino's no longer offers this service, but it was what put the company "on the media map.")

- Rent-A-Wreck (rent-a-wreck.com)—ugly cars that run well rented out at bargain prices
- Old Dog Cookie Company (olddogcookie.com)—dog "cookies" with ingredients that provide arthritis relief and diabetic relief to aging dogs
- White Wave Soy Milk (whitewave.com)—only soy milk to be sold in milk-carton-style packages, plus the first batches delivered by the founder to stores in a little red wagon (Yes, "how the business got started"/"how I got the idea for my product" stories can be newsworthy.)
- Geniusbabies.com (geniusbabies.com)—online source for educational gift/toy baskets for babies and toddlers
- Auntie Anne's Pretzels (auntieannes.com)—rolled by hand, and a thirty-minute freshness guarantee
- The Knot (theknot.com)—first online wedding planner
- Fridgedoor.com (fridgedoor.com)—online store that's the "single largest stop for all things magnetic: novelty magnets, custom magnets, and magnetic supplies"
- Tillack & Co., Ltd. (tillackco.com)—specialist in restoring vintage racing cars
- Coastal Tool and Supply (coastaltool.com)—"lowest possible discount prices" on brand-name hand and power tools

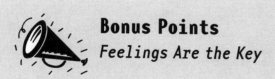

Bonus Points
Feelings Are the Key

As James D. Ericson, Northwestern Mutual Life Insurance executive, said, "If people were really interested in buying policies, I guarantee you that we'd be in the catalog business." He meant that people buy life insurance for the feelings it gives them—the good feeling that their loved ones will be protected should something happen. A good life insurance salesman is really selling reassurance and a feeling of security—benefits that a customer values—not a paper policy.

In publicizing your USA, always present the benefits that your product or service offers to customers and clients—how it will make them *feel* as well as what it will do.

Five USAs That Don't Need a New "Twist"

Clearly, it's worth the time and effort to come up with an original twist. A really great USA makes it much easier to interest the media in your business. If you're lucky, you may not even have to spend much time beneath a thinking cap. That's because if your business offers any of the following USAs, it is a one-of-a-kind enterprise, and you have built-in uniqueness:

- a combination of unique products or services
- broadest selection for a narrow niche
- exclusive source
- first to offer a product or service
- unique product or service that meets a "hole" in the marketplace (i.e., something that no one else offers)

Filling a Hole in the Marketplace: One of the Best USAs

A growing number of entrepreneurs have become savvy niche marketers. They provide a unique product or service that no one else offers. These businesses have a built-in USA; they are often one-of-a-kind.

The idea behind niche marketing is simple. You don't want to be a generalist. You want to be a specialist instead. You don't open a grocery store that sells everything from soup to nuts. You open a store specializing in 1,001 kinds of soup—or nuts.

How to Develop Your USA

Get a writing pad and pen. They will be tools to help you to think through your USA. Begin writing out your USA. Use all the words you need to describe it even if you fill several pages of paper.

State your USA in plain, bold words. Don't weaken it with *ifs*, *ands*, *howevers*, and *buts*. Make it clear and attention-getting. The media (and the public) are bombarded with sales messages every day. Make it easy for them to grasp your USA.

Get all your thoughts on the subject out there. As you're doing this, keep your target customers/clients in mind. What kind of USA will they find of value? Is your USA something your competitors will find hard to copy? Can you explain your USA easily to them? Can you describe it in an exciting way?

The Seattle Caviar Co. (caviar.com), for example, is the only caviar specialty shop in the Northwest. The shop sells luxury foods such as foie gras, fine champagnes, caviar (paddlefish, osetra, sevruga, beluga, etc.), and mother-of-pearl spoons with which to scoop up the caviar.

In select stores in the FredMeyer chain (fredmeyer.com), instructors hold in-store cooking classes where customers can take a break from shopping to learn about new food products or new ways to prepare familiar foods.

Toys Not Just for Kids (toysnotjustforkids.com) markets a "unique mix of toys, games, puzzles, and craft items" at a discount price *and* offers a flat $3.55 shipping charge per item and an "enjoyment guarantee," which allows customers to return items for a full refund within a set time period.

If you can't describe it easily and in language that excites the interest of your target market, keep working at it. You aren't there yet. The same holds true if your USA is something your competitors can easily match.

Once you do come up with a unique, exciting USA, think of a clear and specific one-sentence promise that's compelling and that packs an emotional punch. Before you go public with your USA, test it. Check with your target clients/customers to see if your USA generates excitement—and sales. If it does, congratulate yourself.

Now you're ready to publicize it. Use every publicity channel available to you to get word out on how your USA benefits your customers and meets their needs. Remember to include information on how "top-quality" or "24/7" service or whatever it is you're providing will make them feel. Facts help, but feelings are what really sell products. As your product or service gets used, remember to gather—and use—enthusiastic testimonials. And remember to always deliver on your USA. Advertising expert William Bernbach once said, "No matter how skillful you are, you can't invent a product advantage that doesn't exist." Your USA is *not* a gimmick. It's the foundation for your business and publicity success.

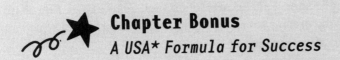

Chapter Bonus
A USA* Formula for Success

focus on a single niche (i.e., a marketplace gap that no one else is filling)

\+

publicize your USA

\+

deliver on your promises/become known as the quality provider of your USA

\=

phenomenal success

*USA = unique selling angle

Part II

Tools of the Publicity Trade

4 Connecting the DOTS (Details of the Story)

News Release How-Tos

"To speak of 'mere words' is much like speaking of 'mere dynamite.'"

—C. J. Ducasse

A news release (also called a "press release" or a "media release") is a one- or two-page text you prepare and send to media outlets. If it's well done, it becomes your key to getting the publicity ball rolling for your business. A good news release can earn you a mention on a news program, an interview on a talk show, or an article in a newspaper or magazine.

Results like that—sustained on an ongoing basis—build your credibility and draw customers. Your news release, therefore, is your most important publicity tool. It's the most-often-used avenue of contact with the media.

Go with the (Information) Flow

Media people appreciate it when you present your news release information in what's called "inverted pyramid" style. In this style of writing, the conclusion, or summary, is presented first, the second most important fact or supporting material is presented second, the third most important fact or supporting material is presented third, and so on.

The inverted pyramid style is the way journalists compose their own news stories—for a very practical reason. Read any news article and you'll notice that as you trim the story from the bottom up, you are cutting out the least essential facts first. As news people have limited space in their papers and on their programs, they often have to shorten a story. The inverted pyramid style allows them to do this easily and quickly while retaining the most important information.

Yes, Looks Do Matter (Formatting Your News Releases)

Media people also expect a certain format, or "look," to news releases.

There are two basic news release formats: the standard news release format and the special events news release format.

Standard News Release Format

Let's first take a look at how a standard news release (see Figure 4.1) is formatted. We'll analyze this release, element by element, to get a better understanding of standard news release format. (My explanatory comments are included.)

Contact Information

Smith's Auto Paint Shop, 401 Main St., Torquay, MI 48167
Contact: Richard Smith, 810-216-1554 or rsmith@ameritech.net

If you don't print your release on your company letterhead, make sure you include a line that identifies your company at the top of your release. The second line provides contact information—the phone number and E-mail address of the person reporters can get in touch with to ask for more information.

Release Date

FOR IMMEDIATE RELEASE

This line is called the "release date" and tells reporters and news producers when they can broadcast or print the story. It indicates the earliest date you think audiences should get your information. "FOR IMMEDIATE RELEASE" means the media person is free to report your information right away.

Figure 4.1 *Standard News Release Format*

NEWS RELEASE

Smith's Auto Paint Shop, 401 Main St., Torquay, MI 48167
Contact: Richard Smith, 810-216-1554 or rsmith@ameritech.net

FOR IMMEDIATE RELEASE
ATTENTION FEATURE EDITORS

"Celebrate Silver" Art Contest Helps Budding Artists Shine

DETROIT, MI, January 20, 2002: Budding artists in Detroit-area elementary schools will have an opportunity to "celebrate silver" this month and win a $250 prize for the top "silver" art work with an automotive theme. Silver is now the top choice in auto colors, and it's a favorite with young artists too. Smith's Auto Paint Shop (www.smithautopaint.com) is sponsoring the "Celebrate Silver" art contest.

Students can submit clay, paintings, or wire sculptures—any media, in fact—as long as it's silver. (To give the kids a helping hand, the paint shop has arranged with an art supply store to provide nontoxic paint to participating schools.)

Richard Smith, owner of the paint shop, came up with the idea when his ten-year-old son, Kyle, and some of his friends asked for silver paint for model cars they were making. "They fell in love with the color, just the way their parents do," Smith says. "We always knew silver was popular with vehicle owners. Now it's officially number one." A just-released survey by DuPont, Smith says, puts silver at the top and sends white, which held that spot for several years running, down to the number two spot. Black comes in third.

"My son and his friends really got into their silver projects and turned out some fantastic art work. Their art teacher even contacted me and said she was amazed at the creativity displayed. A few days later, the results of the survey came out—and the idea of the 'Celebrate Silver' contest was born. Detroit's an automotive town. I think this is a great way to help kids celebrate our heritage—and have some fun too."

-more-

Page 2

Contest rules can be obtained, and requests for the paint made, by calling Robin Carter at Smith's Auto Paint Shop at 810-216-1554.

Smith estimates that his paint shop now applies, on an annual basis, 10,000 gallons of silver paint to car bodies in need of a new look.

Smith's Auto Paint Shop has been in business since 1995 and offers a complete lineup of paint services, including paint chip repair and total body repainting for all types of vehicles.

The deadline for art contest entries is March 31. To coincide with the contest, Smith's Auto Paint Shop is offering a "Celebrate Silver" 15 percent discount to new and returning customers.

# # #

STORY PREP INFORMATION:

Robin Carter—810-216-1554—perky and approachable, paint enthusiast

Richard Smith—810-216-1554—comfortable on camera; offers concise, energetic answers to questions about the "Celebrate Silver" art contest —and everything else you ever wanted to know about auto paint shops—but were afraid to ask

Kyle Smith and friends—810-216-1554—fifth graders at Donaghue Elementary art class are happy to provide kid's-eye views on the "Celebrate Silver" art contest (School location: 900 Ritter Avenue, Torquay, Michigan)

Anne Devon—248-980-3124—upbeat art teacher at Donaghue Elementary welcomes you to an art class with "Celebrate Silver" projects in progress

-more-

Page 3

Website: ("Celebrate Silver" art contest website: www.smithautopaint
.com/silver) ·

Seasonal tie-in: Fifth-grade art teacher Anne Devon will talk about the
need to find entertaining and challenging indoor activities for kids in the
winter months.

Photo opportunity: Donaghue Elementary School art teacher Anne
Devon will hold "Celebrate Silver" art classes, in which students prepare
entries Mondays, Wednesdays, and Fridays, February 12 through March
15, 2002, from 10 to 11 A.M.

Assignment editors: Camera crews welcome.

If there is a reason the information in your release should not be made public
until a certain date, then the release date should state "DO NOT RELEASE
BEFORE [DATE]" or "HOLD FOR RELEASE UNTIL [DATE]."

Attention Line

ATTENTION FEATURE EDITORS

The attention line should be used only if you are distributing your press release
widely—say, if you're using a wire service to send out your release. In this case,
it's meant to alert your targeted media people to a story they might find of interest. You can decide which media people are most likely to cover your story—tech
editors, food editors, start-up editors, and so on—and then mark the release to
their attention. In many busy newsrooms, a departmental assistant is the first to
sort through the news releases that come in—and to toss out any that aren't of
interest. If you make it easy for the departmental assistant to understand which
reporter or news producer should see your release (by including an attention line),
you may help avoid a quick trip to the recycling bin.

Headline

"Celebrate Silver" Art Contest Helps Budding Artists Shine

Drop a space beneath the release date/attention line and then type your headline as shown. Drop another space after the headline.

Like your lead, or opening sentence, headlines are make-it-or-break-it elements of news releases. They should be straightforward. They should also provoke interest. Many media people won't read the body of your release if the headline isn't a grabber. The headline here plays on the words *silver* and *shine* to add interest. Here are some other ways to add interest to a headline:

- Offer tips: "Local Chocolate Shop Offers Six Tips on Making Valentine's Day Memorable"
- Use alliteration: "Farley's Health Foods: Nonfattening Fun Foods"

Dateline

DETROIT, MI, January 20, 2002:

The location from which the release is distributed (usually the city where your office is located or the location of an event about which you're writing) appears next. Immediately after the location, indicate the date the release is distributed. These two elements—the city and the date—are called the "dateline." The body of the release follows the dateline.

Lead

Budding artists in Detroit-area elementary schools will have an opportunity to "celebrate silver" this month and win a $250 prize for the top "silver" art work with an automotive theme. Silver is now the top choice in auto colors, and it's a favorite with young artists too. Smith's Auto Paint Shop (www.smithautopaint.com) is sponsoring the "Celebrate Silver" art contest.

Students can submit clay, paintings, or wire sculptures—any media, in fact—as long as it's silver. (To give the kids a helping hand, the paint shop has arranged with an art supply store to provide nontoxic paint to participating schools.)

The lead is the first sentence or paragraph. It should be written in the inverted pyramid style as it is here. The first sentence provides the gist of the story—the key facts about the "Celebrate Silver" contest. A fact about a current trend (preference in auto colors) follows. This strengthens the news value of the contest. The tie-in to a trend works here because it's relevant both to the contest and to the business sponsoring the contest.

Note: media people don't like to include the phone numbers to businesses they write about in their articles. (It rings too much of free advertising.) Websites, however, are much more likely to be included. Why? Because websites usually include not only contact information but also background information about a business. Therefore, they are viewed as sources of additional information for readers and viewers.

Body

> Richard Smith, owner of the paint shop, came up with the idea when his ten-year-old son, Kyle, and some of his friends asked for silver paint for model cars they were making. "They fell in love with the color, just the way their parents do," Smith says. "We always knew silver was popular with vehicle owners. Now it's officially number one." A just-released survey by DuPont, Smith says, puts silver at the top and sends white, which held that spot for several years running, down to the number two spot. Black comes in third.

The body of the news release provides supporting facts and information that strengthen the appeal of the story.

Note that Richard Smith writes about himself in the third person. Even if you are writing a release yourself, don't write in the first person. A news release should read as much as possible like a newspaper article. By citing a survey—and by noting that it's "just-released" (fresh news), Smith further increases the chances that the media will cover his story.

> "My son and his friends really got into their silver projects and turned out some fantastic art work. Their art teacher even contacted me and said she was amazed at the creativity displayed. A few days later, the results of the survey came out—and the idea of the 'Celebrate Silver' contest was born. Detroit's an automotive town. I think this is a great way to help kids celebrate our heritage—and have some fun too."
>
> Contest rules can be obtained, and requests for the paint made, by calling Robin Carter at Smith's Auto Paint Shop at 810-216-1554.

The personal anecdote about his son adds human interest. Note: this works only if the anecdote is relevant to—and supports—the "news" in your release.

Smith estimates that his paint shop now applies, on an annual basis, 10,000 gallons of silver paint to car bodies in need of a new look.

This fact supports the secondary story here (trend toward the popularity of silver as a vehicle color). Facts, figures, and statistics like this make your news much more attractive to the media than unsupported generalizations or statements of opinion.

Smith's Auto Paint Shop has been in business since 1995 and offers a complete lineup of paint services, including paint chip repair and total body repainting for all types of vehicles.

Include a brief description of your company and what it does, as shown.

The deadline for art contest entries is March 31. To coincide with the contest, Smith's Auto Paint Shop is offering a "Celebrate Silver" 15 percent discount to new and returning customers.

The deadline for the contest encourages the media to move quickly on covering your news. The special offer (designed to draw customers to your business) will probably be included in one sentence at the end of the article.

# # #

Type three hatch marks at the bottom of the release to indicate the end.

The news release is complete without the story prep information section that follows. But the additional information is tailored to media needs and helps "sell" this story to the media. It suggests appealing interviewees and offers up a website as a source of additional information.

Story Prep Information

STORY PREP INFORMATION:

Robin Carter—810-216-1554—perky and approachable, paint enthusiast

Richard Smith—810-216-1554—comfortable on camera; offers concise, energetic answers to questions about the "Celebrate Silver" art contest—and everything else you ever wanted to know about auto paint shops—but were afraid to ask

Kyle Smith and friends—810-216-1554—Fifth graders at Donaghue Elementary art class are happy to provide kid's-eye views on the "Celebrate Silver" art contest (School location: 900 Ritter Avenue, Torquay, Michigan)

Anne Devon—248-980-3124—upbeat art teacher at Donaghue Elementary welcomes you to an art class with "Celebrate Silver" projects in progress

Website ("Celebrate Silver" art contest website: www.smithautopaint.com/silver)

Providing story prep information alerts media people to the fact that you know the process involved in "making" a news story. In other words, you understand their needs and will be easy to work with.

Seasonal Tie-In

Seasonal tie-in: Fifth-grade art teacher Anne Devon will talk about the need to find entertaining and challenging indoor activities for kids in the winter months.

Mention of a seasonal tie-in does a lot to strengthen your news. Think how often you hear stories on the TV news that start with seasonal tie-in openers. The story here could be introduced with something along the lines of "Parents and teachers are always looking for entertaining and challenging indoor activities for kids in the winter months. Now there's a contest that's keeping a lot of fifth graders busy. . . ."

Photo Opportunity

Photo opportunity: Donaghue Elementary School art teacher Anne Devon will hold "Celebrate Silver" art classes, in which students prepare entries Mondays, Wednesdays, and Fridays, February 12 through March 15, 2002, from 10 to 11 A.M.

Assignment editors: Camera crews welcome.

Providing this information in a release signals to TV media that there is a story here that will work well on camera (visuals of appealing kids creating art projects). Adding the "Camera crews welcome" signals that you know how the media operate and will be easy to work with.

Overall Strategy

In the "Celebrate Silver" news release, the business owner has two desired results:

1. He wants to get people who need paint jobs on their cars to consider Smith's Auto Paint Shop. This is done two ways: (a) by presenting the paint shop in a positive light as "giving back" to the community and (b) through the 15 percent discount offer.
2. He wants to create interest in the service that Smith's Auto Paint Shop provides and get people to think about repainting their cars by relating a just-reported fact that ties into the business—the popularity of the color silver as a choice for vehicle paint.

To be attractive to the media, your news release needs to provide information they believe will be of interest and value to the audiences they serve. If Smith's Auto Paint Shop simply sent out a news release that announced a 15 percent discount, the news release would be a nonstarter. Because this release announces a benefit to media audiences—in this case, Detroit-area students—it has a good chance of being picked up as a story.

Special Events News Release Format (the Five W's)

Special events merit their own news release format. The structure that distinguishes a special events news release (see Figure 4.2) is the "Five W's" format, which provides the who, what, when, where, and why of your special event in a highly readable fashion.

Using this format for special events helps prevent your release from falling through the cracks. It allows you to help busy newspeople to decipher your information quickly. Because of this distinctive and clean format, a media person who specializes in your field or industry is more likely to pay attention to the time and date and—if interested—attend or assign someone else to attend.

Public Service Announcement (PSA) News Release Format

The Federal Communications Commission (FCC) requires that radio and television stations provide a certain amount of airtime on a no-charge basis to serve the public interest. This means your local broadcast media will report on meetings and events sponsored by nonprofit organizations, or by for-profit businesses if the event benefits a nonprofit organization.

Figure 4.2 *Special Events News Release Format*

NEWS RELEASE

Holloway Community Center, 8 Grange Road, Parkersville, RI 72183
Contact: Ivy Rendell
(505) 380-1432
rendell@e-camp.com

FOR IMMEDIATE RELEASE
ATTENTION: TECH & FEATURE REPORTERS

"E"-Camp Open House:
Kids Can Build a Computer or Start a Virtual Store

WHAT: "E"-Camp Day Program Open House—an opportunity for kids who want to use summer vacation to learn how to build a computer, launch a Web site, or create an online store.

WHO: The "E"-Camp Open House is sponsored by Rhode Island Parents for Alternative Summer Educational Programs. It's open to all children, ages 8 through 13, who want to learn more about computers and have fun doing so.

WHEN: Saturday, May 13, 2002, 2–4 P.M.

WHY: Because not all kids "take" to traditional summer camp programs. ("E"-Camp is the answer.)

WHERE: Holloway Community Center
8 Grange Road
Parkersville, Rhode Island

# # #

Radio and TV stations publicize these events via public service announcements (PSAs), which are ten- to sixty-second spots read by a news broadcaster.

Figure 4.3 *Public Service Announcement News Release Format*

Szikorski Medical Supplies, 2056 River Street, Pawtucket, RI 45698

Contact: Ralph Szikorski
            453-342-5466
            bromleigh@bac.net

PUBLIC SERVICE ANNOUNCEMENT

:30 Seconds
Asthma Relief Foundation

On June 21, 2002, Szikorski (SHI-CORE-SKEE) Medical Supplies will give out free first aid kits in exchange for a $20 donation to the Asthma Relief Foundation.

Since 1952, the Asthma Relief Foundation has helped in the fight against asthma by providing funds for research on the causes of asthma and methods for relief.

To get your free kit, stop by Szikorski Medical Supplies at 2056 River Street on June 21. Want more information? Call 453-342-5466.

Your PSA news release (see Figure 4.3) should be easy for a news broadcaster to read. That's why the trick of writing a good PSA is to make it sound like something a person would say out loud. Read it aloud to test it. If you find it awkward as spoken text, finesse it until it reads right.

How long should your PSA be? A PSA is usually one minute long or less. You can call the stations you target to ask about the timing.

Speakers generally talk at a rate of 125 words per minute, so a one-minute PSA should be about 125 words long, a thirty-second PSA should be about sixty-two words long, and so on.

Your PSA should deliver the who, what, when, where, why, and how (to request tickets, for example) information pertinent to your event. Be sure to include a contact person and his or her address, telephone number, and E-mail address.

Send your PSA to the stations you target two to three weeks before the date you want the announcement broadcast. Be sure to include a brochure or cover letter that highlights the good work your group or organization is doing, especially if your organization isn't well known.

If you are sending your PSA to quite a few stations and you don't have the time to call and ask who is the appropriate person to receive your PSA, address it to the station's Public Service Director. It's better, of course, to address the release to specific selected media people and then to follow up with a phone call to each asking if he or she received the release and expressing your hope that it will see airtime.

Note: If your release contains any hard-to-pronounce foreign names, include the phonetic pronunciation (in capital letters in parentheses) next to the words.

Overall Print News Release Guidelines

News release writing is an art as much as a science. Some variety in format and approach won't raise too many eyebrows. But, in general, you shouldn't stray too far from what's expected.

The following list provides additional basics:

- No release should be longer than two pages.
- Margins should be at least one inch wide on each side of the text.
- Double-space text throughout.
- Don't carry over a paragraph from one page to the next. (The last paragraph on page one should be complete.)
- When there is more than one page, type the word *more* at the bottom of the first page.
- Create a neat and attractive look.
- Use good quality paper—at least twenty-pound weight.
- Use the inverted pyramid style of writing. (The headline and opening sentence contain the gist of your news release. Supporting facts follow, with the most important supporting fact presented just after the opening sentence, and the second most important fact after that, etc.)
- Proofread, proofread, proofread. If you can, have someone else "eyeball" your release also. (Typos, grammatical errors, and misspellings will undermine credibility.)

How to Make Your Content Count

Let's look at why some news releases get results and others don't.

The clearer your grasp of what news is (as media people define it), the better your chances of successfully generating publicity with your news release. Here's how some leading media people have defined news:

"The departure from normal."

—*Leo Rosten, author and journalist*

"News is anything you find out today that you didn't know before."

—*Turner Catledge,* New York Times *editor*

"Stories that are very current and that focus on what people are talking about."

—*Don Nash,* Today *show producer*

"Anything that makes the reader say, 'Gee whiz!' "

—*Arthur McEwen, journalist*

"A good newspaper is a nation talking to itself."

—*Arthur Miller, playwright*

"Something worth knowing by my standards."

—*David Brinkley, author and news anchor*

One thing all these definitions make clear is that whatever you present to a media person as news needs to be interesting.

Today that's truer than ever. Why? Because in this PC-speeded age, information shoots at us from all directions—radio, TV, newspapers, magazines, and the Internet. We're bombarded with messages. We're becoming more and more "bulletproof" to new information. Our attention spans are shorter than ever before. Reporters are like the rest of us—but more so. In a typical week, a reporter at a major daily wades through a stack of news releases and press kits two feet high. More information comes in via E-mail.

That's a lot of material to sort through—and most of it is unusable! Hard to believe, isn't it? But it's true. Most people (who would very much like to get some notice in the media) simply don't take the time to learn what reporters, editors, and producers are looking for. Sue Doerfler, home styles editor at the *Arizona Republic*, for instance, estimates she throws out "two-thirds or more" of her mail and E-mail.

Mike Sante, business editor at the *Detroit Free Press*, estimates that his section of the paper alone gets five hundred press releases per day via fax, mail, and E-mail. The *Free Press*'s departmental administrator sorts through them, he says, and tosses those that don't pass muster.

Media people don't throw away news releases because they're curmudgeonly or antisocial (well, at least not most of them). Reporters very much appreciate people who bring them fresh, creative ideas for stories and features that they can actually use and who minimize the amount of work they will have to do to use the ideas offered.

This is where your superior grasp of what media people consider news and your well-thought-out, well-written news release enter the picture.

News: What It Is—and Isn't—from a Media Person's Point of View

How can you write a release that snags a media person's attention and keeps it?

How do you write a news release that convinces a media person you've given her "news she can use"?

For one thing, you need a great angle.

So, Just What Is a News Angle?

A news angle, or story angle, spells out what's out of the ordinary about your story. Can you find or create a twist or angle that makes your news different, amusing, extraordinary, or unusual? Can you involve a celebrity? Be first? Biggest? Most environmentally friendly?

A news angle is an approach to a story that makes it timely and newsworthy.

Clever lines can provide your angle. Sometimes the line can be an outrageous claim or a provocative comment. A comedian named Joe Garner might get publicity in a news release that claims, "Joe Garner has killed several people and he's going to pay." The release would explain, a few sentences down, that Garner is a regular at a club called Comedy Tonite, where he has "killed customers with laughter, and he's going to 'pay' by donating 7 percent of his income from an upcoming fund-raiser to charity."

A current event to which you can tie your news also can provide your angle. Immediately after the tragic destruction of the World Trade Center towers in 2001, businesspeople nervous about flying were interested in alternatives to face-to-face meetings. Videoconferencing was one solution. One company that makes a low-cost video camera that you can attach to a computer so that people you're meeting with at a different location can see you while you talk over the phone line earned almost a half-page of ink in *USA Today* and in several other publications.

If you're able to make a living making one-of-a-kind creations—jewelry or shawls or hand-carved chairs and cabinets—that's an angle. People are intrigued by those who somehow manage to escape the 9 to 5 grind by tapping into their own creativity.

Other angles might be the fascinating career you left behind to start your own business. Or the unique hobby that you somehow now bring to bear on the way you do business, like the management consultant who's an avid rock climber, for instance. (He takes his business calls on a wireless headset as he's clambering up and down his personal practice wall. He also used principles he'd discovered in the course of his research on management practices to decide what kind of practice wall he should have constructed behind his home and who would build it.)

News Angles: Strong Versus Weak

Following are some concrete examples of news release content that works or doesn't work, depending on the news angle:

Not a News Angle

A reporter reading the following excerpt from a press release would find little of news value:

> Emily's Tearoom, located at 24 Third Street in Westmore, Iowa, is open from 10 A.M. to 5 P.M. daily. Emily's sandwiches and cakes are nutritious and tasty. The restaurant offers a pleasant atmosphere with a Scottish theme and a variety of teas, lunch items, and desserts.

There just isn't enough news here. Lots of restaurants claim to offer nutritious and tasty meals. A Scottish theme, in and of itself, doesn't make for news.

Improved News Angle

> When Emily's Tearoom holds its Grand Opening on June 1 in Westmore, Iowa, it will be the first restaurant to offer high tea in Stokes County. The fresh-brewed aromas of the largest variety of premium teas in Iowa will fill the dainty tearoom as servers pour steaming tea from China pots, in a decor of lace-trimmed tablecloths and rose-patterned teacups. To celebrate its Grand Opening, Emily's will introduce St. George's Tea Cake, an original recipe that owner Emily MacNeil learned from her grandmother.
>
> Each month, Emily's one-of-a-kind restaurant plans to feature entertainment. From 11 A.M. to 2 P.M., June 6 through 11, Emily's patrons can enjoy the music of The Victorian Flautists, a flute ensemble that will play traditional Scottish tunes. Emily's menu offers treats that include cucumber and watercress sandwiches (crusts trimmed, of course), miniature lemon tarts, and fresh-from-the-oven scones. Emily's is located at 24 Third Street and is open from 10 A.M. to 5 P.M., Monday through Saturday.

This is much more promising. A "Grand Opening" means Emily's is new. The fact that it's the first restaurant in a particular area to offer high tea makes it newsworthy too. The musical entertainment is another distinctive feature, as is mention of the exclusive "family recipe" tea cake. All of these facts reassure a media person that there's substance for a story here.

Not a News Angle

Here's a nonstarter:

> If you want to buy pillows that add pizzazz to your decor, visit the Pillows Aplenty website (www.pillowsaplenty.com). You can choose from a huge variety of pillows, and you'll be sure to find something you like.

This reads like an ad. News releases that read like advertisements are at the top of the list of turnoffs for newspeople. They signal to media people that the writer doesn't understand what makes for news.

Improved News Angle

And here's the improved version:

> Launched today, www.PillowsAplenty.com offers the widest variety of decorator pillows in the United States—with more than seven hundred designs to choose from.

Shoppers can select pillows by theme (floral, animal, juvenile, etc.—or any combination thereof). Owner Cheryl Cruchon also offers personalized service offering suggestions and answering any and all questions related to decorating with pillows.

"There's nothing like unique and original pillows to complete a home's decor," Cruchon says. "But finding that just-right pillow always seemed to take countless hours scouring countless stores. I launched PillowsAplenty.com to change all that.

Hmmmm. Much better. "Widest variety" makes this business unique. Stating that there are seven hundred designs seems to back up that claim. The quote, however, would be stronger if it came from a customer or an interior decorator who patronizes the store and is ready to rave.

Not a News Angle

The following information won't excite most media people:

The Walk Kindly Shoe Store offers a variety of nonleather shoes, sandals, and accessories. There's something that's sure to please everyone in the family.

Again, this reads like an ad—and it would find a quick home in the circular file.

Improved News Angle

Walk Kindly Shoe Store is the first cruelty-free shoe store to open in North Dakota. Vegetarians who shun shoes and accessories made of animal hides can now find stylish and comfortable shoes, belts, and handbags made of plant fibers and synthetics at Walk Kindly. The store is located in Rockaway, North Dakota, where the number of people adopting a vegetarian lifestyle has risen by 15 percent over the past three years.

Store owner Arless Corey is a dedicated vegetarian. She and many of her friends find leather shoes and accessories objectionable for their personal use. Her new store offers stylish and comfortable alternatives to leather items.

Corey is a passionate and outspoken defender of animal rights and is willing and able to mix it up verbally with vegetarian-bashers. "I know I'm right, and it's a pleasure to speak for creatures that can't speak for themselves. I'm ready to rumble," Corey declares.

Rewritten, the "cruelty-free" shoe store information presents some interesting possibilities to a media person. Walk Kindly is the first shop of its sort in the state. It answers a need for the growing number of vegetarians in the area it serves. And broadcast media, especially talk shows that enjoy controversial guests, will welcome an "outspoken" guest who's "willing and able to mix it up."

And What Exactly Is "Timely" News?

You'll hear it over and over again: presenting media people with "timely" news is key to achieving success in the publicity process.

What exactly is timely news? Well, let's look at what's *not* timely. Any news that can be described as "old," "stale," or "tired" is not timely. To be timely, your news must be, or appear to be, fresh and new.

That said, what then qualifies as timely news? Anything new about your business or organization is a start—new products, new hires, a new location, or a new building.

Or, you can release the results of a survey or a poll you've conducted. Media people consider statistically valid survey results to be real news, especially if the results are surprising or unexpected. If your survey clicks with the media and you conduct it annually, you can earn a lot of ink this way. Why not conduct a survey on consumer attitudes on issues related to your business? You can then provide the results to the media including a line in your press release like: "According to a survey conducted by Your Company, etc."

An award, contest, anniversary, celebration, or special event can be news. You can initiate your own award. December is an especially good month to send out a "Top Ten of the Year" list. For the past few years, for example, Nell Minow, author of *The Movie Mom's Guide to Family Movies*, has picked the "ten best family movies of the year." She issues her list in December. The list is a great way for Minow to keep her book in the public eye and to continue her crusade for good family films as well. Minow also reviews movies each week on several radio stations and maintains a website (moviemom.com) that reviews current movies and videos.

If you don't have the time or resources to issue your own award, why not sponsor an existing awards program? The Athena Awards, for example, are given annually by the Athena Foundation (athenafoundation.org), an international organization to recognize leadership in women. Because the organization seeks sponsors in communities throughout the United States, small businesses have an opportunity to garner "piggyback" publicity by sponsoring an existing and increasingly prestigious award.

Awards and contests can be particularly valuable as timely news items because they lend themselves to "twofer" news coverage. You can announce them when they begin—then report on results when they wrap up.

A donation of money to a good cause is also news. Philanthropy makes you feel good—and it's great publicity. Highlights of your—or your employees'—volunteer activities or new twists on charitable endeavors are especially newsworthy.

The Four Magic Media Words

What are the four magic media words? *One of a kind.*

Just as unique businesses are more likely to get publicity, one-of-a-kind news releases are more effective with the media. So what can you do to make your release one of a kind?

Present reporters with opportunities for experiences that involve them. Invite a reporter over to watch your gourmet chocolate chip cookies being made. Offer to clean or "calm" a reporter's office using your company's new aromatherapy-scented spray cleaner or your feng shui expertise.

Be as visual as possible. Send your media contacts a photograph that drives your story home in a compelling way. Recently, one mother active in the Mothers Against Drunk Driving (MADD) campaign called a press conference. At the press conference, she sat behind a table stacked high with a mound of beer six-packs her underage daughter had purchased easily from unscrupulous or careless liquor stores. A photo with a caption explaining the significance of the display might have been as effective.

News Angles—from Fizzle to Sizzle

Present a weak news angle, as in the news release in Figure 4.4, and you won't earn more than a small calendar item in the media or a short mention on broadcast news.

In Figure 4.5 on page 74, the same story is presented with a different and much stronger angle. The rewritten news release—same story as in Figure 4.4 but with a stronger angle—scored an invitation to appear on a TV talk show and landed feature articles on the front page of the Lifestyles section, including huge color photos, in the *Seattle Post Intelligencer* two years in a row.

Figure 4.4 *News Release with Weak News Angle*

Men of Ebenezer A.M.E. Zion Church, Seattle
Contact: Steve Adams, 212-412-4238
FOR IMMEDIATE RELEASE

Ebenezer Church Hosts "Fishers of Men" Day

Ebenezer Church will host the annual "Fishers of Men" day to honor men in the church. The event is organized by David H. Dudley III, the president of the Ebenezer men's group. Dudley has organized this event for three years in a row. This year the church will honor Webbie Jackson, Hal Raines, Kenneth Archie, Charlie James, Bobbie Wooten, and Robert Williams, Ph.D.

# # #

Source: Talion.com "Red Dog" Publicity (talion.com)

Notice how the release in Figure 4.5 gives the media a timely and compelling reason to cover the event (an opportunity to counterbalance negative media and honor men whose quiet heroism often goes unnoticed and unrewarded), ties the story into an upcoming event (Father's Day), and mentions an interesting variety of individuals who can be featured in the story.

How to Hype-Proof Your News Releases

Here's an entrepreneurial nightmare: you actually have a breakthrough new product—the next Coca-Cola, or safety pin, or headphone radio. But every time you try to interest the media, you get a cold shoulder.

Why? It's possible you're using language that comes across as hype.

What exactly is hype?

Hype is the attempt to interest people in a product through overblown claims and unsubstantiated praise. For example, you're a shoe store owner who is launching a new line of boots and you write a news release with phrases like, "most com-

Figure 4.5 *News Release with Great News Angles*

Men of Ebenezer A.M.E. Zion Church, Seattle
Contact: Steve Adams, 212-412-4238
FOR IMMEDIATE RELEASE

Local African American Men Who Are Everyday Heroes to Be Honored on Father's Day, June 18

The media sometimes misses opportunities to portray black men in positive roles. Here is an opportunity to make a positive statement.

Unsung heroes in Seattle's African American community will be given awards on Father's Day, June 18, at 3 P.M. Six men—devoted fathers, community leaders, entrepreneurs, and steady, dependable blue-collar workers, will receive awards that recognize their roles as "Fishers of Men." The event seeks to honor ordinary men who help to provide young black males with a positive image of who they are.

"Fishers of Men" refers to a biblical passage that exhorts men to become role models in a manner that will capture the attention of others, who will then follow.

The program is sponsored by the Men of Ebenezer A.M.E. Zion Church. The men traditionally honored are mainly nine-to-five workers, many of whom are ignored when heroes or role models are honored. "This was the first time my dad has ever been recognized for anything," said Marvin McWilliams Jr., after his seventy-four-year-old father, Marvin McWilliams Sr., received the award last year.

Coverage of this event provides important weight to counterbalance the frequent negative press about African American men. Impromptu camera crews welcome.

# # #

Source: Talion.com "Red Dog" Publicity (talion.com)

fortable boots you'll ever wear," "hikers will be wowed," "fit your feet like a glove," and so on. But you don't back up any of these claims.

That's hype.

Now, let's say you are the owner of that same shoe store and you write a release about a new product—Aussiclogs, a hiking boot made using a new Australian-processed leather that adapts to the wearer's foot instantly and requires no breaking in. The boots are comfortable from day one—even if you trek ten miles in them the first day you wear them.

You know the Aussiclogs story has a lot of potential. But you also know it'll be ignored if the media think it's just hype. You know your job is to convince them it's news, not hype. To do this, you supply facts—from credible sources—to back up and "prove" your news release's claims. These facts can include the following:

- **Scientific proof**—a report, say, of the results of a test by an objective and credible organization—The International Foot Health Institute, for example (If the manufacturer doesn't provide this kind of information, you don't necessarily have to commission a study yourself. You can do some research. Has any organization tested the properties of the new type of leather used in Aussiclogs and found it superior? You can quote the findings in a sentence or two.)
- **Results of a survey collected objectively**—input, for example, from hikers who have trial-tested the boots
- **Testimonials**—quotes by celebrity hikers, foot doctors, and professionals like forest rangers, cashiers, and so on who walk or stand a lot in the course of their work

You collect these facts, and you're more than halfway there. To doubly ensure that the media will be receptive, *tie your news into a trend*. Let's say you've done a little research and you know that the number of people hiking wilderness trails has increased 24 percent over the past two years. Cite the authoritative source for this data in your release. Then note that although more and more people find hiking an appealing pastime, some people still shy away from it because they tried it once and their feet blistered. Present Aussiclogs as a solution to the problem—a way to enable people to join the crowds flocking to newly popular wilderness trails.

Then send your release to media people who specialize in business, lifestyle, fashion, and health.

In addition, contact a select group of key media people—a hiking columnist for a hiking magazine, a foot doctor who writes a syndicated column on foot health, a travel writer who regularly reports on fantastic new gear, and so on. Offer them a free evaluation pair of Aussiclogs. (See Figure 5.18 on page 142 for an example of a product request postcard you can enclose with your pitch letter.) Contact them early enough so that you can use excerpts from any positive reviews/mentions that result in your ongoing publicity efforts.

Congratulations! You've hype-proofed your media efforts.

Target, Target, Target

Is there a particular local publication that writes about your industry? Or a radio or TV program that deals with related issues? Figure out which reporter at a particular media outlet is most likely to cover your business. Is it the small-business editor? The home decorating reporter? The food columnist? The producer of the automotive news talk show? Give them a call and let them know who you are and where your expertise might be helpful to them. Share your expertise. Share your information. Tell them about websites where they can find statistics about your industry. Tell them about trends developing in your area of expertise.

Ask the media people you contact for the names and numbers of local freelancers who write about and report on your industry. Give the reporters and freelancers you select a call and offer to be a resource for them as well.

Establish yourself as a source, an expert that newspeople can call for a quote or information when they're working on a story about your service or industry.

"This is more important than anything else," says Mike Sante, business editor at the *Detroit Free Press*. "Even if the reporter rejects your idea for a story, get yourself onto his or her Rolodex. Are you an expert on entrepreneurial financing? The pet care industry? Become a source. Establish relationships with the reporters who cover those industries. Ask them directly, 'Can you put me in your Rolodex? I'll be a good source for you.'

"Good reporters are always looking to build their list of sources," Sante says. "Later, when they write a story and it touches on your area of expertise, they are likely to call you and you'll end up quoted in their stories." Sante adds, "Keep in mind when you call a reporter that they are probably getting calls from at least ten other people that day. Be efficient. Have your pitch down. Present your credentials and tell them your idea."

Maintain contact. Be friendly, upbeat, businesslike, and brief. Always respect their time.

Checklist for Producing a News Release That Gets Results

If you're going to take the time and effort to put together a news release, make sure it benefits your business. Think strategically. Don't make news for the sake of making news. That's a luxury that businesspeople can't afford. Your news release should tie back to—and support—your marketing efforts.

Here's a checklist to help you do that:

✔ *Target your news release.*

Every newspaper, magazine, E-'zine, and radio and TV program operates with a specific audience in mind. Look for the media outlets your potential customers read and listen to. These are the ones you should approach.

If you are located in a small town or suburb and run a local print and copy shop, a hairdressing salon, or a landscaping/lawn service, and so on, sometimes all the business you need can be drawn from your local area. For businesses that draw from a local customer base, your target media outlets will include the local newspapers and local TV and radio programs and talk shows.

Send your news release to the appropriate local media people. To make your release "newsworthy"—in their judgment—first analyze their publications and programs to find out what kinds of stories they favor. Tailor your news to their preferences.

If you need to look beyond the local area for clients/customers, then you also need to look beyond the local media for publicity. Plan accordingly.

Note: Interestingly, sometimes it's easier for a small business to place a story in a large metropolitan daily than in a small hometown paper, which can be idiosyncratic in its editorial policy. If you continue to strike out with your hometown newspaper, don't hesitate to approach your city daily—which, in all probability, will be as well read by your target market as your hometown paper. Exceptions: the *New York Times*, the *Los Angeles Times*, the *Chicago Tribune*, the *Boston Globe*, the *Washington Post*, and other newspapers of this caliber draw a national and international readership, so they are really "national" newspapers. If one of these newspapers happens to be your "hometown" daily, you will need a very strong, well-angled story that ties into national trends to make a placement work with them.

✔ Tie your news release to a trend or upcoming event.

Whenever possible, tie your news into other current news and trends, upcoming events, holidays, anniversaries, or other celebrations. This greatly increases your chances for success.

✔ Be creative.

During the Bush-Gore presidential campaign, NBC's *Today* show gave a free plug to the California Pizza Kitchen. Why? Because the chain baked pizzas shaped like the two presidential contenders. Don Nash, supervising producer of the show, says creativity is essential to businesspeople hoping to feature their products on the show. A new brand of potato chips won't be featured on the *Today* show, Nash says, just because it's new. But if the chips are made to look like the *Today* anchors, Matt Lauer, Katie Couric, Ann Curry, and Al Roker, "that's something we could get interested in."

✔ Plan ahead.

Once you target a newspaper or magazine, call or E-mail its advertising department and request a copy of its editorial calendar. (Tip: sometimes you can find these online.) Many publications plan special sections that focus on particular topics throughout the year. Your news will be easier to "sell" to media people if it's a good fit for an upcoming special section.

✔ Write an attention-getting news release headline.

Your news release headline should grab and hold a reporter or assignment editor's attention. It should make them want to read on. Use active sentences that convey action and get to the point. Be simple and straightforward. Try to include the benefit to the media's audience in your headline.

Following are some examples:

- "Six Ways to Make Tax Season Pain-Free"—for an accounting business. Time your release, of course, to be sent out just as tax season is about to start.
- "Boost Your Property Value with Trees"—for a landscaping service. Time this one for release in the spring or fall, which are top tree-planting times.

- "Three New Ways to Keep a Car Rust-Free on Salty Highways"—for a release announcing a new car wax. Provide the three tips and then include a line noting that these tips are provided by you (the manufacturer of the new wax). Time it for release just before heavy snows start falling.
- "Blue: the Hot New Color for Room Decor—and for Picture Frames"—for a frame shop announcing a new collection of picture frames. This headline enhances the news value of the release by tying it into a color trend.
- "New Dessert Helps You Lose Weight"—for a health food restaurant that's launching a new low-cal dessert. This would be especially effective in January when most people are trying to lose extra holiday pounds.

✔ Make the lead (first sentence/paragraph) deliver on the promise of the headline.

After you attract their attention with a magnetic headline, your lead (the first sentence of your press release) should deliver on the promise of the headline.

How? Read your daily newspaper. Notice how the first sentence of each news article tries to grab your attention. Notice how the writers use simple and clear language. Notice how the reporters offer unique and interesting information. That's the way media people like their information packaged. That's the way to write your releases.

Note: you don't always have to answer the who, what, when, where, and how questions in the lead (or opening) sentence of your news release. You can do that in the second sentence. Be strategic. Open with a sentence that keeps a media person's attention and engages his or her interest.

✔ Brag (but only in quotes).

Press releases can express enthusiasm and excitement about your product/service/event, but words of high praise should be presented in quotations. Why? Testimonials, quotes, and impressive statistics ring truer in quotations than if you appear to be tooting your own horn. That's why the only acceptable way to "brag" in a news release is to have someone else do it—in a quote.

Examples:

"Customer service isn't just a couple of words in a brochure at Friendly Fred's Print Shop," says customer Caroline Harley. "Traffic around the store is hectic, and parking is sparse. But Fred Morris, the store manager, will actually wait on the curb so that his regular customers can make 'drive-by' pickups."

"The real beauty of Lester's leather furniture is its fantastic versatility. Lester's offers every style of leather sofa and chair, including traditional, rustic, or contemporary," says decorator Ann Hollaway, who shops frequently at Lester's Leather Seating Shop.

Note: Include the phone numbers of people you quote. Reporters may want to verify your information or call and get original quotes.

✔ Let them know who you are.

In the last paragraph of your press release, include a "thumbnail sketch" describing your company. This can highlight (very briefly) a recent key achievement. Also, point reporters in the direction of additional sources of information about your company, such as a Web address.

✔ Lighten reporters' workloads.

Make it easy for reporters to cover your story. Include a fact sheet (see Figure 5.11 on page 126) and/or a list of suggested story angles (see Figure 5.7 on page 120), or add a Story Prep Information section to your news release (see Figure 4.1 on page 55, a standard news release sample that includes this information). You can also include talking points or suggested questions for radio/TV/Web broadcast talk show hosts and interviewers (see Figures 5.8 and 5.9 on pages 122 and 123).

✔ Observe protocol in approaching the media, and format your news release properly.

Time-pressed reporters often are grateful for news releases from which they can pull chunks of material. It's not unusual for a reporter to include whole paragraphs of a well-written release in an article. If you write your release to read like a news article, you make it easier for a reporter to use your information.

✔ Include the whens and wheres.

Always include the time and location for any special event, seminar, conference, or speech that you're publicizing.

Twelve Tips to Help You Write More Effective News Releases

1. **Tell the "story behind the story."** For example, if you want to promote your bakery, don't just talk about the kinds of cakes you bake, profits you make, and so on. Talk about how you got the idea for your business after you were laid off and you couldn't repay a loan a friend made to you. The friend was kind and told you not to worry about it. He knew you'd get back on your feet soon. Your wife wanted to show her appreciation for his understanding. She baked one of her special-family-recipe pineapple upside-down cakes and took it to the friend. He loved the cake and told his friends about it. Word spread and people started asking if they could buy one of your wife Marianne's wonderful cakes. Soon you had to quit your new job to help your wife bake her cakes, and a thriving business—Marianne's Wonderful Cakes—was born (and you repaid the debt, too).

Kevin Salwen, small-business editor for the *Wall Street Journal*, offers another fictitious story-behind-the-story example—this one of a small business that has tried to find a company that will back its new product for several years. Finally fed up, the entrepreneurs convince family and friends to put up the needed capital. Then, within weeks, the business is purchased by Microsoft. As Salwen notes, the story-behind-the-story approach makes for a more interesting story than one that simply focuses on the product.

2. **Don't use jargon.** Jargon words will be readily understood only by people in your business. Here's an example:

> The obverse ratio of the new Scanalon 2000 3-D Scanner is a delightful feature of its subtuned loading capabilities, ensuring crisp, clear datalog captures in seconds.

This sentence contains several words I made up. It makes no sense. When you use language loaded with "shop talk," the words fall on outsiders' ears just as confusingly as these fake words. Let's say the Scanalon 2000 is a new scanner and this is what you've been trying to say in the jargon-loaded sample sentence:

> The Scanalon 2000 takes two-dimensional scanners to the next level. It scans three-dimensional objects as easily and accurately as regular scanners scan pictures and photos.

Say so, in just those words!

Media people are impressed with, and grateful for, industry spokespersons who can explain complex concepts in clear and simple language. Spew what sounds like gobbledygook, and they will run—in the other direction.

3. **Provide only the key information.** Simple is better. Provide only enough information to support and illuminate the promise your headline and lead sentence make.

4. **Skip statements that smack of sales pitches.** That means avoid sentences like: "Our prices are unbeatable," "We stand for excellence," and so on.

5. **Don't tease.** If you're a seismologist predicting that a major earthquake will hit a big U.S. city, you need to mention your credentials and tell how you came to that conclusion. Are you a professor of geology at a major university? Did you invent a "better seismograph"? A new way to read existing data? If you don't provide facts and credentials to back up your claims, you will be ignored.

6. **Write simply but with flair.** The average newspaper is written at a fifth-grade reading level—short sentences and short words. Stick to that style, but use those simple words and sentences effectively. Many of the news releases that cross reporters' paths could be ground up and sold as sleeping pills. That includes news releases written by high-priced professionals. Keep it simple. Simple writing is like cold water splashed on busy readers' faces. Simple writing shouldn't mean dull writing. It does mean carefully chosen words. Mark Twain said, "The difference between the right word and the almost right word is the difference between lightning and the lightning bug." Make lightning!

7. **Eliminate all typos, bad spelling, and poor grammar.** They are sloppy and unprofessional. If you can't write well, hire a writer or editor. Search the Web or the Yellow Pages for "editorial services." Or call your local newspaper and ask the business or feature editor to recommend a freelancer.

8. **Include a contact name and phone number on each page of your release and on all other elements of your press kit.** Make it easy for media people to get in touch with you—and to reassemble your kit after parts have been spread out over a cluttered desk.

9. **Always send your news release to a specific reporter or producer.** The *Wall Street Journal* is a business publication, so it might seem that any editor at the *WSJ* should be interested in any business-related story. But the *Journal* has specific columnists and reporters for *each* of these areas of interest: upcoming events, reviews of store catalogs, film, autos, sports, wine, home features, travel, and more. The *Journal* assigns its reporters to "beats"—specific areas of interest. So do most other publications.

If you plan a small campaign (contacting twenty-five to thirty media people) and don't know whom to contact at a particular media outlet, call and ask. Tell the person who answers the phone the kind of newspaper section in which you think your news fits best (business, home style, sports, etc.), and ask him or her for the name and title of the person you should send your release to. Also, ask how that person would prefer to receive your information—by mail, fax, or E-mail. You can attach a Post-it Note to releases you mail, or jot a line on your faxes that says, "I'll call in a day or two to see if you have any questions. Thank you." Sign your name. Like the rest of us, media people respond more positively to the personal touch.

10. **Double-check to make sure you have correctly spelled the names of reporters, editors, and producers to whom you're sending your release.** If you aren't annoyed when someone misspells your name, that's unusual. Don't go to the trouble of personalizing your press contact material only to have the personalization backfire because of a typo.

11. **After you send the release, be available.** Try to be as flexible as possible when reporters call. Bend your schedule. Don't ask them to bend theirs.

12. **Follow up with reporters.** Call three to four days after you send the news release. Prepare your "pitch" before you call. It should be something like this:

> Hello. This is _____. I sent you a news release a few days ago on _____. I just wanted to make sure you received it. I think your audience would benefit by knowing something about _____ because (*state benefits of your product/service*). I'll be happy to chat with you about it.

Say you've invented a new golf product and you've requested the publication's editorial calendar to check on upcoming special golf sections. Your pitch can be more specific, as follows:

> Hello. This is Dan Dolan. I sent you a news release a few days ago on the Ace Putting System. I just wanted to make sure you received it. I understand the *Chicago Tribune* will run a special section on golf in the May 20 edition. I think a story on the Ace Putting System will be a good fit. Your audience includes thousands of golfers who would be interested in knowing there's a new putting practice system that provides computerized feedback on their putting game—and that they can use it all year 'round. I'll be happy to chat with you about it.

Important: call radio and TV stations in the morning to follow up on a news release. Don't call in the afternoon. That's when they're scrambling to prepare the evening news program. When you call, always ask, "Is this a good time for you to talk?" If the answer is no, ask when you can call back.

Go Online, Young Man (and Woman)— E-Publicity Is Low Cost and Effective

If you've used E-mail to send your clients or customers an update about a new product or service you've developed, or to let them know about your company's opening a new facility, you may not realize it, but you've sent out an E–news release. Some people call them E-mail alerts or just plain E-mail. But news releases announce news and special events—and if that's what your messages did, they fit the bill.

The Internet has opened up a tremendous new realm of publicity possibilities for small businesses. Small and home-based businesses can set up websites that rival those of much larger companies in style, content, and appeal. In many ways, although the Internet hasn't quite leveled the playing field, it does smooth down a few of the bumps.

Web commerce is the subject of a whole other book. Let's concentrate here on the fantastic publicity opportunities offered by the Web. These include the ability to send press releases with ease and efficiency (and at ultra low cost) via the Internet.

Tell Me More About "Virtual" Publicity

"Virtual," or Internet-based, publicity—publicity communicated via Web pages or E-mail—evolved naturally as the Internet grew.

The Internet began as something called ARPANet. It was designed late in the 1960s to link military bases, research universities working with the military, and government research facilities. The idea was to find a way to keep these institutions, vital to national defense, linked and up and running in case of outside attack. Today, the Internet is an immense electronic network—a global system of computers connected in order to share files.

The Web, simply put, is a worldwide collection of files that are linked to each other. Files are any of the documents, applications, pictures, and data that can be found on the Internet.

At this writing, 59 percent of the U.S. population, more than 160 million people, go online to keep updated on the news, to search for information, to send and receive E-mail, to participate in online discussion groups, to post messages to online bulletin boards, and to shop. This translates into vast numbers of people who are increasingly more comfortable turning to their PCs to gather and exchange information—including information about products and services that you might offer. You can now sit in your living room, tap a few keys on your laptop, and communicate in "real time" with potential customers in all fifty states and across the globe for the cost of a local phone call. What's more, if you're able to post information or create a website that offers news of value to your target market, *they* may well seek *you* out.

How Can I Begin My E-Publicity Efforts?

At this writing, the chances are very strong that you already have Internet access—and perhaps even a website of your own, either personal or for your business. If you are Web savvy, great! All you need to do is marry your Web smarts with your publicity strategy. The rest of this chapter outlines some of the ways to do that.

If you're an Internet newbie, that's great too! You have a whole exciting "virtual" world to discover. There is nothing daunting about learning to log onto a computer or to send or receive E-mail. The ability to work with E-mail in and of itself will boost you to a whole new level of efficiency and productivity.

What about designing and setting up a website? If you're a newbie and you're planning to pick up HyperText Markup Language (HTML) from scratch, you have a learning curve ahead of you. However, programs like Microsoft's FrontPage allow you to post professional-looking Web pages with almost turnkey ease. Netscape's Composer also has much to offer to website newbies—and Composer is free.

Don't be intimidated. Jump in. Get your feet wet and splash around. It won't be long before tweaking Web pages and uploading files is business as usual.

Why Go Virtual? Because Media People Are Increasingly "E" Inclined

Speaking of business as usual, reporters increasingly prefer to access press releases and press kit materials online. Send them a news release and—if they're interested and want additional information (bio, fact sheet, photos, suggested questions, etc.)—they want to be able to find the text documents online and to download any photos they need from your website. And, actually, it's pretty cool to be able to respond to their request by giving them a uniform resource locator (URL—website address) that they can visit to collect the information. Not to mention how it saves you the time and trouble of printing, packaging, and mailing the additional materials. (One little added benefit: it also saves a tree—or at least a twig or two.)

Media people work under tight deadlines. That's why so many of them have taken to the Net like animatronic ducks to code-laden waters. They like the instant access that the Internet provides. They also like the paperless aspect of it. (In an increasingly complex and cluttered world, it's good to know you don't have to throw yet another pile of paper on your desk or in your files.)

This "E" inclination on the part of media people is good news and bad news. It's good news because it means you can now create and update press kits at a fraction of what it costs to create hard copies. It's bad news in that if you are serious about your publicity efforts, you really need to take the time to master some basic HTML or to get a handle on a program like Microsoft FrontPage or Netscape Composer, which allows you to create your own website.

Note: if you're averse to learning techie-type things, don't despair. HTML is not quite as easy as learning the ABCs, but even the technologically challenged like myself have been able to pick up enough of it to get by. Basic HTML is within the grasp of most people. Organizations like the HTML Writers Guild (hwg.org) offer inexpensive (although fast-paced) classes to help newbies. Many community colleges offer HTML courses as well. You can, of course, hire someone to design a website and your online press kit materials. But software programs like FrontPage and Composer may be a better alternative if cost is an issue.

But Before You Make Your Web Debut . . .

Use your good judgment. If you know your sense of design and "what looks good" is weak, get help. Your website, like your press materials, should reflect positively on you.

What's in a (Domain) Name?

An easy-to-remember Web domain name is one of your best marketing tools. People will increasingly use the Net to gather information on products and services before they buy. This is opening up great opportunities for small-business owners.

Let's say, for example, you run a bee farm and you sell the honey you harvest as Sally's Honey. If you register Sallys-Honey.com as your Web domain, you can integrate all your marketing communications, tying them back to a website. Your business cards, brochures, and honey jar labels—maybe even a billboard that drivers going past your farm could see—all would have your Web address on them. "Sallys-Honey" is easy to remember—even for a driver passing your sign at sixty miles per hour.

Anyone who's interested can log onto the Net, find your site, read about your wonderful honey, and—if he or she wants some—find your prominently displayed contact information, call, and order from you.

Websites extend and enrich all your other marketing efforts.

The Wonderful World of the Web—Congratulations! You're Interactive

Once you create a website for your business, you can provide basic contact information online and set up an E-mail link. Congratulations! You're now interactive. Your Web visitors can use the Internet to contact you and/or provide feedback. You can also create an online catalog and a link to it from your website's home page, providing product information and order forms.

In addition, you can launch a newsletter that you regularly update on your site or even create a discussion group that you host. Why? To draw visitors back to your site. When people return to Sallys-Honey.com to join in the bee-related discussion group, they "pass by" your sales information as they log on. They're reminded of your honey. They might recommend your site to other honey lovers. A reporter specializing in farm issues might check out the discussion group and eventually decide to write an article about you and your business.

An online newsletter serves the same purpose. You provide content of value—in the case of Sallys-Honey.com, to bee and honey lovers, fellow farmers, and honey aficionados. If you update your newsletter regularly, they have a reason to return.

Note: think through how much time you want to devote to maintaining your site. If you build it, they will come. But if they come, you don't want to disappoint them. It's better, for instance, to start out with a very modest newsletter that you update quarterly than with a long, ambitious effort that is simply too demanding to maintain.

Because your newsletter or discussion group would present information of value to people interested in your product or service, it is meant to attract customers to your business. But these uses for the Net fall under the umbrella of marketing. And that's another book. Our focus here is publicity.

Online Press Kits and Other Electronic Wonders: How to Publicize Your Business 24/7

Outside of Internet service provider (ISP) failures and power outages, the Internet never shuts down. It's operational twenty-four hours a day, seven days a week. That's where online press kits come in. Once you get your website running, you can post your press kit online and put the power of the Internet to work for you 24/7.

How?

On your home page, create a link called "Press Room." This is what media people can click on to access your online press kit. (You may want to have the links to each of your press kit elements on your home page. My preference, however, is to keep the home page uncluttered.)

On your "press room" page, post links to all the elements from your press kit. The links should be labeled in a straightforward manner. News release headlines can be posted as links, and visitors can double-click on them to access the texts of the news releases.

Upload and post all the elements that would go into a hard copy press kit: your latest news releases, bio, fact sheet, backgrounder, brochure, testimonials, and even the texts of speeches you've presented that add to your credibility or prestige or that illuminate some aspect of your company or industry. Each of these elements can be a separate page on your website. In addition, you can post scanned copies of magazine, newspaper, newsletter, and trade journal articles about you, your company, or your products and/or services or provide links from your site to the sites where these articles appear online—with each of these also being separate pages.

To see examples of online press kits, visit the IBM Press Room site (ibm.com/press). It contains links to press releases, photos, bios, and a backgrounder, and it includes contact information for media people and others who wish to contact IBM's PR department. In addition, it includes a feedback link for those who wish to send an E-mail to the company. Or take a look at General Motors' home page (gm.com), which has a Company Information area that offers extensive information about the company, including the company history and profile, upcoming events, latest news releases and executive speeches, and a virtual tour of the company's headquarters. And you're welcome to take a peek at my site (hatchigan.com), which I set up using Web publishing software and a little help from my friends.

Online Mailing Lists and Discussion Groups

Another way to get media attention for your business is to participate in online mailing lists and discussion groups, although this is, admittedly, an indirect way to do it. But the fact is that journalists do participate in online groups pertinent to their beats (the areas they cover). There are more than fifty thousand Internet mailing lists, covering every topic imaginable, and many are open to the public. Between ten and ten thousand subscribers participate in each list.

A word of caution here: don't expect much to happen if you are blatantly self-promotional when you interact with these groups. Actually something may happen, but it won't be good. Blatant self-promotion is actively discouraged on the Net. You need to be prepared to offer information of value if you participate in these groups. Answer questions and share your knowledge. If you do that, you may just attract a customer or two, and even a reporter. To find a discussion group related to your business or industry, visit liszt.com.

Make sure you take the time to become familiar with the group and its ways of communication by reading other people's posts for a while before you begin to participate. You'll get a feel for the unwritten rules. When you do post, include your contact information below your signature.

Fun (and Publicity) with E-Mail

E-mail allows you to reach hundreds or even thousands of media people, no matter where they're located—from Texas to Timbuktu—simultaneously and instantly. It is low cost, convenient, and efficient.

Grab 'Em from the Git-Go

Pyramid style is especially important in composing your E-mail pitches and news releases. It's incredibly easy for people on the receiving end to zap an unwanted E-mail to the recycling bin. The subject line and the first sentence of your message will probably be all a media person looks at in order to decide the fate of your message.

Don't risk losing credibility with poor grammar, sloppy punctuation, or bad spelling. Be professional. Read your message out loud to check for tone and to catch mistakes. If anything needs fixing, change it. Check and double-check before you hit Send.

No Spam Please

Remember that there is a downside to the good news about E-mail. Because it's so cheap, many companies and individuals have abused E-mail with the practice of "spamming"—sending unwanted and annoying advertising materials to people who have no interest in what they have to sell. Just as spam mail annoys most people, newspeople who receive E–press releases that deal with subjects outside their area of interest—tech press releases going to a food reporter, for instance—also are justifiably miffed. Sending an E-mail release about your new debugging software to Julia Child is bad. But more subtle miscues also can put reporters off. E-mailing a news release about your new California winery to a wine reporter who specializes only in writing about rare European vintages shows you didn't do your homework. So does misspelling a reporter's name in the body of a news release. Doing this kind of thing annoys a reporter and makes it harder to get her or his attention the next time you try.

E-Mail News Releases: HTML Versus Plain Text

Let's look at how you can use E-mail to create electronic press releases—both plain text and HTML.

A "plain-text" E–news release is just what it sounds like—a news release sent in unadorned type style (see Figure 4.6). You can send your news releases in this way. Or you can use the HTML message formatting option available with most E-mail programs to create something more elaborate. The HTML formatting option allows you to format an E-mail news release to look like a Web page and lets you send graphics, including logos.

This raises a simple question: Which is better to E-mail to media people—HTML news releases or plain-text news releases?

One advantage of plain text is that it's a smaller file size and so doesn't make the reporter wait a long time for the text to come in. Also, it can be read online or offline once it's in a media person's Inbox.

The advantages of HTML news releases are that you can embed your logo in them and use fonts in an eye-catching way.

One problem with HTML news releases is that some of your media recipients' E-mail programs may not be able to "read" HTML. Another problem with HTML news releases is that they are larger-sized files than plain-text E-mails. HTML messages take two or three times longer to download, especially if you've embedded a graphic (like a logo). Reporters (who are often rushing on a deadline) find this longer download irritating. Another drawback of HTML is that a reporter may have to go online each time he or she wants to read your release. And not all E-mail programs can display HTML releases properly. In worst-case scenarios, all they display is the HTML code. This defeats the purpose of using HTML in the first place.

Figure 4.6 *Plain-Text E-Mail News Release*

Subject: Survey: "Scooping" Tops List of Most Annoying Chores
Date: April 2, 2002
From: "Monica Hartwick" <monica@tesh.com>
To: "Reporter's Name Here" <reporter's E-mail address here>

FOR IMMEDIATE RELEASE

4/2/2002

CONTACT: Monica Hartwick, 515-456-7703, monica@tesh.com

SURVEY REVEALS "SCOOPING" TOPS LIST OF MOST ANNOYING CHORES

SANTA CLARITA, CA—A just-released survey conducted by TheErrandStopsHere shows that cleaning up litter boxes and backyards after pets tops the list of "most disliked" chores. The next two most disliked chores, in the order they were rated, were: taking the car in for repair and taking the car in for an oil change.

TheErrandStopsHere is a newly launched errand service available to people in the Santa Clarita business district. "Runners" from TheErrandStopsHere perform chores like booking airline tickets and rental cars, addressing holiday cards, picking up dry cleaning, picking up prescriptions, taking the car in for an oil change, shopping for and delivering groceries, shuttling pets to the groomers, taking the dog for a walk— and, yes, cleaning up after pets—anything, in fact, that saves busy businesspeople time and helps unfrazzle nerves.

- more -

Page 2

TheErrandStopsHere surveyed 430 businesspeople and asked them to rate ten chores on a scale of one to ten, with one being "don't mind" and ten being "dislike extremely."

Here are the results, and the scores received, listed with the most disliked chores at the top of the list:

SANTA CLARITA BUSINESSPEOPLE'S MOST DISLIKED CHORES
1. Cleaning up after pets (9.5)
2. Taking the car in for repair (9.5)
3. Taking the car in for an oil change (9)
4. Booking airline tickets (8)
5. Shopping for groceries (8)
6. Booking rental cars (8)
7. Picking up/dropping off dry cleaning (7.5)
8. Calling in/picking up prescriptions (7)
9. Taking the car in for a wash (7)
10. Waiting for furniture to be delivered (7)

TheErrandStopsHere errand runners are equipped with cell phones and pagers. Charge for errands run is $30 per hour, including travel time. Flat fee arrangements are available. To sign up, Santa Clarita businesspeople can call 515-456-7703 or log onto the company website at http://www.TheErrandStopsHere.com.

For more information about TheErrandStopsHere, please visit: http://www.TheErrandStopsHere.com.

TheErrandStopsHere
27 Palmview Drive
Santa Clarita, CA 91504

Phone: 515-456-7703
Fax: 515-456-7704

In addition, some people have E-mail programs that accept only text posts. And if you are mailing to media people in other countries, you should be aware that it's often very expensive for them to connect to the Internet, and HTML attachments including imbedded graphics add to their expenses.

Due to concerns about security, many people install filters that block incoming HTML E-mail.

One more thing about HTML: you can E-mail an HTML release that looks pristine on your end only to find that the document takes on a life of its own on the receiving end. Line breaks are strange, and some of the characters (bullets, hyphens, fractions, ampersands, etc.) become gobbledygook. This, again, is because some E-mail programs aren't able to read HTML E-mail. There is a solution to this. Most E-mail programs allow you to send your E-mail messages as both plain text and HTML, so that your recipient's E-mail program displays the version it can read best. It's not a perfect solution, however, as some E-mail recipients have to scroll down through garbled HTML to get to the readable plain-text message. In addition, the plain text, which has been extracted from the HTML, may not look well formatted.

My strong personal preference is to send—and receive—plain text. My feeling is that for most media people content is the main concern. And speed is a close second. A recent survey found, in fact, that most people won't wait more than eight seconds for a Web page to download. Imagine how thrilled a reporter is when a cumbersome E-mail clogs up his or her PC long enough for tumbleweeds to blow across wide prairies.

In general, simpler is better. Until universal standards are adapted that enable HTML releases to live up to their potential, plain text is a safer bet.

Two Tips for Producing More Effective E-Releases

Here are two things it's important to remember when communicating with the media electronically:

- **The "Subject" line of your E-release is critical.** Make sure your subject line contains an enticing headline. Reporters receive hundreds of E-mails each day. Make yours stand out.
- **Don't send news releases as attachments to an E-mail.** Many viruses are transmitted as attachments. If a reporter doesn't know you, chances are your attachment will remain unopened.

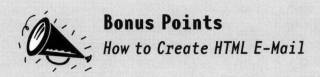

Bonus Points
How to Create HTML E-Mail

The two main Internet browsers, Microsoft Explorer and Netscape, both provide their E-mail users with a basic HTML editor you can use to compose HTML news releases.

To compose HTML news releases in Netscape, take the following steps:

1. Click on Communicator in the menu at the top of the page.
2. On the drop-down menu that appears, click on Messenger.
3. Click on Edit in the new menu that appears.
4. Click on Preferences in the drop-down menu that appears.
5. In Preferences, click on Mail & Groups.
6. Click on Messages.
7. In the box that says "Wrap long lines at," enter the number 62.
8. Now Click on Formatting (which is also in Mail & Groups).
9. Under Message Formatting, select "Use the HTML editor to compose messages."
10. Click on New Message in your main menu.
11. Compose your message. Or, if you've already written your news release, cut it from your Word or text editor document and paste it to constitute the body of the E-mail message you're creating. Use the HTML toolbar you'll see above the message box to select your fonts and font options and to create lists and tables. Note: your recipients won't see the fonts you select unless those fonts are also installed in their computers. Safe bets are Arial, Times Roman, and Helvetica, which are mostly universal.
12. To insert an image (like your company logo), upload the image you want to insert to a Web page. Then click on Insert and select Image. In the Image Location box that appears, enter the URL (the "http" Internet address) for the image you want to insert. Note: the media person to whom you're sending the E-mail will need to be online to view the image this way. Another way to send

images via E-mail is to insert a graphic. Here's how: Click on Insert Image. Click on Choose File. Select the graphic you want to send from your computer files. Netscape will embed the graphic into your E-mail message. Note: this increases the size of the message you are sending—something most reporters do not appreciate, so use this option with care.

13. Double-check to make sure the HTML news release file you are sending is less than 25K. To check your file size, click the Save As option in your E-mail program. (This is under File in Netscape Messenger.) Save the E-mail HTML news release you've created to your PC's desktop as "check.html." This should create a check.html icon on your desktop. Right click on the icon and select Properties from the menu that appears. The Properties window will indicate the file size. If your news release is more than 30K or 40K, change it to reduce the size.

The process for composing HTML news releases is similar in Microsoft Outlook:

1. Click on Tools, then select Options.
2. Click on Send.
3. For Mail Sending Format select "HTML."
4. Click on HTML Settings.
5. To send graphics, select "Send pictures with messages."
6. Click on New Mail in Inbox.
7. Compose your message using the HTML toolbar to achieve HTML effects.
8. To send a graphic, click Insert and select Picture. As in Netscape, you can type in the URL for your graphic or click on Browse to select a graphic from your computer files. The same caveats apply as in sending graphics with Netscape.

Note: in each iteration of Netscape and Microsoft's E-mail programs there are slight changes to the sequence and placement of drop-down bars, icons, and so on. Therefore, your E-mail program might have a slightly different sequence from the ones indicated here.

How to Send Your Electronic News Release to the Media

There are three ways you can distribute your E-releases.

• **Method #1:** If you have a small, targeted group of media people to contact (twenty-five to thirty people), you can prepare your own E-mail media mailing list. Make use of the BCC (blind carbon copy) function of your E-mail to send out a simultaneous multiple mailing to your target media. Here's how: E-mail the news release to yourself, and simply BCC the media people you want to reach.

Using the BCC function for an E-mail sent simultaneously to a large group is more courteous than simultaneously sending the E-mail to the group using the To function. In the latter case, the first thing each recipient sees is twenty-five or thirty other E-mail addresses when they open your message. This distracts from your information, looks unprofessional, and makes the recipient feel as though he or she is reading the electronic version of junk mail.

• **Method #2:** You can purchase media mailing lists and use them to send out your E-releases. Most of these mailing lists are on CDs, with programs designed to streamline the process of selecting your target media and of sending out the E-release. These prepared lists allow you to quickly contact media people who have special interests (automotive, financial, sports, etc.) that dovetail with the news you wish to publicize. E-mail media mailing lists are provided by companies like Bacon's (bacons.com) and Gebbie Press (gebbie.com).

• **Method #3:** You can hire an online news service to E-mail your E-releases for you. Companies like PR Newswire (prnewswire.com), Business Wire (businesswire.com), Internet Wire (internetwire.com), Xpress Press (expresspress.com), and OnlinePressReleases (onlinepressreleases.com) provide this service. Most of these news release services also will write your release for an additional fee.

Use E-Mail to Make Friends with Reporters

There's one additional and often overlooked way to use E-mail to build relationships with reporters. When a media person who reports on your business area or industry writes a substantive article or one you found particularly helpful, send him or her a short E-mail with a detail or two about what you particularly liked, content- or style-wise. This is a good way to make a positive contact with a reporter. Like all of us, they work hard at what they do, and praise is rarer than you might imagine. They will appreciate your comments.

If you have constructive criticism, offer that tactfully as well—but only after you've noted at least two things you found good to excellent in the article. You can also add a bit of information you may know of that's related to the story but that the reporter may not know. This demonstrates your expertise and it may end up in a future article, with attribution to you. The reporter may not even respond to your E-mail except with a curt thank you (if that), but he or she will notice.

Important: remember that everything you "say" to a reporter in an E-mail is "on the record." Don't write anything you'd be uncomfortable seeing in print.

If a reporter does contact you for more information as a result of an E–press release you've sent or a previous contact of another sort, remember that they are always on deadline. Respond quickly to provide whatever she or he needs.

Tip: you may want to consider pitching your feature story exclusively to one media outlet. Many print, broadcast, and online media outlets are highly competitive and exclusives appeal to them.

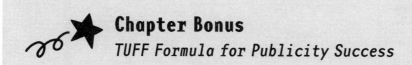

Chapter Bonus
TUFF Formula for Publicity Success

To successfully publicize your business, remember to be TUFF:
- **T**argeted—aim at the right audience and media.
- **U**nusual—give the media new information.
- **F**ocused—present your information clearly and effectively.
- **F**actual—use statistics and/or statements from experts to back up your claims.

5 Package Your News like a Pro

Press Kits That Get Results

"I've never advertised, even though I have a degree in advertising. I don't need to spend money when I'm able to give my business exposure at no cost."

—Lisa Kanarek, founder of HomeOfficeLife.com

A "kit" sounds like something that should be hefty, doesn't it? Certainly press kits can be that. There are companies that create press kits as thick as telephone books. (These, by the way, are not particularly welcome by the time-pressed media.)

In the world of publicity, a press kit is usually as simple as a folder containing a news release and a photo. Remember the nine-by-twelve-inch folders with one or two pockets from your school days? Take a slightly more elegant folder (of about the same size), tuck in the most fascinating and newsworthy information you can produce about your product, service, or company, and you've got a press kit. The kit is usually accompanied by a pitch letter that's paper-clipped to the top of the folder. The pitch letter should "sell" the media person on the story—and get him or her to open the folder.

A well-done press kit can be one of your best tools for selling your news to the media. The key words are *well done*. The reason is simple. Newspeople are naturally skeptical. They wade through floods of hype every day. You need to be savvy in preparing the materials that tell them your story.

Most people can create a press kit. The trick is to create a press kit that successfully tells your story. That's what this chapter will show you how to do.

A well-done press kit should do two things. It should make your story appealing to the media, and it should make media people's work easier.

So, Just How Important Is the "Look of the Book"?

Before we get into what is contained in a press kit, let's consider, for a moment, the importance of how the kit looks. Information is the only thing that matters, right? Unfortunately, it's not quite that easy. The "look of the book" counts too. In fact, it counts very much. Poorly presented material loses credibility.

If you use a standard two-pocket folder, what impression does the opened folder make? Is it balanced? (Don't put all the components in the right-hand pocket, for instance, and leave the left-hand pocket empty. Some people do this and it always looks as though something's missing. Use one-pocket folders if you truly have no use for the other pocket.) Does what's showing above the pockets make a neat and attractive impression? If so, great. If not, perhaps you need to reformat the top pages of your materials.

The paragraphs that follow go into more detail on each of the individual components of a basic press kit: pitch letter, folder, news release, and photo.

Keeping It Simple: Basic Press Kit Ingredients

As mentioned, a press kit can be—and most often is—as simple as a pitch letter attached to a two-pocket folder. Open the folder and inside you'll find a photo on the left side and a news release or two on the right.

Or, you can cram a press kit full with multiple releases, photos, slides, videos, pamphlets, brochures, and product paraphernalia.

To the media, however, thin is in. Don't overcomplicate things. Three-inch-thick press kits are a turnoff. Include only what's necessary to tell—and sell—your story. Package and present your press kit and its contents—no matter how many or how few—attractively.

Pitch Letter

A "pitch" is a brief and polished attempt to sell something to someone. When a salesperson pitches a product to you, he or she tells you what's great about the product or service and why you need to buy it now. If the salesperson is good at his or her job, you buy the product or service. Your goal in pitching your story is to make reporters "buy" the news you're selling—in other words, report your story.

The pitch letter makes the best case possible to media people for why their audiences *need* to hear about you or your product or service *now*. It points out the news value and key news angle(s) of your story.

Before we get into the content of the pitch letter, let's talk about first impressions. Usually paper-clipped to the top of the press kit, the pitch letter is the first thing the media person will see. Make sure it presents the kind of image you want to project—crisp, professional, upbeat. Use your company letterhead for your letter. This should be nice-looking, good-quality bond paper. Use a laser printer or laser-quality inkjet printer to print the text of your letter.

Unless you've known the media person for twenty years and she's named her first child after you, don't handwrite your pitch letter. Sure, it might be easier if you're on the run. But it will cause an immediate strike against you. Why would you want to do that?

Now, let's talk about content. Because the pitch letter is one of the make-it-or-break-it elements of your press kit—again that's because it's the first thing the media person will see—your first sentence must make a case—immediately—for why the person reading what you've sent should read on.

As noted in Chapter 4, media people appreciate inverted pyramid style construction. That means you invert what is considered the normal logic—of presenting several points and then adding them up to a conclusion. Instead, you present the conclusion—the tip of the pyramid—first. Inverted pyramid style aims to grab the reader's attention right away and then provide supporting facts, figures, and arguments. So, in your pitch letter, sentence one should clearly state the problem you're proposing to solve for the media person's audience and present your creative solution to the problem. For an example of inverted pyramid construction, take a look at the sample pitch letter in Figure 5.1 on page 102. Notice how the first sentence expresses the main point the writer wants to make.

Key supporting information follows—starting with the most important fact first, second most important next, and so on.

Figure 5.1 *Snail Mail Pitch Letter*

Educational Alternatives

768 Woodham Road
East Point, MO
342-890-3456
trudy@ealtco.com

May 6, 2002
Anne Whelker, Features Editor
Largetown Herald
235 Dorset Street
Largetown, MO 65167

Dear Ms. Whelker:

Now there's an alternative to traditional summer camps for kids: e-Camp, a first-of-its-kind summer day camp in which kids as young as ten learn how to build their own computer, set up Web pages, and even participate in operating an online store.

Kids who may not have "taken" to the traditional summer camp routine in the past may just "connect" with e-Camp. Parents who are looking for ways to make their children tech-savvy will recognize this as an "electrifying" opportunity.

The attached release provides more details about our alternative to traditional camp programs. Please give me a call if you'd like additional information. I look forward to hearing from you.

Sincerely,

Trudy Juneau

Trudy Juneau

Pyramid style is an effective way to communicate with media people for the following reasons: (1) because they work in a hectic, time-pressed environment; (2) because this is the way they present news; and (3) because if you don't catch their interest immediately, chances are your pitch letter will take a fast trip to the circular file.

Here are some additional ways to strengthen your pitch letter:

Keep your pitch letter short—no more than one page. It should look—and be—easy to grasp. Simplicity is a plus. So is a lively writing style. Be businesslike, but don't be stiff or formal. Keep the reader awake. As kids, we may have been impressed with long words and with stilted words and phrases like, "Notwithstanding . . ." or "I have given consideration to . . ." or "A matter has come to my attention that. . . ." People don't talk like that. With maturity, most of us recognize that these are awkward and awful constructions. Read your letter out loud. Would you speak those words to someone? If not, start rewriting. Write in a breezy conversational tone—or as close to that as you can get.

You're ready to write your pitch letter when you can sum up what your product or service offers in brief punchy prose—one simple, clear, but enticing sentence or short paragraph.

If there's a seasonal tie-in, mention it. This gives timeliness to your story. In the sample pitch letter in Figure 5.1, for example, the seasonal tie-in is the approach of summer camp season.

In the pitch letter in Figure 5.2 on page 104 (composed, by the way, in faxable format), the seasonal tie-in lies in the postholiday devotion to getting back into shape.

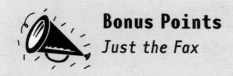

Bonus Points
Just the Fax

If you choose to fax your pitch letter to your target media, you can use the format in Figure 5.2 on page 104. Send your fax on company letterhead or plain paper. Be sure to include your contact information in your fax. Your pitch letter outlines the very basic elements of your story—and tells a media person why he or she should care. Fax a news release along with your pitch letter to provide additional details.

Figure 5.2 *Fax Pitch Letter*

Health Bounty, 47 Wembly Avenue, Plymouth, MI 48167
Contact: Carter Holmes, 734-235-9981

VIA FAX
No. of pages to follow: 2

To: Sylvia Adams, Food Editor, *Plymouth Times*
From: Carter Holmes, Owner, Health Bounty Restaurant, 734-235-9981
Subject: Restaurant Cooks Up New Way to Lose Postholiday Pounds

Now your readers can enjoy delicious desserts, win great prizes (by losing unwanted pounds), and help the community—all at the same time.

According to a study recently released by the Moreland Dietary Research Center, more people start diets in the first week of January than at any other time of the year. But most stop dieting before they achieve their weight loss goals. The reasons: not enough motivation and feelings of deprivation.

Starting January 4, the Health Bounty Restaurant in Plymouth, Michigan, is sponsoring the "Indulge Yourself and Win by Losing (Pounds)" contest. All proceeds from the contest will be donated to the Westmoor Presbyterian Soup Kitchen in Detroit to feed homeless people. Patrons who purchase one of the new fruit-based desserts (less than 150 calories each and exclusive to our restaurant) will get a ticket for a raffle that will be held February 1. Prizes include a pearl necklace and a Montblanc pen.

Our new desserts mean no one has to feel deprived while dieting—and the opportunity to help the homeless gives area dieters that extra motivation.

The following release provides more details. Please give me a call if you'd like additional information. I look forward to hearing from you.

# # #

Let Them Know Why They Should Care

It doesn't hurt to highlight a positive fact or two about your business. The focal point of the Health Bounty Restaurant pitch letter is the raffle. But the pitch letter also mentions that the restaurant will donate income from the raffle to a local soup kitchen. This establishes Health Bounty Restaurant as a good citizen of the community—and makes it more likely that the promotion will be covered. (Reporters are usually good citizens themselves and are inclined to help businesses help charities.)

Keep It Clean

When you've finished the first draft of your pitch letter, double-check your spelling and grammar. There is nothing that will undercut your credibility like a misspelled word or poor grammatical construction. You don't have to write Shakespeare-like prose. Simple is good. In fact, simple is best. Just make sure the simplicity is underpinned by flawless grammar and spelling.

Reshuffle the Deck (Until You Win)

Revise mercilessly. Cut out all the words you don't need. Use the active voice ("Customers can purchase discount tickets," not, "Discount tickets can be purchased"). Ruthless editing and elimination of the passive voice will help make your pitch letter as effective as it can be.

Cool It

If time allows, set your pitch letter aside for a day or two, then check it again. A "cooling-off" period helps you see any mistakes you missed on your last read-through.

Use Pinpoint Precision

Send your pitch letter to the specific person at a newspaper who's likely to cover the kind of story you're suggesting—food stories to the cooking reporter, exercise equipment stories to the lifestyle reporter, and so on. A reporter's enthusiasm for a story will determine whether the story (1) gets pursued, (2) gets published, and (3) gets good play. Yes, you could approach an editor rather than a reporter. But editors often bend to the inclinations of reporters and their assignment editors. It's better to try to sell the story to the person who'll report on it.

Important: while this holds true for newspapers, the dynamic is different for other media outlets. For magazines, send your pitch to the managing editor. For TV and radio, send it to the assignment editor for news programs and to the talent coordinator for talk shows.

Check media lists like Bacon's and Burrelle's to find the names, mailing addresses, and E-mail addresses of the reporters, assignment editors, and so on at the media outlets you decide to contact. Almost all major city newspapers and many print-based newsletters and magazines have online editions, and these also offer up-to-date information on how to contact media people.

A pitch letter you send by U.S. postal mail should be typed on your business stationery or company letterhead. See Figure 5.1 on page 102 and Figure 5.3.

If you don't have any business stationery, print some up using a laser printer. The quality of today's word processing programs and laser printers is high enough to turn out printed letterhead that makes a professional impression.

If you're sending to more than one person at a particular media outlet, it's a courtesy to attach a handwritten Post-it Note, as follows:

> *Please note that I've also*
>
> *sent this information to*
>
> *(name of the reporter,*
>
> *editor, etc.) at your paper.*
>
> —*(Your Name Here)*

If you personally know a reporter or have had contact with him or her, mention it in your pitch letter. Write something like, "I enjoyed meeting you at the (Press Club meeting, Rotary awards dinner, sports banquet, etc.) last week." Then proceed with your note. Media people are just like most of us. They respond to the personal touch. An additional benefit: at large metro newspapers, a note like this will help your news release get past the departmental assistant who may be the first person to sort through all the pitch letters, news releases, and so on and who may be looking for reasons to throw as many as possible away.

If you haven't made personal contact with the media person to whom you're writing, simply stick to the inverted pyramid style and get straight to the point in your opening sentence.

Figure 5.3 *Snail Mail Pitch Letter*

Health Bounty Restaurant

"non-fattening delights"
47 Wembly Avenue, Plymouth, MI 48167
734-235-9981, cart@healthbounty.com
www.healthbounty.com

December 12, 2002
Sylvia Adams
Food Editor
Plymouth Times
600 West Main Street
Plymouth, MI 48932

Dear Sylvia:

I enjoyed meeting you at the Plymouth Food Expo last month. I've got an idea for a story that I think your readers will find interesting.

Now your readers can enjoy delicious desserts, win great prizes (by losing unwanted pounds that have piled up over the holidays), and help the community—all at the same time.

According to a study recently released by the Moreland Dietary Research Center, more people start diets in the first week of January than at any other time of the year. But most stop dieting before they achieve their weight loss goals. The reasons: not enough motivation and feelings of deprivation.

Starting January 4, the Health Bounty Restaurant in Plymouth, Michigan, is sponsoring the "Indulge Yourself and Win by Losing (Pounds)" contest. All proceeds from the contest will be donated to the Westmoor Presbyterian Soup Kitchen in Detroit to feed homeless people.

- more -

Page 2

Patrons who purchase one of the new fruit-based desserts (less than 150 calories each and exclusive to our restaurant) will get a ticket for a raffle that will be held February 1. Prizes include a pearl necklace and a Montblanc pen.

Our new desserts mean no one has to feel deprived while dieting—and the opportunity to help the homeless gives area dieters that extra motivation to get serious.

The attached release provides more details. Please give me a call if you'd like additional information. I look forward to hearing from you.

Sincerely,

Cart

Carter Holmes
Owner
Health Bounty Restaurant

Note: we're discussing pitch letters as part of a press kit here. Pitch letters can also be sent as stand-alones to your target media person to initiate interest. You may choose to send your pitch letter first and then follow it up with your press kit later.

You can send your pitch letter by U.S. postal mail (see Figures 5.1 and 5.3 on pages 102 and 107), or you can fax it (see Figure 5.2 on page 104) or E-mail it.

Ask About Pitching Preferences—Paper or E-Mail

More and more reporters prefer E-mail communications. Paperless pitch letters are fast, efficient, and environmentally responsible.

But it's best, if you can, to try to find out the preferences of the media person(s) you've targeted. (There are still techophobes among us.) This can be done with a quick phone call. Be businesslike and brief. Say something like, "I've got an idea for a story I think you might find interesting. I'd like to send you a short letter with the details. Would you prefer an E-mail, a fax, or snail mail?" Calling and asking is a good way to begin building a relationship.

With larger campaigns—say if you plan to contact more than thirty media people to publicize a particular story—you have to forego the nicety of asking a media person what his or her preference might be. It's simply too cumbersome. This is where news release distribution services like PR Newswire and Internet Wire, which send your news release out to targeted media for you, can come in handy (see the Resources section).

Note: if you are an "unknown quantity" to a media person, include materials that will help establish your professional standing with your pitch letter—your business card, a brochure about your business, and perhaps clips of articles written about you by other publications.

Tip: For small campaigns, address your pitch letter envelope in your own handwriting. It's unprofessional to handwrite the pitch letter itself. However, in our junk mail age, one thing that seems to capture our attention is an envelope with a handwritten address.

Folder

Folders serve a practical purpose. They help keep the elements of your press kit together and prevent photos, news releases, and so on from getting dog-eared and damaged. From a strategic standpoint a folder offers media people the basis for forming a first impression of you and your business. A well-chosen folder should create an image that's upbeat and professional.

Some people opt for custom-made folders with elaborate graphics. But simple, low-key folders cost less and can be just as effective—if not more so. Fortune 500 companies know this. Their press kits often are enclosed in folders that feature a very simple graphic element and logo—or just a logo. The look is tasteful and professional.

If you don't have the budget for personalized folders, it's acceptable to print up adhesive-backed labels on a laser or high-quality inkjet printer and stick these onto the front of plain folders. One businessperson I know buys inexpensive adhesive-backed two-by-three-inch see-through plastic pockets from an office supply store, affixes them to the top of her press kit folders, and slips her business card into the pockets—a neat and inexpensive way to "brand" her folders.

Many of the presentation folders you can purchase in office supply stores have prepunched slits on the cover or on one of the inside pockets into which you can insert your business card. Or you can simply slip your card under the paper clip you used to fasten the pitch letter to the top of the folder.

Tip: Some folders are made of paper that batters easily in transit. Test how your press kit folder "travels" by mailing one to yourself. One entrepreneur solves the problem by placing her press kits in sturdy nine-by-twelve-inch clear vinyl envelopes she buys from office supply stores. She then puts the vinyl-packaged press kits into Tyvek envelopes. The stiff vinyl envelopes keep her press kits pristine.

Note: school supply–type folders are fine—for the schoolroom. Don't use them for your press kits. They look amateurish. You'll find modestly priced, attractive business folders at any well-stocked office supply store. If you're operating on a shoestring budget, it's acceptable simply to mail your press kit elements (photo, news release, bio, etc.) in a large envelope (without a folder). If you go this route, invest in a professionally made rubber stamp that attractively prints your business return address on the envelopes. Or, print some neat and attractive return address labels on your laser or laser-quality printer.

News Release

See Chapter 4 for information on preparing news releases.

Photo

Good photographs are a press kit must. They help sell your story to the media—and when your story runs alongside an interesting photo, it's more likely to attract the attention of the reading public. Let's say you're announcing that you're the exclusive distributor of an innovative new hiking boot. A photo of the new hiking boot, sent along with your release, would increase the chances of the story being used. A photo of a celebrity wearing the boots would (because we are a culture that is fascinated by celebrities) increase your chances of coverage even more.

For your press kit, you will need one or more of the following:

- A good head-and-shoulders shot of yourself
- A good product photo (if you sell a product)
- Good action shots (if you provide a service, want to show a product in use, or are promoting an event)

How do you find a good photographer—and make the most of your photos? While some photographers can "do it all" (head shots, action and product photos), most specialize. If you don't know photographers who specialize in high-quality portrait/product/action-shot work, here are a few ways you can locate good people:

- **Method #1:** For product or action shots, call your local major daily newspaper and ask for the photography department. Explain who you are and tell them you are looking for a good freelance photographer. They usually know several freelancers who do great work and are willing to take on new assignments.
- **Method #2:** For head-and-shoulder shots, call the theater departments of nearby colleges or universities. Ask to speak to the chair of the department or his or her assistant. Introduce yourself and explain that you are looking for a photographer. Ask for a recommendation. (Actors-in-training have to put together portfolios that include high-quality head shots.)
- **Method #3:** If you are operating on a shoestring budget, call the journalism department of your local college or university and ask if they can recommend a reliable student who takes good photos and who is willing to take on freelance assignments.

Ask your photographer if he or she wants a photo credit. If the answer is yes, include a credit in the caption.

Important: photographers own the rights to any photos they shoot. Before you finalize arrangements with a photographer, explain to him or her that you are preparing publicity materials and that you will need to print multiple copies of your photo(s). Request a signed letter on his or her business stationery granting you permission to do so. You will need to present this to the photo lab that prints your photos.

Following are the specs for press kit photos:

- Press kit photos should be five by seven inches or eight by ten inches—sizes considered standard by the media.

  Tip: don't send snapshots or snapshot-quality photographs. Send nothing smaller than five by seven inches. Send nothing grainy or poorly composed. Don't send "action" shots with boring backgrounds (brick walls, for example). If you're publicizing a product, a photo and/or video of the product in use is a strong plus.
- Color has become standard, but black and white is still acceptable for most media.

- You should almost always include a head-and-shoulders shot of yourself. You can also send shots of yourself in your environment (office, podium, retail outlet, etc.) or in action—addressing a large audience (for a speaker), tossing a salad (for a chef), overseeing installation of new windows in a home (for the president of a construction company)—you get the idea.
- Your photos *must* have captions (see Figure 5.4). Your press kit photo can easily end up with umpteen others somewhere amid the clutter on a reporter or producer's desk. Make it easy for the media to identify the photos that go along with your story.

Captions ease a reporter's workload. If the photo you send to a media person has no caption, someone will have to call you to get input and may have to fax you the photo to confirm it's yours. Then the media person will have to write the caption. Creating this kind of extra work for a media person doesn't make sense. You want to make sure your material is easy to use.

Following are examples of caption write-ups:

Caption for an action shot:

Emily MacNeil, owner of Emily's Tearoom, pours an Earl Grey blend for guests at one of the restaurant's monthly tea-tasting brunches. Photo by Jared Walker.

Caption for a head-and-shoulders shot:

Brandon Welch, president of the Light Fantastic Lamp Company. Photo: Lena Antonelli.

Here's how to attach captions to your photos:

- **Method #1:** Work with a print lab that can print your caption directly onto your photo. (This method adds to your expense, complicates the printing, and isn't any more impressive than Method #2.)
- **Method #2:** Print a caption on a piece of plain typing paper. Cut the paper into a five-by-two-inch or an eight-by-two-inch strip—depending on the size of your photo. The words you printed across the long side should be centered about one-quarter inch from the top of the strip. Fold the strip about one-quarter inch under the typed caption. Tuck the

Figure 5.4 *Photo with Caption*

Author and publicity expert Jessica Hatchigan speaks to a group of elementary school students about careers in writing and communications in Holly, Michigan.

Photo: Hugh Trundle

photo into the fold you've just created so that the caption appears at the bottom of the photo viewed from the front. On the back of the photo, tape the folded strip to the photo with a piece of clear tape. It's plain and simple, but many major corporations go this route because it's also quick and easy.

- **Method #3:** Use a laser or laser-quality printer to print a caption onto a sticker. Place the sticker on the back of the photo.
- **Method #4:** Use a waterproof fine-tip felt pen to write the caption on the back of the photo.

Important: do not use a ball-point pen to write your captions. Ball-point ink rubs off slick paper easily and can smudge other photos—something media people won't appreciate.

And, by the way, don't expect media people to return your photos.

Bonus Points
To Gimmick or Not to Gimmick

Be careful with gimmicks. Some are wonderful and appropriate and can strike a responsive chord in media people. This happens when you include an item that intelligently and (best case) humorously or whimsically reinforces a point you make in your press release. The idea is to be creative and witty but to be so in a businesslike way. Convey the spirit of your endeavor appropriately.

Here are some gimmicks that have worked or might work well:

One software company launched a new accounting program by sending bullwhips out with cowboy-themed press kits that announced it would "whip business into shape."

Publicists who organized the Sydney Opera House celebrations for New Year's Eve 2000 included a digital clock that counted down the seconds to the new millennium in the press kit announcing the event.

An ice cream shop owner can announce a new flavor by including an ice cream scoop with her press kits and proclaiming, "Here's Our Latest Scoop." A garden supply company owner can send out miniature Slinky toys with his press kits in early spring and announce a "We're Springing into Action" campaign. A software developer with a cool new software program to promote can burn a sample CD, print a snazzy CD label using precut adhesive-backed paper (available from office supply stores), and include it in the press kit. A cruelty-free (nonleather) shoe company that caters to vegetarians can send out a shoe horn with an animal-shaped handle stamped with the motto, "Let Our Cruelty-Free Shoes Fit Your Lifestyle."

Other gimmicks *don't* work for a variety of reasons. The main problem: gimmicks that fail to refer back to what a company is promoting.

A common and very bad ploy is to enclose glitter, confetti, or accordion-folded paper snakes that work on spring coils and jump or fall out of a press kit as it's opened, the idea being, I suppose, that the exciting "moment" created will succeed in getting the attention of the person on the receiving end. The only excitement you should create for the person on the receiving end is with your story ideas, news angles, and so on.

One editor told me that when she unsuspectingly opened a press kit once, glitter showered over her desk, chair, and office floor—and that much of it remained in the carpeting for ever afterward, defeating the repeated efforts of the building cleaning people. "Every time the sun hit at a certain angle in that office, I could see this blinding glitter," she said. Needless to say, the sender of the glitter kit didn't score any points.

The moral of the story: think things through and don't do anything that is potentially annoying. This includes sending food items that have a limited shelf life, anything gooey or gluey (chocolate included), and (please!) all living creatures. In short, use good judgment and good taste. And when in doubt, don't.

One more caution: don't include expensive gimmicks. One publicist, working to promote a high-tech product, included expensive handheld PCs as giveaways with her press kits. She justified it by claiming that the handhelds underscored the high-tech content of her client's product. But she was criticized by fellow publicists for making many media people feel uncomfortable. (Items this costly appear to be bribes.) A rule of thumb: if it costs more than thirty dollars per person, it costs too much—and, actually, thirty dollars is way more than you should pay per person for a gimmick.

Going to Town: Expanded Press Kits

You can create very effective press kits quite simply, as already noted, using the four basic ingredients: a folder, a pitch letter, a news release, and a photo. However, you can put together press kits that are more elaborate too. If you want to expand your press kit beyond the four basic elements, here are some things you can add.

Table of Contents

If you send out press kits containing several elements, you can include a table of contents (TOC) sheet. This is an added convenience. Slip the TOC into the left-hand pocket of a two-pocket folder, or simply include it as a cover sheet with your materials if you don't use a folder.

The table of contents in Figure 5.5 lists quite a number of elements. Yours can be simpler, depending on what elements you choose to include.

Note: suggested story angles and talking points elements need to be included only in mailings to broadcast media.

Tip: a quick and easy way to create a TOC is to print one out as a bulleted list on a three-by-four-inch label and affix it neatly to one of the pockets of your press kit.

Bio

A bio (biography) presents your credentials and your most recent and/or key accomplishments—as they relate to the story you're pitching (see Figure 5.6 on page 118). What makes you different—and what makes you the right person to interview for this story? What makes you an authority in your field? Your bio should answer these questions.

You can include an interesting quote in your bio, one that shows that you understand what makes for a lively news story—and that you're quotable. This is one time when you can quote yourself at your wittiest, most profound, or most engaging best.

Your bio should be written in the third person. It should be one to one-and-a-half pages long at most. A well-done bio should present you as an appealing personality. Like a well-written news release, the first sentence of your bio (your lead sentence) should grab the reader's attention immediately.

Figure 5.5 *Press Kit Table of Contents*

Robindale Boot Shop
12 Albemarle Lane
Sandy Point, IL 60321

PRESS KIT CONTENTS

Contact: Will Robindale
                412-433-0980
                will@robindaleboots.com

**NEW HIKING BOOTS
NEED NO BREAKING IN**

- News Release: Revolutionary New Boots Need No Breaking In
- Bios

  ✔ Will Robindale, owner of Robindale Boot Shop
  ✔ Kent McClurg, inventor of Aussiclogs Boots

- Robindale Boot Shop Brochure
- Aussiclogs Company Newsletter
- Aussiclogs Fact Sheet
- Backgrounder
- Testimonials
- Product Sample Request Postcard

# # #

Longer bios, seven to ten pages, written in feature article form (like a short story) are popular in publicity circles these days. They can be peppered with your punchy quotes and with anecdotes that convey your distinctive personality and highlight your accomplishments. However, a longer bio does require a great deal of writing skill. If you aren't confident of your ability to pick and choose the right quotations and anecdotes, and if your creative writing abilities fall short of excel-

Figure 5.6 *Bio*

Taste of Provence Restaurant, 6 Main Street, Stanhope, WI 58573

Contact: John Wiedermeir, 456-345-2342, john@tasteofprovence.com

Biography—John Wiedermeir

John Wiedermeir, owner of the Taste of Provence Restaurant, says he "strives to bring the best of southern French cuisine to Main Street." If the reviews are any indication, he must be succeeding. The Taste of Provence rated five stars in a column written recently by the *Stanhope Journal*'s Anonymous Diner. The reviewer noted, "If you've ever had your doubts about southern French cuisine, stop by the Taste of Provence and have them dispelled—tastefully. This is authentic, and great, southern French cooking."

Wiedermeir earned the right to cook southern French cuisine authentically. After graduating from Wisconsin State University with a journalism degree in 1988, he moved to southern France (Provence) to work as a correspondent for the International Press Syndicate. His two-year stay in Provence helped him appreciate French food and wine and its artful preparation and presentation.

After two years with IPS, Wiedermeir decided to switch career tracks and to study cooking at the Provence Culinary Institute under chef Michel Toulaine, who is considered legendary in French cooking circles.

"I began cooking as a hobby in Provence, and my wife raved about the dishes I turned out. The career switch was Stella's idea. She told me I was a good journalist—but she knew I would be a *great* chef."

While studying the preparation of traditional and modern Provençal main dishes and desserts at the Culinary Institute, Wiedermeir also worked alongside chef Toulaine in Toulaine's Restaurant, renowned for its beef in pastry dishes and cream-based desserts.

When he returned to Wisconsin in 1991, Wiedermeir worked for two years as a line cook at the Pan European Grill, a popular Madison restaurant known for its international cuisine, under the direction of chef Monty Thomas. In 1994, Wiedermeir was promoted to sous-chef and stayed on in

- more -

Page 2

that position for another two years. During that period, he innovated several new main dishes and desserts based on his knowledge of Provençal cuisine. In its June 1995 issue, *Wisconsin Diners Guide* called the Provençal dishes at the Pan European Grill "the best European food in Wisconsin."

Wiedermeir opened Taste of Provence in 1997, with encouragement from Thomas, who also helped fund the new restaurant. Since then, Taste of Provence has been featured in *Food and Wine*, *Chef's Report*, and *European-Style Dining*.

When he isn't supervising the preparation of coq au vin or selecting the just-right *fume blanc* to serve with *Framboise Anouille*, the restaurant's signature raspberry dessert, Wiedermeir coaches his son Jack's eighth-grade soccer team, serves as president of the Stanhope Rotary Club, and is a leading voice in the state legislature for Wisconsin farm groups on food-related issues. He was named Volunteer of the Year by the Stanhope Chamber of Commerce in 1998 for his help in organizing a food drive to help flood victims in Wenoway County, Wisconsin.

# # #

lent, hire a pro or wait until you can afford to hire a pro before you opt to go this route.

Suggested Story Angles

Media people won't always have in-depth knowledge about your field or industry. Your job is to get them to see how the story you are trying to sell them is indeed "news." An excellent way to do this is to provide a suggested story angles sheet. The example in Figure 5.7 on page 120 outlines some suggested story angles that a stained glass artist could use to accompany a news release announcing an open house. You can use the same format for your own suggested story angles.

Notice that the story angles suggest several approaches and possible intriguing leads that a reporter might not know of without doing some research. For more on story angles, see "So, Just What Is a News Angle?" in Chapter 4 on page 67.

Figure 5.7 *Suggested Story Angles*

Glass by Virtecki, 23 Charles Street, Boston, MA 10353

SUGGESTED STORY ANGLES

Contact: Rick Virtecki
756-432-1223
virtecki@glassart.com

**Award-Winning Glass Artist Bridges the Centuries:
Work Will Be Featured in New Music Building**

Great Story Angles!

Story Angle: Stained Glass Today: Medieval Art Goes Modern at Open House

No one knows how the manufacture of stained glass began—it's that old. The first stained glass windows appeared in the tenth century. They replaced books in a day when most people weren't taught how to read. People learned the stories in the Bible by looking at their depictions in windows. Today artist Rick Virtecki uses stained glass symbolically to modernize ancient stories of faith. Selected works will be on display at the open house alongside photos of classical windows from French, German, and English churches.

Story Angle: Award-Winning Artist Shines in Glass

Virtecki's just-completed "Faith in Action" series of stained glass wall hangings were awarded the prestigious Glass Artists Guild top honor, the Gerstner Award, last week. The "Faith in Action" hangings will be among the artworks on display at the open house.

Story Angle: Virtecki Uses Time-Tested Technique to Create Timeless Art

About 1100 A.D., the monk Theophilus described how to make a stained glass window. Amazingly, stained glass window makers use basically the

- more -

Page 2

same techniques today. Virtecki will demonstrate how to make a stained glass window using these ancient techniques at the open house.

Story Angle: Glass Shimmers with Mystery

Glass is mysterious. It's a form of matter that has some of the properties of gases, liquids, and solids. Made from an ordinary substance, sand—one of the most abundant substances in the world—it has, all the same, some almost mystic qualities. It's solid, yet transparent. It allows light to shine through it. "Staining" adds to the mysterious allure of glass because when you add minerals to glass, the glass is altered to capture certain portions of the spectrum. This enables the human eye to see vivid—although transparent—colors. Rick Virtecki will demonstrate how cranberry glass is created by adding gold and how blue glass is created by adding cobalt.

Story Angle: Stained Glass Creates Unique Windows for Homes and Businesses

Contemporary glass art uses light and color to transform the ordinary into the mystical. Virtecki's "Contemplation" series—window art in restful shades of blues and greens—exemplifies this. The series has been chosen by the Cranhope Music Conservatory for their innovative Serenity Concert Hall. The construction of the new hall will be completed in June of this year. Several of the windows to be used in the hall will be on display at the open house.

# # #

Talking Points/Suggested Interview Questions

Talking points and suggested interview questions are sent only to radio, TV, and online interviewers. They are meant to demonstrate that you would make a great guest on a talk show or interview program (i.e., that audiences would find you interesting). The talking points/suggested questions highlight what's fascinating and newsworthy about the story you are offering up. They help a TV, radio, or Web broadcast interviewer see at a glance what shape an interview with you might take. See Figures 5.8 and 5.9 on pages 122 and 123 for examples.

Figure 5.8 *Talking Points*

TimeSaver, Inc., 88 Resley Lane, Trudeau, LA 48743

TALKING POINTS

Contact: Martha Hampton
             412-554-0098
             martha@timesaverserv.com

TIMESAVER—CLEANING SERVICES
YOU CAN ORDER ONLINE

- **TimeSaver Cleaning Services,** a new Internet-based cleaning service, offers the public several unique benefits: services **can be requested by E-mail**. Services are offered "a la carte." And clients do not need to sign up for regular weekly or monthly services.

- Recognizing the growing trend to save time by turning to the Web to order products and services, TimeSaver has become **the first completely Web-based cleaning service**. (An 800 number is maintained for customer service, but all requests for service are expected to be made via the TimeSaver website, www.timesavercleaning.com.)

- TimeSaver services are offered "a la carte." In other words, customers can **order only the particular service they need** and have it done at any time specified between 8 A.M. and 6 P.M.

- Since its inception two months ago, **more than two thousand people have signed up for** TimeSaver services. An additional fifty people are signing up every day.

- How it works: TimeSaver contracts with various local cleaning services to share resources and to ensure **there is always someone available to provide the service clients need *when* they need it**.

# # #

Figure 5.9 *Suggested Interview Questions*

Mama Mia, Ltd., 703 Angel Avenue, Woskosh, NH 45321

SUGGESTED INTERVIEW QUESTIONS

Contact: Sal Fabrizio
202-564-9800
sal@mmsauce.com

Mama Mia's New Basil Profundo Spaghetti Sauce

• You claim to have come out with a new kind of spaghetti sauce, but realistically, what can you do with spaghetti sauce to make it "new"?

• Basil is a common herb. You claim that the kind of basil you grow is different. How can you substantiate that?

• You've managed to get a lot of celebrity endorsements for your new sauce. Isn't that just a gimmick you've arranged with some PR firm to get your new product some exposure?

• We all know that vegetables are good for you, but you claim your sauce has twice the nutritional value of your nearest competitor. That sounds improbable. Aren't you stretching it?

# # #

These press kit elements save interviewers work because they provide a ready-made list of points to get across to audiences. Therefore, they reduce the amount of prep work that media people need to do if you are booked for a program. I'm sure you've noticed talk show hosts glancing down at their desks while conducting interviews. They may well be looking at a talking points/suggested questions sheet.

Notice in Figures 5.8 and 5.9 that "ad" language isn't used in the talking points and suggested questions. People aren't rushing to sign up for the "unbeatable," "fantastic," etc. service. The unique pluses of each business are described as factually as possible.

To create your own suggested interview questions, make a one-page list of the ten best questions a radio or TV interviewer could ask you about yourself, your business, or your product or service—the ten best questions, that is, to elicit the kind of information the audiences would appreciate most. To do this, think through the key newsworthy points you would like to make, and then rephrase them as questions.

Note: media people pride themselves on being more like Mike Wallace and Sam Donaldson (tough, no-nonsense guys) than like Clark Kent (the "mild-mannered" reporter). They look down on what they call "softball" or "puffball" questions that are meant to elicit only positive information. These include infomercial-type questions like, "What's great about your company/your new product?" "How fast have your sales grown?" "The new spaghetti sauce your company makes is so flavorful. What's the secret?" Wallace and Donaldson would shudder.

Your suggested interview questions should show that you understand news. The best way to do this is to try to think with a reporter's mind-set as you compose your questions. Imagine you're Sam Donaldson or Ted Koppel. Make your questions sound coolly objective and even a little hard-nosed (the way the real Sam or Ted would write them). The suggested questions example (Figure 5.9 on page 123) gives you a flavor of the tone your suggested question list should take. You would, of course, have great (and substantive) answers to all the questions you propose. The benefit of posing questions in this no-nonsense way is that your answers will come across as more credible when you actually are interviewed on radio and TV. Preparing tough questions this way is also an excellent warm-up for actual interviews. (You will be able to think through your answers before you hit the airwaves.)

By the way, talking points are simply suggested interview questions with the questions left out. Which format you choose to use is a matter of preference.

Reminder: again, don't send suggested interview questions or talking points to print reporters. Print reporters don't operate in the "hot" environment of broadcast media. They don't need memory joggers to prevent "white spaces" in a broadcast, which is the essential function of the suggested interview questions or talking points sheets.

Note: in the talking points example in Figure 5.8 on page 122, I've made some of the key information bold. It's another way to make information "pop" for reporters.

Figure 5.10 *Brochure*

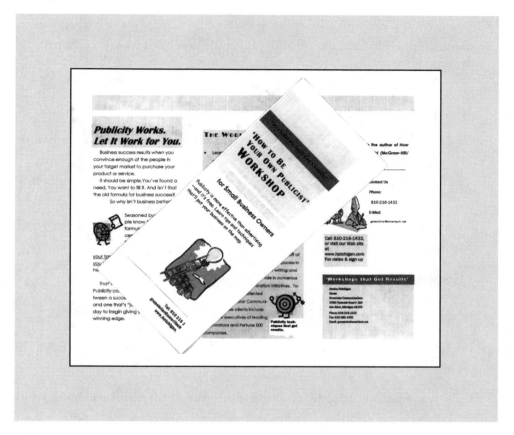

Brochure/Newsletter

A brochure or a newsletter can help explain what you or your company, or a particular product or service you're offering, are all about. (An example of a brochure is shown in Figure 5.10.) In addition, if you are a small, brand-new, or not-well-known business, a well-done brochure or an issue or two of a company newsletter can add to your credibility.

Fact Sheet/Backgrounder

If you are an "unknown quantity" to the media, you can make yourself a "known quantity" and position yourself as an expert in your business or industry, with a helpful and informative fact sheet. (See Figure 5.11 on page 126.)

Figure 5.11 *Fact Sheet/Backgrounder*

Greenbriar Communications, 3588 Plymouth Rd. #286, Ann Arbor, MI 48105

FACT SHEET

Contact: Jessica Hatchigan
810-216-1432
jessica@hatchigan.com

Microbusinesses Pour Billions
into the U.S. Economy Each Year

Small and home office (SOHO) businesses contribute billions of dollars to the U.S. economy every year. Some useful information on the SOHO market follows:

What do SOHO businesses contribute to the U.S. economy?

- Each year, the self-employed produce more than three-quarters of a trillion dollars in economic activity in the United States.

- In the United States, non-farm sole proprietorships accounted for revenues of $757 billion in 1994, according to a Small Business Administration self-employment study.

- The self-employed generally earn more money than those who work for wages or salaries. In 1996, the median annual income for non-farm self-employed individuals was $23,754, compared to $22,287 for wage and salary workers. Approximately 5 percent of self-employed individuals earned more than $100,000 in 1996 compared to approximately 3 percent of wage and salary workers. About half of the self-employed work part time. An average home-based business generates $36,000 in annual sales.

- more -

Page 2

Who are the self-employed?

- The self-employed represent more than one out of eight workers. In the 1996 tax year, 16.4 million Americans, or 13.1 percent of all workers, filed sole-proprietor returns, a 16 percent increase over 1988. In the same time frame, there was only a 12 percent increase in wage and salary workers.

- Approximately 10 million Americans are self-employed full time.

- Half of home-based business owners work full time at their businesses, with the remaining half working part time for an average workweek of twenty-three hours.

- More and more of the self-employed are women and minorities. In 1996, there were about 4.2 million self-employed women. Approximately 676,000 African Americans and 663,000 Hispanics were self-employed in 1996, increases of 37 percent and 30 percent, respectively, from 1988. The number of self-employed women grew five times faster than the number of self-employed men and three times faster than the number of salaried women between 1988 and 1996.

How many home-based businesses are there?

- About 6.1 million U.S. households have home-based businesses, according to a 1998 U.S. Department of Labor survey. That figure represents about 6 percent of all U.S. households. Most home-based businesses (4.1 million) are operated by self-employed people. Home-based business owners include 1.7 million managers and professionals, 726,000 construction industry professionals, and 532,000 people in retail trades.

- more -

Page 3

- Home-based business ownership is split evenly between men and women.

- About 6.5 million self-employed people, almost 5 percent of the entire U.S. labor force, do some work at home.

- More than 12 million workers, or 9 percent of the total U.S. workforce, work part time or full time from their homes. That's one worker out of every eleven in the United States. The number of people working from their homes for wages or salaries about doubled, from 1.9 million to 3.6 million, between 1991 and 1997.

Call Jessica Hatchigan, 810-216-1432, for more information.

# # #

Your fact sheet should provide substantive information on your industry or target market. It can also include some key information about yourself and your company. But a much heavier emphasis should be given to the industry/target market information.

Media people collect and file well-done fact sheets on various topics and industries. If your fact sheet is little more than a thinly disguised ad for your company, it will be thrown away. However, if you provide solid overall information on your industry or market segment—information that can save a media person some drudgery—the chances of your information being kept and referred to later are good.

Because you've included a bit of information about yourself and your business, that keeps you on the media's radar. Because you've included your contact information and a line that says, "Call (Your Name Here) for more information," you've upped your chances of getting a call the next time a media person is working on a story about your industry.

Articles

Copies of Articles About You or Your Business

Articles about you or your business add to your credibility (see Figure 5.12 on page 130). You can make eight-by-ten-inch copies of the articles and include them in your press kits. Photocopies are perfectly acceptable, although some people choose to have particularly impressive articles reprinted on glossy stock paper. (Reporters aren't more impressed by the latter. Save your money.)

Important: don't include clips of the exact same news story that you are pitching—use clips of other news stories about your business instead. You don't want to give an impression that the story you're selling has been "done to death"—in other words, is no longer news. For example, let's say you are the owner of the Spring Fever Garden Tools Company. You're launching a new EZ-grip trowel you've developed. You might want to include clips you've garnered on your company's participation in a recent charitable event, your record sales in the previous quarter, and the EZ-grip rake you launched last year. These will add to your credibility—without giving the media the sense that the EZ-grip trowel story is old news, which could happen if you include articles on the EZ-grip trowel that have run in several other publications lately.

Copies of Articles You Have Written

If you're like most people, you prefer to buy from knowledgeable salespeople. You want to buy furniture from people who can explain why a sofa or chest of drawers is well constructed. You want to buy your computer and the software you load on it from people who are up-to-date on the latest in PCs and in the programs that run them.

People are much happier buying from experts. As someone who is knowledgeable in your field, you can position yourself as an expert by writing articles for newspapers, magazines, E-'zines, and trade publications.

It's tough to get published in *Reader's Digest* or *Good Housekeeping*. But it isn't necessary to get published in these well-known, large-circulation publications to build your business. If you own a Seattle-based plumbing supply company, the *Plumbers' Quarterly Newsletter* and the *Seattle Plumbers* magazine might be the publications to target.

How do you write an "expert" article? Experts solve problems. Get a pen and a pad of paper. Think of a particular problem your company helps resolve. Draw

Figure 5.12 *Copies of Articles About You or Your Business*

a worst-case scenario of what happens if this problem isn't solved. Then provide five to eight tips pulled from your area of expertise to solve the problem. Write a summary paragraph. In your final paragraph, include your contact information.

Because electronic publications are easier to launch than their print counterparts, there are quite a few E-'zines. Many are open to new writers. Almost all are open to E-mail queries. Contact the editors of publications that make a good publicity fit, present your credentials, and ask if you can send in an article.

Print publications often have specific guidelines for submitting material. Contact the managing editor at your target publication and ask for guidance. The *Writer's Digest* magazine site lists contact information for hundreds of magazines and newsletters in its online Writer's Guidelines pages. These can be found at writersdigest.com. Or check to see if a given publication offers submission guidelines on its own website. When you purchase a copy of your target publication—which you should do to study it for content, style, and so on—you also can look for contact information within its pages.

Writing articles for publication is an excellent way of establishing yourself as an expert. If writing isn't your strong suit, you can hire a freelancer to ghostwrite for you. Bill Gates, Jack Welch, and Lee Iacocca all did, so you can rest assured that it's an accepted practice. Note: ghostwriters for corporate executives who are national icons may charge fees in the nosebleed range. Call the business editor at your local daily and ask him or her to recommend a freelancer in your area.

If your work isn't accepted for publication anywhere, you can always print up your own "Special Reports" on your company letterhead. Good, solid writing and a clean, simple look for these reports will work fine. Dull writing won't. Content is what's important, yes. But a little pizzazz—such as a catchy headline, an attention-getting lead-in sentence, thought-provoking statistics, punchy quotations, and so on—goes a long way.

Tip: if you've chosen to write your own articles, have someone you know who is a good writer read and edit your work before you send it out into the world.

Tip Sheets

A tip sheet is a one-page list of useful advice and information that people in your target audience (your potential clients and customers) will find valuable. Figure 5.13 on page 132 shows an example. The media will be open to running your tip sheet, or excerpts from it, if the information it contains is of value to their readers.

Figure 5.13 *Tip Sheet*

Greenbriar Communications
3588 Plymouth Road #286
Ann Arbor, MI 48105

For more information, call: Jessica Hatchigan, 810-216-1432, or E-mail
jessica@hatchigan.com

Seven Ways to Survive a Speech You Didn't Plan to Make

Impromptu speeches happen. Sometimes it's miscommunication—you simply weren't informed you'd be called on to speak. Sometimes the meeting chair or event emcee, carried away by enthusiasm for the subject at hand, decides no one else can quite explain a particular issue just the way you can at right this moment. However it happens, next time you have to give an impromptu speech, here are some tips that can help:

1. **Make a quick "laundry list"**—Many people "freeze" (think "deer in headlights") when faced with an audience. It helps to do a quick think-through of the key points you want to make and jot down short "memory joggers" on anything handy. Even a nearby napkin or the back of a receipt you've kept in your wallet will do. Usually you have a moment or two while the meeting chair or event emcee is wrapping up his or her remarks. Use the time to draw up your on-the-spot laundry list.

    Example: You're the head of the New Members Committee at your local reading club, and you've been asked to report on the status of new members. You know there are ten new members. You know there would be plenty more except for the high cost of dues and the fact that not enough people know about the club. Your laundry list could be: "ten/high dues/get word out."

    If you don't have a chance to write the laundry list, try to memorize it quickly.

2. **Get centered**—Breathe, breathe, breathe. The first thing Yoga masters learn is how to breathe deeply to relax. The Lamaze method of natural

- more -

Page 2

childbirth (without anesthetics) teaches women to use deep breathing to control pain. It works. Take a deep breath in through your nose. Part your lips slightly and exhale slowly. Repeat. Repeat again. No one will notice. It's tremendously calming. (And it's legal.)

3. **Remember that it's OK to be rough around the edges**—Unless you are delivering a eulogy or have a naturally wooden style, smile. Be friendly and be yourself. No one will notice if you are a little nervous. If you are very nervous—and you think it shows—don't worry about it. Keep in mind that "slick" people—people who are too polished and sure of themselves—rub a lot of people the wrong way. They're often considered untrustworthy. (Remember the many "just-a-little-too-smooth" characters Phil Hartman portrayed on *Saturday Night Live*?)

4. **Don't comment on your own nervousness, lack of preparedness, etc.**—It will only make you feel more awkward. And it will make the audience uncomfortable.

5. **Don't worry about any "technical" errors in your impromptu speech**—Focus on informing the audience and on making eye contact with them. Scientists say it's impossible to hold two ideas in your mind at the same time. By focusing on your message and on them, not on your fears, you will greatly reduce your jitters.

6. **Play it straight**—Don't go for laughs (unless you are one of the blessed to whom wit and humor are as natural as breathing). Don't add to your stress level by telling a joke that could bomb.

7. **Give it "shape"**—Begin by thanking the emcee or chair, greeting the audience, and summarizing what you're going to tell them.
   Example: "Thank you, Joan. Good afternoon, everyone. It's a pleasure to be here. I'm going to talk a little bit about the status of our membership drive."

- more -

Page 3

The facts and thoughts that are the gist of your speech are the middle. Your ending should consist of a summary of what you just told them, followed by positive and upbeat (if appropriate) closing remarks and a thank-you.

Example: "So that's where we're at. I hope I've clarified what we need to do to increase our membership. This is an energetic group and I'm confident we'll do what needs to be done. Thanks for the opportunity to talk to you today."

One of the best ways to sharpen your impromptu speaking skills: join a group that provides an ongoing opportunity to practice and get feedback. Toastmasters International (www.toastmasters.org) is one of the best.

Jessica Hatchigan is the owner of Greenbriar Communications, a public relations company that specializes in publicity strategy and executive communications. She is the author of How to Be Your Own Publicist, *and also is available to speak to business audiences.*

For more information, visit www.greenbriar.biz or www.hatchigan.com, or contact Jessica Hatchigan at 810-216-1432 or via E-mail at jessica@hatchigan.com.

There's a temptation you must avoid here. Say you are an accounting firm. You may be tempted to write your tip sheet as a self-promotion piece ("Five Reasons to Do Business with Crunch-it! Accounting"). But remember, publicity is not about you or advancing your interests. It's about how you can help or inform audiences or solve their problems. (Of course, in taking this approach, you position yourself and your business in the kind of positive light that attracts clients and customers.)

Media people are much more likely to run a helpful tip sheet like "Five Ways to Make Your Tax Return Painless"—and credit Crunch-it! Accounting as the source (usually done in a few lines at the end of the article)—than they are to run an article on "Why People Should Do Business with Crunch-It! Accounting."

The fact is, the non-self-serving publicity will be much more effective at drawing customers to your business than the blatant "sell" piece could have been. The sell piece would read too much like an advertisement—and most of us are conditioned to tune those out.

Note: numerals in the headline are part of the appeal of a tip sheet—perhaps because by numbering your tips you make people feel you've really nailed the key points. How many tips should you include in a tip sheet? If there are too few, your article will seem thin. If there are too many, a reader's concentration will waver. Five to fifteen seems about right.

Cautionary note: one problem with tip sheets is that they're what media people call "evergreens." There's often no compelling reason to run them in an upcoming issue. That means they can sit in media limbo indefinitely. One way to reduce the chances of this happening is to connect your tip sheet to an upcoming holiday or event. For example, the tax return tip sheet mentioned previously might get good play if sent out in early March, just before prime tax return time.

Another way to make your tip sheet more timely is to send it with a news release announcing an imminent event. For example, if you are announcing the launch of a firm that specializes in establishing tax shelters for individuals, you can include a tip sheet on "Eight Ways to Decide If a Tax Shelter Makes Sense for You." A media outlet might run a story on your upcoming event and run the related tips as a "sidebar" (an accompanying piece).

Media List

A list of the radio or TV shows that have featured or interviewed you reassures broadcast media that you are a pro and is a definite plus when you are trying to line up future broadcast media coverage (see Figure 5.14 on page 136). A track record of TV and radio interviews reassures TV and radio producers that you are an experienced—and probably personable—guest. (And broadcasting credentials reinforce, for print and E-media people, that you're an established professional.)

If you have only a handful of broadcast media experiences, forego preparing a separate list and simply include the information in your bio with a line like "John Robbins has appeared on radio and TV programs, including WXYT TV's *Good Morning, Kenyon County* and WBBT radio's *River City Morning Talk.*

Testimonials

Testimonials are enthusiastic, positive endorsements made by experts, authorities, or media reviewers about you and/or your business or about your product or ser-

Figure 5.14 *List of Your Media Appearances*

Organize It!, 77 Laurel Street, Jacksonville, FL 29174
Contact: Sabrina West, 213-435-3444, west@organizeit.com

Media Appearances-Sabrina West

Television

- *MSNBC News*, "New Trends in Office Life" (June 12, 2001)
- *CBS Evening News*, "A Better Way to Work" (June 6, 2001)
- *ABC Nightly News*, "Clutter Buster for the Fortune 500" (June 14, 2001)
- Fox News, "Organization Guru Revamps Cubicle Life" (June 7, 2001)
- C-SPAN II-Speech, "Organizing (Work Spaces) for Power," delivered at conference of National Association of Human Resource Executives (May 12, 2001)
- WJXX-TV (Ch. 25-ABC), Jacksonville, FL, "Local Organization Company Has Better Ideas" (May 2, 2001)
- WTLV-TV (Ch. 12-NBC), Jacksonville, FL, News Segment (May 1, 2001)

Print

- *USA Today*, "Changes in Work Spaces—More Efficiency?" (May 31, 2001)
- *BusinessWeek*, "Office Guru Makes a Clean Sweep with the Past" (May 29, 2001)
- *Washington Post*, "Future Offices Will Be Paperless (Well, Almost)" (April 28, 2001)
- *St. Louis Post-Dispatch*, "Progress on the Office Front" (April 12, 2001)
- *Florida Today*, "Florida Office Guru Sets Trends" (April 2, 2001)
- *The News-Press*, Fort Myers, FL, "Just When You Thought It Was Safe to Go to the Office" (March 15, 2001)
- *Pensacola News Journal*, Pensacola, FL, "West Intends to Set Direction for Offices of the Future" (March 4, 2001)

- more -

Page 2

Radio

- NPR, "West Coast Live with Jules Stebbens"
- WBAL Baltimore, MD, "The Steve Brightmore Business Talk Show"
- WMAC Georgia, "Your Money"
- KINA Kansas, "Tom Darcy Show"
- KEYL Long Prairie, MN, "Vivian Southender Show"
- WTLN Florida, "Jonathan Stallings Business Minute"

# # #

vice (see Figure 5.15 on page 138). Collect the strongest endorsements you've gathered and group them together on one sheet in quotation format (with attribution) as in the following:

> "Last year when a recession in auto manufacturing caused a sales slump for most auto suppliers, we achieved a record 55 percent growth in sales due to the help Alternate Market Adapter software gave us in quickly tailoring our products to meet the needs of new markets."
>
> —*Joe Vance, president, Ace Auto Carpeting*

Note: enthusiastic praise is appropriate and convincing in a testimonial. This strong language coming from happy clients and customers lends credibility to your marketing and publicity efforts. However, if a businessperson writes a press release and uses this same emphatic language *without* identifying the specific customers and clients it came from, it will read like hype.

Generic statements like "Our customers and clients say we're the greatest thing since sliced bread" just don't work in press kit materials. In fact, they weaken your efforts overall because without a link back to the people who made the statements, they ring false. Facts that can be checked up on are what convince reporters. You need to identify the source of praise so that a reporter knows she or he can, if she or he chooses to, check to make sure it's true.

Figure 5.15 *Testimonials*

Inn on the Lake Bed and Breakfast, 12 Silver Lake Rd., Verdant, OR 53987

Contact: Lisa Bontemps, 987-345-2345, lisa@iotl.com

What Our Customers Say

"Bob and I just returned to Illinois, having been guests at your wonderful bed and breakfast. There aren't enough superlative words to describe what a pleasure it was to stay at the Inn on the Lake. You were so caring and personable. The breakfast was a pleasure to wake up to, especially the smell of Lisa's wonderful coffee. Bob and I are still raving over her homemade Paradise Jelly and breakfast rolls. The country-style decor is comfortable and homelike but with those special touches that made it unique. Thanks for a wonderful visit. We are telling all our friends."

—Bob and Carol Champion
Champaign, Illinois

"Looking back at my wonderful weekend, I realize that the food was some of the finest I've ever been treated to—better than what I've had at some five-star restaurants. Is there any way I can convince Lisa to share her recipe for Lasagna Lite? I still dream about it! Kudos to you, Jeff and Lisa!"

—Sandy Millefiore
Rockport, Florida

"Jeff and Lisa, your sense of humor made us feel right at home at the Inn on the Lake from the first moment. You were both so sweet and efficient, helping us plan our outings to the art museum and the spa-in-the-city meticulously and even providing hand-drawn maps and directions. Now that's attention to detail! You obviously love your guests—and you love your work as hosts because it shows. You're both so good at your jobs and just so very caring. We had a WONDERFUL TIME! Thank you! We hope to see you again, same time next year!"

—Andrew and Liz Wheeler
Beauport, Louisiana

# # #

Note: if you get a glowing testimonial in an unsolicited note or letter, can you use it in your press materials? Yes, but contact the client/customer first to be sure it's all right to reprint the testimonial and identify him or her as the source.

Client List

If the companies you do business with are prestigious or recognizable to the media, include a list of your clients (see Figure 5.16 on page 140). It's another source of credibility.

Video

Producing an effective publicity video can be pricey. But there are some real benefits to video. It's an effective way to demonstrate how a new product works. And a well-done product video will make it easier for TV stations to run a story on your product. If you're trying to book yourself as a speaker or as a guest on a TV talk show, a video can highlight your professional presence and communication skills. See Figure 5.17 on page 141 for an example of a publicity video.

Note: on the other hand, an amateurish video may hurt your chances of getting press coverage on TV or speaking engagements. As with all your publicity materials, don't send it out unless it's good.

To produce a video about you or your business, you need to learn enough about video to be able to create a good-quality tape (or you need to work with a good recording studio). If you choose to produce your own video, get Hal Landen's *Marketing with Video*. It contains excellent advice and tips on how small-business owners can create professional-quality videos on a shoestring budget.

If you have the budget to hire professionals, here's one way to find a reputable studio. Check out the websites of the International Association of Business Communicators (iabc.com) or of the Public Relations Society of America (prsa.org) and find a chapter of one of these organizations that's close to you. Call and ask for the phone number of a member who works in the broadcast media area and who will be able to recommend a good recording studio.

Note: if you are sending a product demo video to TV stations, they will ask for "B-roll." B-roll is video shot with Betacam equipment (broadcast quality as opposed to VHS, which is not suitable for broadcast). To obtain B-roll, make arrangements with the local recording studio of your choice. It's costlier to dub B-roll than VHS. Therefore, the usual procedure is to send out a VHS-format product demo to TV stations with a note saying "B-roll is available" and to provide a contact number to call to request it.

Figure 5.16 *Client List*

Hogarth Accounting, 451 Trimble Avenue, Indianapolis, IN 98124

CLIENT LIST

Financial	Indianapolis Savings & Loan
	Esterbrook Financial
	Western Pacific Bank
	Katersky Financial
	Southern Pacific Bank
	Union National Savings
Real Estate	Indiana Realtors
	Hi-Mark Realty
	J&N Enterprises
Retail	Bluebells of Indianapolis
	The Fashion Shoppe
Food	Kentucky Sparkling Water
	Spring Clean Drinking Water
	Fast Burger Restaurants
	Bella Italian Products
	Tuscan Sun Pasta
	Aunt Wendy's Bakeries
	Landward Farms Foods

For more information, call: Sam Hogarth, 504-312-9880, or E-mail shogarth@hacorp.com

# # #

Product Sample or Product Sample Request Card

Product samples can be enclosed if they are of a size and type that makes sense—a small new widget (if you are a manufacturer), a book (if you are an author), and

Figure 5.17 *Video*

so on. Otherwise, you can include a prestamped postcard that can be filled out to request a product sample (see Figure 5.18 on page 142).

Electronic Press Kits: They're Inexpensive and Effective

Before the Internet and the widespread use of PCs, most press kits were printed. Things have changed.

The first computer, built in the 1940s (the ENIAC), was the size of a room. But it couldn't come close to doing what an average household PC can do today.

Since 1984, the percentage of U.S. homes that have computers has increased more than fivefold. Census Bureau statistics show that, in 2000, 54 million U.S. households (51 percent) had one or more computers, and more than 80 percent

Figure 5.18 *Product Sample Request Card (Front and Back)*

The Aussiclogs Challenge: "Walk a Mile in Our Shoes"

Wearing Aussiclogs is the best way to test what we say about their instant fit and comfort. Fill in the required information below, and we'll send you your free evaluation pair of Aussiclogs right away.

_____ Yes, please send me an evaluation pair of Aussiclogs shoes.

Name _____

Street Address _____

City, State, Zip _____

My shoe size is: _____
I prefer the ____women's walking shoe ____men's walking shoe
The color I prefer is (check one): ___black ___tan

[PRESTAMP]

To: Aussiclogs Central
73 Michigan Avenue
Chicago, IL 60901

of those households had Internet access, which represents 95 million people in the United States able to use the Internet.

Today almost all journalists are online and computer savvy. That means it's possible to create an "electronic press kit"—a website or CD that contains all of the elements you would put into your printed press kits.

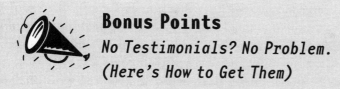

Bonus Points
No Testimonials? No Problem.
(Here's How to Get Them)

• **Method #1:** On an ongoing basis, mail recent customers/clients a one-sheet survey that asks them to rate you "on a scale of one to five" on overall satisfaction and quality, and on any of the specific areas of performance (speed, reliability, etc.) that you are particularly trying to track. At the end of the survey, write: "If you've been completely satisfied with our performance, please take a moment to write a one- or two-sentence testimonial we can use in our marketing materials."

Provide a space at the bottom of the survey where the survey taker can jot a signature under a sentence that reads, "This is to affirm that _____ may use the endorsement provided above in his or her marketing and publicity materials."

Enclose a self-addressed, stamped envelope that the survey taker can use to mail the survey back to you.

• **Method #2:** Make a list of clients or customers you know have been pleased with your products and services within the past few months. Phone or write them. In the course of your conversation, bring up some of the details of how your product or service "came through" for them. Tell them you're preparing some new marketing materials and would love to include their testimonials. Then ask, "Would you consider giving me a testimonial I can use?" Then tell them that you know they're busy and to make it easier for them—if they prefer—you can draft a testimonial for them to sign off on or edit as they please.

If your customers/clients indicate that they will gladly write their own testimonials, thank them and tell them you'll look forward to receiving them. If you don't hear from them within two weeks or so (via the post office or E-mail), courteously write or phone to remind them.

• **Method #3:** If you operate a retail outlet, restaurant, or dealership, give your customers a card that asks them to write what they like about your service or products. Make sure the card has a space where they can provide their signed approval for you to use their input in your marketing efforts.

There are some great benefits to creating your press kits in electronic form. The biggest benefit of electronic press kits is that you can use them to provide "instant" information to the media. In addition, once you've paid for your initial Web page setup and design, E–press kits are very economical. Once you upload (post on the Web) pages that include the history of your company, your bio, photos, descriptions of your products and services, and so on, you can write pitch letters and news releases that refer media people to your additional online materials for more information (e.g., "For more information on SummerKids Summer Camp, visit the SummerKids online press room at www.summerkidsonline.com").

You can always opt to use both printed and online press kits or variations thereof—perhaps sending the printed kits to key media people and sending others on your mailing list a news release that refers them to your additional online material.

Want Low-Cost, Power-Packed Publicity? Burn Those CDs

CD "burners" (also called CD "writers")—the hardware that creates CDs—are relatively inexpensive (around three hundred dollars or less), as are the blank discs used to make press kit CDs (less than one dollar each). CD burners allow you to reproduce and distribute your printed press kit on a CD.

You also can include a CD containing all of your printed press kit materials as an element of the "hard copy" press kit you mail to media people. It represents

Bonus Points
How to Get Great (and Low-Cost) Feedback on Your Press Kit Before You Start Using It

If you want valuable feedback on your press kit before you start using it, have it reviewed by the students in a university or college marketing class. Contact the business department of a local university or college and ask to speak to a professor who teaches marketing classes to arrange this.

an extra convenience for them. They can pull photos and whole paragraphs of text from the CD to cut and paste into their stories.

Make sure you purchase CD labels (available at most office supply stores) and print them out for your CD press kits. An unlabeled CD easily gets lost in a stack of other unlabeled CDs.

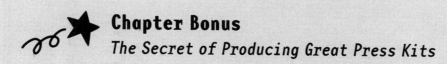

Chapter Bonus
The Secret of Producing Great Press Kits

A well-done press kit doesn't just rattle off facts (what your story is about/what's new about you or your business). Here's the formula for a winning press kit:

feelings
(vivid, lively language that tells your story with flair and makes it appealing)

+

useful benefits
(why media audiences will care/what's in it for them—entertainment, information, money, timesaving tips, etc.)

+

the news angle
(what makes this story news/what's timely about this story)

=

a great press kit

6 Who're They Gonna Call? You!

Establish Yourself as an Expert

"A good message will always find a messenger."

—A. E. Barr

To successfully publicize your business you must develop relationships with the media people most likely to run a story about your business or industry. With a large city daily newspaper, for example, "If you have a tech story, look for a tech writer," Mike Sante, business editor of the *Detroit Free Press*, advises. He adds, "It's the reporter who deals with a certain industry most often who's the most likely to be intrigued by a new story affecting that industry. Send a press release or letter that says: 'Here's why I think you're going to love this idea,' and present your credentials."

Note: all newspapers, but especially large city papers, guard their credibility vigilantly. The larger the paper, the more skeptical a reporter will be. Expect tough questions to reassure the media person of your credentials. This includes questions relating to your track record, what other businesses you or your partners have started, what kind of expertise you have, what your business plan is, and how profitable you've been.

"Business reporters on large city dailies will want to know why you have an edge—why you are not going to fail," Sante says. There's a good reason for this. They don't want to write a glowing story about a company only to turn around the next week or month and have to report that it's going bankrupt, or that its principals have been convicted of fraud, or that it's being sued by an unhappy customer.

Credibility, in other words, is vital. Once you establish credibility, media people accept you as an expert in your field or industry. And it's to the experts that they turn when they need information or a quote for their stories and news reports.

Tips and Techniques for Establishing Your "Expert" Status with the Media

So how do you establish credibility and get media people to recognize you as an expert in your field? Here are some ways:

Send a "Please-Think-of-Me-as-a-Source" Letter

Contact editors, reporters, and local freelancers who specialize in writing about your industry with a letter explaining your area of expertise (in your industry, not in your product or service), and offer to be a source (media speak for "expert" or "resource") if they are doing an article on that industry. ("This is who I am. This is my area of expertise. If you need information about my industry, please give me a call.") You can include a short (100- to 250-word) bio that establishes your credentials. Three or four days later, you can follow up with a phone call and remind them that you are available and will be happy to help if they need to tap into your expertise.

Do you have a fact sheet (see Figure 5.11 on page 126) about your field or industry (not your business) that you've prepared? Or some other information about your field or industry that a reporter might not ordinarily have access to but would find of substance or value? This can be a special edition of an industry or trade newsletter, perhaps one packed with vital statistics, or a "future trends" report prepared by a professional association to which you belong—anything that provides good rich data a reporter would need to make an effort to find on his or her own. Share it with your target media people.

Offer to make a quick stop to drop off the fact sheet, special report, and so on in person at their newsroom or station. Try to convey the fact that you will make the drop-off short and sweet. Be sensitive to their reactions. If they signal that they prefer not to take the time to meet face-to-face, offer to mail your information instead, and do so cheerfully.

If you get a go-ahead on the drop-off, be sure you're dressed and groomed in a way that conveys a successful and professional image for someone in your field of work. Shake hands, present your materials, restate your willingness to act as a source, and leave. Make it painless, and don't wear out your welcome.

Suggest a Story

Again, you are positioning yourself as the answer to a reporter's problem (the problem of coming up with great story ideas that please his or her boss and the reading public). Your story suggestions don't need to be about your own business each and every time. The point is to make contact with reporters at least three or four times a year—in other words, to stay on their radar in a positive way (as someone who is genuinely interested in helping them do their jobs better and more efficiently).

If you are generous in suggesting stories that relate to trends in your industry (again, not just stories about your own business), you will boost your credibility with media people. And, sooner or later, the law of reciprocity will go into effect. A reporter will quote you, for example, making an insightful comment related to a story you helped develop. Even if it's only an inch or two of ink, a steady drip-drip-drip of this kind is a powerful way to position yourself well in the eyes of media audiences (the target audiences for your products and services). You're building a reputation for yourself as an authority in your field—and the "halo effect" extends to cast a positive glow on your business. Remember: a subtle approach can be the most effective.

Note: take time to think things through before you call a reporter with any story idea. Study the kinds of stories the reporter favors. If your story idea doesn't have the same substance, be cautious. The worst thing you can do is to repeatedly demonstrate to a reporter that you have a poor understanding of what he or she is looking for. This is the opposite of what you're trying to accomplish. You don't want to become the reporter's equivalent of "the boy who cried wolf" as a media source. If you're sloppy about the story suggestions you offer up, you'll find your future calls (justifiably) ignored.

Call, Fax, or E-Mail When There's Breaking News

When important news related to your area of expertise is breaking, call, fax, or E-mail a news release. Call the media outlets you've targeted to find out which method the media people you want to contact prefer.

Do a Little "Face Time"

Play it by ear in developing relationships with media people. Like people in general, some are gregarious in nature, and others are retiring. (Writers, in general, tend to be the latter.) Some media people enjoy an occasional lunch or meeting at a coffee shop at which you can update them on trends and developments in your neck of the business woods. Others prefer that you contact them by phone and E-mail and stick to the facts.

One way to meet the media people you've targeted is to join an organization like the Public Relations Society of America (prsa.org) or the International Association of Business Communicators (iabc.com). These organizations often host "meet the media" events. Check the websites of their local chapters for their schedule of upcoming events.

Note: as you develop relationships with your key media people, you may get invited to lunch—or vice versa. If you share a meal with a media person, split the check or let the media person pay. Many media outlets have ethics rules that don't allow reporters to accept free meals or gifts.

Keep Building Your Relationships with Reporters

As your relationship with a media person develops, abide by the same rules you'd apply to any business relationship. Be gracious and well mannered. People remember. Publicity success is not about gimmicks. It's about being genuine. Some publicity newbies are intimidated by reporters and the press. Don't be. Remember, they're just people too. They like to chat every once in a while (when they're not on deadline). They like a good laugh. As you get to know media people, make notes in a contact file. This is a technique many politicians use. It may seem like extra work, but do it anyway.

When you get back in touch with a reporter, months later, she will be impressed—and flattered—that you remember and ask about how her three-year-old is doing in preschool and whether he's gotten over his fear of escalators. (Wouldn't you be flattered if the shoe were on the other foot?) Her responses will open the door to additional small talk. Of such little exchanges professional friendships and great working relationships are born.

One low-tech way to keep this information from fading from your memory is with an alphabetized index card system (total investment: less than five dollars). Or you can buy a software program that organizes your contact information. Two of the better-known contact tracking programs are ACT! and Microsoft Outlook.

Important: if you opt for the electronic system, be sure to back up your data regularly by saving it to a Zip or Jaz disc or a rewritable CD.

Note: you have to foster detachment in working with the media. It's part of the game. If in your role as a source you convey any sense of entitlement (to a story or coverage), that's bad form. And if you come across as aggrieved or resentful when the "payback" is slow in coming, you will be pegged as "immature" and dropped as a source.

Send a Letter to the Editor

Another way to reinforce your expert status with the media is to send a letter to the editor of your targeted media publication. If you notice an error in an article dealing with your area of expertise or have something to say about a developing trend in your field, write an articulate and well-argued letter. Or, if the publication runs an article about your industry to which you can add pertinent facts or share valuable insights, write and do so.

To increase your chances of getting your letter published, study the letters that the publication regularly does run. What are the common elements? New facts? Corrections of erroneous information? Thoughtful commentary? Expressions of concern? Write your letter accordingly.

Note: While it's acceptable to convey enthusiasm or strong feeling in your letter, don't overdo it—and don't express negative emotions. Conveying a sense of concern about an issue is different from conveying a tone of anger or contempt.

Write an Op-Ed Piece

You can also establish yourself as an expert by writing an article for the op-ed (opinions and editorials) section of a newspaper or magazine. In newspapers the editorial pages are easy to spot. Not all magazines feature op-ed sections. Those that do usually limit them to a page with titles like "My Turn," "Readers' Voice," or "In My Opinion."

Study the style of other op-ed pieces that are run in the publication you've targeted. Get a handle on the tone and substance the editor is looking for. Write your piece to match, or hire a freelance writer to help you shape your thoughts into publishable prose.

Note: you have the best chance of getting a piece accepted when there's breaking news or a developing trend related to your area of expertise. That's when you write an insightful piece that offers a fresh point of view or helps people better understand what's happening. If you do it well enough, you'll see your byline in the op-ed pages.

Tip: it's essential to get your op-ed piece to an editor fast—when there's breaking news, newspapers have to respond quickly.

Here's one way to position yourself to move quickly: even before any breaking news story occurs, think through what key insights you've acquired working in your industry—especially those insights you have that are not common knowledge. Can you come up with any thought-provoking statements along these lines?

Say you're the owner of a photography studio. Among the tidbits of knowledge you've learned along the way: when catastrophe threatens a home (once people are sure their family members and pets are safe) they run to rescue family photos. That's because they're one-of-a-kind treasures that can't be replaced.

Work up an op-ed piece or an editorial along these lines, adding two additional pertinent insights and/or facts that make a case for how people value memories second only to life itself. This is a subtle way to say that investing in high-quality studio photos is a worthwhile purchase. Then, when there's breaking news that relates to the theme of "how valuable memories are to us," add a paragraph or two to your prewritten essay to tie it into the breaking news, and send it to the op-ed editor. (Make sure you find out the name of the op-ed editor and that you mail your work to a specific person.)

A good breaking news story on which to piggyback the studio photos op-ed piece, for example, would be the death of a well-regarded public figure (like actor Jimmy Stewart) whose passing evokes many positive memories in people.

Exercise good judgment and good taste. Trying to piggyback the same op-ed piece on a natural disaster story or a house fire story might seem to make sense at first blush, but it would appear to be (and would be) crass and opportunistic. The same would be true of writing this piece to tie into a tragic and premature death (like that of Diana, princess of Wales).

Tip: in the weeks just before and just after Christmas, editors receive the fewest letters to the editor and op-ed submissions. Most people—including the writers who usually fill these pages—are traveling and visiting family and friends. That means you might have more luck placing your letter to the editor or your op-ed piece at this time.

Write a Column

Another way to get known as an expert is to write a regular column for your local daily or weekly newspaper. A column writer regularly offers advice and insights on a specialized theme—legal issues, home repair, food, and so on.

There's a lot of competition for spots as a columnist with large city dailies. The competition includes syndicated professional columnists. As more business-people are becoming savvy about the great publicity opportunity a column provides, it's getting harder to become a columnist at some suburban weeklies and dailies too. However, there is a lot of regional variation. Some papers are hungry for columnists. Others might be open to a columnist with a unique business background who can offer fresh ideas and specialized advice.

Note: while a regular column is an excellent way to reinforce your status as an expert, writing the column can be time-consuming. Unless you can write quickly and well, or have the resources to hire a freelance ghostwriter (someone willing to allow you to have the byline, or writing credit) to help you shape your thoughts, column writing may not be for you.

Hold Workshops or Teach Seminars

Media people are always looking for story ideas and often pay attention to special interest seminars, workshops, and speeches. Once you're advertised or listed in a catalog as a speaker or workshop facilitator, send a copy of the ad or catalog, with the section advertising your seminar or workshop flagged with a Post-it Note, to your target media people along with a short note inviting them to attend. Indicate that you are available to interview before or after your workshop or seminar.

Note: if you can think of a punchy title for your workshop or seminar, you'll increase the chances of sparking a reporter's interest—not to mention the general public's. Here are some examples:

- "Everything You Always Wanted to Know About Indoor Plumbing—but Were Afraid to Ask" (plumbers' seminar)
- "The Little Engine That Could (but Didn't)—and How He Went Wrong" (auto repair shop's workshop)
- "What a Weigh to Go! Tips for Dieting" (weight loss consultant seminar)

Write for Trade and/or Professional Publications

If you can write clearly and effectively, why not get published in the magazines and newsletters that are important to your field or industry?

Study these publications. What kinds of stories and articles do they run? Do they use staff writers, or are they open to freelance submissions? If you can't tell from studying the publication, check the guidelines in *Writer's Market*, a publication of *Writer's Digest*. *Writer's Market* is available at most bookstores. Or you can check guidelines listings at writersdigest.com. If you can't find the guidelines for the particular publication you're interested in, call or E-mail the editor, introduce yourself, and ask if his or her publication accepts freelance submissions. You can also ask which sections of the publication, in particular, are open to freelancers. Then ask how you can get a copy of the publication's guidelines. When the editor has answered your questions, say thank you and bring the conversation to a close. Don't ask what kinds of articles they're looking for. It's unprofessional. It's your job to come up with story ideas. To form story ideas, study the publication to see what they are looking for—and what you can add that's new and useful and that fits into the publication's theme and style.

Many trade publications pay for freelance contributions. If they offer to pay, why not check to see if they will provide free advertising for your business (in the issue in which your article runs) instead? Also, confirm that their editorial policy will allow you to include a short paragraph at the end of your article that mentions your business and includes your phone number and E-mail address.

Get a Pager and (Gulp!) Establish a Hot Line

Today all of us are into instant everything. Reporters are just as rushed as the rest of us. If two sources offer their expertise, which one will the reporter call? The one who's instantly available.

If you are willing to step up to this level of dedication, buy a pager or a cell phone and be willing to respond within fifteen minutes of a reporter or producer's call. Let them know you are giving them your "hot line" number.

Note: this is not for the fainthearted.

Speak the Speech! (What Public Speaking Can Do for You)

Public speaking merits special attention. It's one of the most powerful ways to establish your expert status with the media. A word of caution here though: not all of us are natural extroverts who take to the idea of public appearances with relish. And few of us are naturally gifted speakers. In fact, *The Book of Lists* places public speaking at the top of the list of common fears—higher even than death.

Human potential seems at times unlimited. And I believe that anyone who seriously wants to be an effective speaker can become one. Some of the best speak-

> ## Bonus Points
> ### *What's This I Hear About Speakers Bureaus?*
>
> Speakers bureaus agree to represent prominent experts in a variety of fields. Most small-business speakers don't need the services of a speakers bureau. Speakers bureaus require that you prepare a video that highlights your strengths as a speaker. This is a convenient way for them to assess your skills, and it also is one of the key selling tools they have to market you as a speaker. But producing a video of the quality required is expensive. (You can't "go cheap." A bad video will only hurt your efforts.) If you're just starting out as a speaker, it probably doesn't make sense to invest the kind of money required. Why? Because even if you are accepted by a speakers bureau as a client, the bureau—unless you are already in demand as a speaker—will probably do little to actively market your services. It most likely will simply include you in a catalog with scores—or hundreds—of other speakers. Until you become established as a sought-after speaker, you are probably better off lining up your own speaking engagements.

ers in history had to overcome fear, trepidation, and even speech impediments before they conquered the podium. However, your time, resources, and energy are limited. No one can do it all. And no one knows better than yourself what your capabilities and potential are. If you weren't born with the "gift of gab," are you prepared to commit to acquiring and polishing your speaking skills? If you are intensely uncomfortable speaking in public, is this a state of mind you can overcome?

A halfhearted effort will fizzle where public speaking is concerned. If you aren't enthusiastic about the prospect of communicating to large audiences (no matter what the benefits), then skip this section. Pour your energies into the many other avenues that can generate publicity for your business.

If, on the other hand, you find the prospect of public speaking appealing—or at least not totally intimidating—great! Public speaking can be very good for you—and for your business. And the really good news is that, with determination, even speakers who start out a bit wobbly and knock-kneed can become highly poised and effective communicators.

How exactly does public speaking open doors of opportunity for entrepreneurs? Public speaking gives you instant credibility—both with the media and with your customers and clients. Your audience assumes you are an expert in your business or industry. Why else would you have been invited to speak? And because public speaking is something that creates a good deal of jitteriness, even in the best of us, the fact that you are boldly taking your place behind the podium causes audience members to view you as gutsy and capable. Public speaking also enhances your publicity chances. Here's how:

• **"Pulls" media to you:** Just as it boosts your credibility with your audience, public speaking boosts your credibility with media people as well. They know, just as your audience does, that you must have some expertise or valuable insights to share—the kind they can tap into the next time they need information about your business or industry. Media people have even been known to contact people who are highlighted as upcoming speakers in service club flyers or association newsletters or who are listed in speaker's bureau directories—to work up a story on the subject matter of the speech (if it's fresh or timely) or to ask for input or a comment on a story involving the speaker's area of expertise. In short, getting out there as a speaker is a great way to come to the attention of the media.

• **Provides "before-during-after" publicity opportunities:**

Before—About two weeks before your speech is scheduled, you can send a news release to the print and broadcast media in the region in which you'll speak. This should result in at least brief mentions.

Day of—Call or E-mail key media people the day of your speech to remind them about it and to invite them to attend and cover the event. Make your pitch short and interesting. ("I'll be speaking to the Wentworth Astronomy Club this afternoon on 'Comets of July,' and we'll hold a viewing. The Parker-Gell comet, which passes by every twelve years, will be visible by telescope in the sky over Wentworth. I have a photo of the comet I can provide to you. I'm the owner of Barnes Telescopes, by the way, and several of my articles on summer comet viewing have appeared in the *Stargazers' Newsletter*. I hope you can attend or send someone to cover the event.")

After—E-mail or fax a news release reporting your speech highlights to local media. Include the most interesting and gripping nuggets of information. (You'll have prepared this beforehand, of course.) This gives you a third chance to get some ink or airtime and get your message out to the public.

- **"Pulls" customers to you:** Public speaking also presents you with direct marketing opportunities. Because you are talking to people who are interested in your area of expertise, there might be one or more people in the audience who approach you about your products or services. Your speech, of course, will not include any overt advertising for your business. Odd as it may sound, directly soliciting business while you are in your "speaker" role will undercut both the effectiveness of your speech and your chances of getting business. It's considered bad form to pitch your business services in your capacity as a speaker. However, it's perfectly appropriate to mention that if anyone in the audience belongs to a group or association that is looking for a speaker, you might be available. (Be selective about which offers you choose. Accept only those that enable you to best reach your target market and/or to publicize your business—in other words, that make sense from your overall marketing strategy point of view. In short, "stay on message.")

Polish Your Speaking Skills (for Fun and Profit)

Given all the benefits of public speaking, what do you need to do to become a good public speaker?

If public speaking doesn't come naturally to you, make up your mind to acquire the needed skills. The best way to do that is by practicing in front of audiences. Organizations like Toastmasters (toastmasters.org) and Dale Carnegie (dale-carnegie.com) have been created to provide you with just such opportunities. At Toastmasters meetings, for instance, fellow members are your audience. You get the opportunity to address them from a podium regularly. And they provide feedback, suggestions for improvement, and occasional applause. This kind of active practice and ongoing feedback is invaluable and provides insights that remove barriers to successful communication.

By the way, check to see if your local college or university offers acting classes. If it does, consider taking one or two, especially classes on improvisation. You will learn how to be conscious of body language and make it match your verbal messages; how to express yourself with gestures; tips and tricks for controlling on-stage jitters; how to vary the pitch, volume, and tone of your voice to best effect;

and how to think on your feet—in short, all of the things that really good speakers have mastered.

Seven Ways to Pump Up Your Podium Skills

As you practice and hone the craft of public speaking, your presentation skills will become more and more polished. To help the process along, here are some insights I've collected while coaching some of our nation's top executives in their roles as public speakers.

K.I.S.S.—Keep It Simple, Speaker

Big and technical words won't impress the audience. It's naive to use big words in a mistaken notion that they boost credibility. Jargon, technical language, and long, dry "ten dollar" words (where "dollar" ones would do) turn audiences off faster than a speeding bullet.

In her book *On Speaking Well*, Peggy Noonan, former speechwriter for Presidents Reagan and Bush, talks about the emotional impact of "good hard simple words." When soldiers take a bullet, she says, they don't say, "I have been shot." They say, "I'm hit."

Winston Churchill was one of the best speakers of all time. In his most memorable speeches, rallying his countrymen to war, he didn't use weak, multisyllabic words and say things like: "We are determined never to negotiate surrender at any enemy battlefield invasion point." Instead, he chose short strong words that still ring with power: "I have nothing to offer but blood, toil, tears, and sweat." . . . "We shall fight on the beaches. We shall fight on the landing grounds. We shall fight in the fields, and in the streets. We shall fight in the hills. We shall never surrender!"

A "Just the Facts, Ma'am" Approach Won't Cut It

Although statistics are useful to add credibility to your speech, the audience won't be swayed by facts and statistics alone. If cold, hard data were that powerful, mathematicians, accountants, and statisticians would rule the world. That's not the way it works. Studies repeatedly show that although people like to believe they make decisions based on the facts, they actually make decisions based on feelings. Say you're the CEO of a company that's trying to distinguish itself as the "high-quality provider." If you're going to talk to a group of potential buyers about why they should purchase your widgets, don't just give them the cold, hard figures on your process-improvement efforts. Throw in a punchy quote that summarizes your company's approach to quality—something like Debbi Fields's "Good enough never is." Or, if you're talking to them about major changes you're instituting at the company, give them a joke or an anecdote that provides an insight into, say, the difficulty of change, like: "How many psychiatrists does it take to change a lightbulb?" "One . . . but the lightbulb has got to want to change."

Audiences are won over when you make them laugh or move them emotionally. They're also more receptive to your message when they like you. Which brings us to the next thought . . .

Get Real!

Effective speakers don't always act serious and authoritative or talk in a steady, unvarying tone of voice.

William Safire, editor of *Lend Me Your Ears*, a collection of all-time great speeches, says a good speaker begins by "shaking hands with the audience." He means that the speaker connects emotionally. The best speakers sway audiences by appealing to their hearts as much, and probably more so, as to their minds. Look at clips of two of our country's greatest speakers—Ronald Reagan and John F. Kennedy. Or, watch Katie Couric in action on the *Today* show. These communicators set the standard. How? They're the opposite of wooden. They're animated, natural—real. They're masters of "connection." They smile, project warmth, and seek eye contact with the audience. They send the message "I like you" to their listeners. And they vary the cadence and pitch of their voices—as appropriate—to match the subject matter at hand. They also use humor well.

"But what if I tell a joke and it falls flat?" Not a problem. Just make sure that the joke has a point that ties into your speech. That way you'll raise at least a few smiles, and the lack of belly laughs won't be noticed.

The Zen of Speaking: Silence Adds Zing

If you stop for a moment in the middle of your speech, do you think the audience will think you're losing it?

They won't. Actually, one of the most powerful things a speaker can do in the middle of a presentation is to . . . pause. A few beats of silence peppered throughout your speech can serve many purposes. A pause adds suspense. A pause rivets the audience's attention. A pause acts as a graceful bridge for a change of topic. And—finally—a pause builds an image of you as a sophisticated and masterful speaker. Why? Because most beginning speakers are scared to death of those power-packed moments of silence. Use them.

If you pepper your speeches with nervous verbal tics—"uhs" and "ahs"—start replacing those tics with power pauses. That single change in your speaking style will boost you into a whole new category of polished speakerdom.

Remember: They're Rooting for You

Audiences generally are foursquare behind a speaker. They also are a very forgiving bunch. The reason? Most of us know it takes guts to get up there and hold forth. There's definitely an empathy factor at work. So keep that in mind if you stumble getting on stage, knock over your water glass, or commit some other gaffe. Unless you're speaking to an odd group—like the Society of Hard-Core Curmudgeons—the audience will be sympathetic.

There are a few commonsense exceptions here, however. If you get up to speak and your mistakes are a result of poor preparation, the audience will—justifiably—think you're wasting their time. Or, if you're the CEO of Really Mean Company, Inc., and are announcing a 10 percent salary cut to employees following a year of record profits, the sympathy factor will not apply.

Should You Wing It?

Are the best speeches always unrehearsed, spontaneous, and "from the heart"?

Yes, the best speeches are "from the heart." But a speech doesn't have to be spontaneous to be genuine—and to come across that way. Churchill is famous for his line: "I'm just preparing my impromptu remarks." He was an excellent speaker who appeared to be talking off the cuff, but the reality was he worked very hard on his speech texts beforehand.

A great speech appears to be unrehearsed and spontaneous. But if it's good, the chances are the speaker—or his or her speechwriter—worked hard at the content. Some of the most effective Fortune 500 CEO speakers around are effective because they devote tremendous care to their speeches. There is no substitute for doing your homework.

"Soup to Nuts" Speeches Give Audiences Indigestion. Don't Do It!

Don't try to lay it all on the table. A speech should be only one key element of an overall communications plan. To keep it effective, keep it short. Ronald Rea-

Bonus Points
Should You Read Your Speech from a Text?

Politicians and corporate chiefs generally speak from prepared texts written by speechwriters. They read the speech from a teleprompter or from a text they take with them to the lectern. If you take this route, learn how to write the pseudo-conversational prose that professional speechwriters have mastered. It's not as difficult as you might think. Simply read the remarks you prepare aloud. Do they sound conversational? If not, change your speech so that they do.

Conversational: "It's great to be here in Kansas City. I really appreciate this opportunity to talk to you about some of the problems you're facing—and to offer up a possible solution or two."

Nonconversational: "It's my humble pleasure to stand before this august audience here in Kansas City this fine morning. The situations causing you problems are a cause for grave concern among all of us citizens. Perhaps I may offer up a solution or two in the course of my remarks."

Some people are more comfortable without a prepared text. They simply outline the speech they'll give in bullets that include key words or phrases. Take this route and you may end up with an awkward construction or two, but if you present confidently and if your content is valuable, no one will notice or care.

gan, a master at gauging audiences, told his speechwriters to keep his speeches to twenty minutes or less. He had it right. Twenty minutes is more than enough time to make one to three key points. That's all you need to do. That's what you should aim to do if you want to get a reputation as an effective speaker. It's a mistake to try and tell your audience everything they need to know about a subject. Pick a few important points and convey what you have to say in a punchy, memorable way.

In speeches, shorter is sweeter. As Franklin Delano Roosevelt, another top presidential communicator, said, "Be sincere, be brief, be seated."

By the way, although the competition is stiff, speaking can be a lucrative career in and of itself. If the public speaking bug bites and you want to learn more, Dottie and Lilly Walters's book *Speak and Grow Rich* is an excellent place to start.

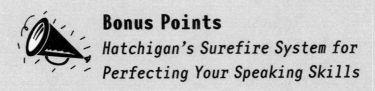

Bonus Points
Hatchigan's Surefire System for Perfecting Your Speaking Skills

Let's say you've polished your skills, prepared your presentation, and are raring to go. How do you launch your speaking career?

Take a methodical step-by-step approach. Here's how:

1. **Zero in on your area of expertise.** You will succeed in landing speaking engagements that strategically promote your business when you find a way to overlap two sets of interests: the interest of a particular group in enhancing their knowledge in a particular area and your interest in spreading awareness of your company, product, or service.

Say your product is a new kind of pill container—one that's especially small and discreet. You probably won't interest your target audience—people who take medications regularly—in a speech on pillbox manufacturing. But they certainly might be interested in a speech on "Ten Health Tips Your Doctor Never Taught You (but Should Have)." Do a little research. Offer ten creative, information-packed health tips—including one on "How to Take Good Care of Yourself—and Not Look Like a Hypochondriac" (and mention carrying any medication you need to take in a—you guessed it—discreet container).

Or, if you're the owner of a shop that specializes in repairing scratches, dents, and nicks on auto bodies, you probably won't find much interest in a general audience for a speech on "How We Repair Dents at Ace Body Shop." But a speech on "Eight Ways to Save Money When You Return Your Lease Car" might find a wide audience. (You'd mention that repairing blemishes on the car body is one way to save a bundle, and you could add something that's not an overt sell like, "And you can find some shops that will repair scratches, dents, and nicks so well that they really do become invisible. For instance, at my shop—the Ace Body Shop—we've even developed a new technique for paint repairs so effective that one of our customers thought we'd returned the wrong car to her.")

Note: it's considered bad form for you to distribute your business card to an audience that came to hear a speech, say, about improving their golf stance (not about how to buy new clubs from your golf club company). However, one way to get your contact information tastefully out is to prepare a tip sheet (see Figure

5.13 on page 132) that lists some of the tips you're offering plus some additional information of value. You can arrange to have a copy of your tip sheet waiting on each seat before the audience arrives. The tip sheet would, of course, include your contact information and your company name. Or, alternatively, you can tell the audience you've prepared a tip sheet and tell them that if they leave their business cards with you, you'll be happy to mail them a copy. (You can enclose some information about your company with the tip sheet.)

2. **Think through which target audience you want to reach.** Your target audience is the group of people most likely to buy your product or service. This will vary, of course, depending on your business. The people who come to hear your speech will probably be only a small part of your target audience. However, if you get good coverage for your speech (newspaper, radio, and TV news coverage) you will reach additional members of your target audience.

Tip: another way to extend the audience for your speech is to write an article based on your speech text and submit it for publication to magazines, newspapers, and newsletters likely to be read by your potential customers and clients. Very often speech texts lend themselves easily to this kind of double duty. And because speeches often touch on timely subjects, your recycled speech may be an easy sell.

3. **Find a winning topic for your speech.** Ask yourself the following questions:

- What do I feel strongly about in my business or industry?
- What have I earned a right to talk about?
- What do audiences need to hear/want to hear about my business or industry?
- What challenges is my business or industry facing?

A successful speech presents a solution to a problem or concern facing an audience. Here's a good formula for doing this: find an interesting way to introduce the problem. (Cite some surprising statistics, for example, or briefly tell a story from your personal experience or that of others.) Once you've stated the problem, suggest a solution and/or provide insights that expand the knowledge base of the audience. Make your solution/insights as unique and fresh as possible if you want to wow the audience. Provide at least three arguments/examples that support your solution or develop your insights. Summarize what you've just said. Offer to answer any questions (or your emcee can step in to let people know you will take questions for ten or fifteen minutes).

4. **To line up speaking engagements, call groups in your area that meet regularly and are always looking for speakers.** These include clubs and service organizations like the Jaycees, the Rotary, Kiwanis, Soroptomists, and other local chapters of national associations. Contact your area chamber of commerce or the visitors and convention bureau of the closest large city to pick up a list of local clubs and associations like Women Business Owners, the Association of Independent Realtors, Franchisees International, and so on. Or check to see if your chamber of commerce posts the information online. (Most do.) If it makes sense, consider talking to college and university audiences. You are not, of course, limited to your local schools and organizations. Try to line up engagements in other towns and cities within driving distance. As your speaking skills are honed—and if your overall marketing strategy calls for it—work your way up to the national audiences.

To line up a speaking engagement at a given organization, contact the program chairperson. To find out who this is, call the organization's main phone number and ask for his or her name and direct dial number. When you contact the program chairperson, introduce yourself. Be friendly and professional. Have a prepared script (that doesn't sound like a prepared script when you say it) that presents your credentials convincingly. Then ask if the organization is presently signing up new speakers. If the answer is yes, give a short, interesting summary of what you propose to speak on and throw out a speech title that has wit and pizzazz. Your goal is to capture the program chairperson's imagination and to convince him or her that you'll present an information-packed talk that his or her audience will enjoy. Here's a sample:

> "Hello. This is Janis Jones. I'm calling to ask if the Rain Valley Homebuilders Association is presently signing up speakers. [Pause to hear reply.] Oh, great. I'm the owner of Pineland Designs, a landscaping firm. I help homebuilders boost the value of the properties they sell by making smart choices in landscaping. The title of my speech is 'Tree Ways to Boost Your Bottom Line.' I explain the three things a homebuilder can do to ensure he'll double his money on every dollar he invests in landscaping."

Be aware that organizations often book speakers several months, even a year or so, in advance, so think in that time frame.

Note: to ensure good results, adopt the rule of thumb that telemarketers use—for each hour you devote to calling prospects, dial at least twenty phone numbers and make it your goal to talk to at least four decision makers (people who have the final say on hiring a speaker). The more speeches you want to line up, the more hours you will have to devote to calling. (Get used to rejection. Lining up speaking engagements is a selling job. Expect to "fail forward" to success.)

A little bit more about titles: a great title for your speech builds interest. It also boosts attendance—and the chances that the media will cover your speech. The best titles promise a benefit, create curiosity, and even use humor to entice attention—and attendance. Go to the library and look through *Books in Print* and *Forthcoming Books in Print*. This will give you ideas for titles. (You can't copyright titles, by the way, so don't worry if your title gets close to someone else's. But don't steal another person's title outright either.)

Use That Speech to Leverage More Publicity!

There are several ways to "recycle" your speech to maximize its publicity value. Here are some of the best ways:

- Find additional organizations—clubs, associations, universities, colleges, and so on—to which you can give the same speech. (Modify it slightly each time to fit the needs of the new audience.)
- Rewrite the speech as an article. Submit it to appropriate publications.
- Send key excerpts from your speech in news release format to your target media. (You can also include the news release format speech with information you send to potential customers and clients and include it in your future press kits as appropriate.)

Sixteen Ways to Make Your Speeches Sparkle

Public speaking requires commitment and an investment of time and energy. Make your hard work pay off by attending to the details that ensure a smooth and pleasant experience for your audience and host organization—and a highly effective presentation for you.

1. **Write a one-page introduction.** This will be for the use of the person who is introducing you. The introduction should mention your career highlights as they pertain to the subject of the speech. Don't be humble. Think in terms of your audience. If you were in the audience, wouldn't you like to hear that you were about to be treated to a talk by an exciting, dynamic, accomplished individual? Write your intro that way.

2. **Prepare a tip sheet** (see Figure 5.13 on page 132). Your tip sheet can provide information that relates to your speech content but extends it in some valuable way. It should not recap your speech. Somewhere in your speech, where it fits, let the audience know that the tip sheet is available and that you'll be happy to send it to anyone who leaves a business card. When you mail the tip sheet, you can include a flyer with information about your product or service. This enables you to build a mailing list of people who may be seriously interested in your product or service.

3. **Rehearse, rehearse, rehearse.** If you have a friend or family member who will give you honest and helpful feedback, ask him or her to listen to you rehearse. Another effective way to polish your presentation is to videotape yourself rehearsing. Videotape tells no lies. You might be pleasantly or unpleasantly surprised and enlightened, and you will know what to work on—facial expressions, gestures, body language, voice quality (varying tone and pitch, pauses, projection, etc.).

4. **Ban verbal tics.** "Uhs" and "ahs" can creep into a speech without your being fully conscious of them. These verbal tics can grate on an audience's ears. Get rid of them. How? See the previous rehearsal tip.

5. **Time your speech.** Don't plan to speak for longer than twenty minutes. Polished, professional speakers know that this is the optimal time an audience can listen and fully enjoy a speech. Rule of thumb: 125 words equals one minute of speaking time. (Most word processing programs can count the number of words in a text.) If your speech is longer than twenty minutes, prune it ruthlessly. Remember: your goal is not to examine every possible aspect of a problem or situation. It is to cast a keen light on one, two, or three particularly interesting solutions or insights you have to share.

6. **Make friends from the git-go.** Find some words of sincere appreciation for the organization you're addressing and/or for the city in which

you're speaking (if you have an out-of-town engagement). Do a little research beforehand so that you can be specific. Generic praise is weak ("this fine city," "an audience of accomplished professionals like your-selves," etc.). It sounds trite and insincere. Be concrete. ("I understand the Hampton Grove Rotary has sent more than five hundred underprivi-leged kids to summer camp," "Plum City's championship high school swim team is the envy of the country.") A little research goes a long way. It can be as simple as asking the program coordinator for details on what is a particular source of pride for the organization/city/town.

7. **Love your audience.** Let them feel that in your body language and eye contact. Your content should reflect this also. Even if you have a generic, all-purpose speech, learn about each audience and the problems it's facing beforehand to tailor your speech to fit.

8. **If you're nervous, don't comment on it.** It won't make you less nervous. For some reason the only effect of commenting on a negative feeling is to escalate it. Don't get swept up into the vicious spiral. Use controlled breathing techniques to steady your nerves. Take a long deep breath, filling your diaphragm, then slowly expel it. (Natural childbirth coaches teach breathing techniques to help women in labor control pain. It works.)

9. **Present yourself as a pro.** If this is your first speaking engagement, don't share that information with the audience. They don't want to know. They think you're a polished speaker. Don't push the "halo" off from over your head.

10. **Arrange for a photographer.** Get permission from the organization to have yourself photographed giving your speech. Contact the photo department of a local major daily newspaper several days in advance of your speech. Tell them you are looking for a freelance photographer to take some candids (action shots), and ask for a recommendation. Photos of you addressing an audience will look great in your press kits and accompanying your news releases in the future. By the way, the fact that a photographer is taking your photo while you're speaking may just impress the audience. It confers a bit of celebrity status on you. (And you may even feel a bit like a celebrity yourself.)

Note: make sure the photographer understands that you want to use the resulting photos for publicity purposes and that he or she is willing to give you the negatives and a signed letter of permission indicating you have the right to reproduce multiple copies of the photos for publicity purposes.

11. **Show up!** Never be a no-show at a speaking engagement. No-shows create really bad word of mouth. Think about it. Ten, fifty, a hundred or more people show up to hear you speak. Each has carved out time from a busy schedule to listen to what you have to say. You don't show up. No matter how graciously the emcee tries to cover for you (and some won't), you look bad. Be reliable—always.

12. **Check on audio arrangements.** Will a mike be provided? What kind? You need to know beforehand. If there's no mike, practice projecting your voice. It's disconcerting to launch into a speech only to hear shouts of "We can't hear you" from the back of the room.

13. **Claim your rights.** Will the organization that's hosting your speech audiotape or videotape it? If so, courteously let them know that you own the copyright to any presentation you make that day. Tell them they can make an agreed-upon number of copies for their organization's use. Once you are a polished speaker and your tapes are in demand, you may want to ask them to pay you a royalty of perhaps a dollar or so per tape. Ask for a copy of the tape and the master when they are finished dubbing.

14. **Prepare feedback sheets.** Arrange for these (and pens) to be placed on each chair. Tell the audience this is an important way for you to keep getting better at what you do and that you look forward to their feedback.

15. **Spread the word.** When you make the arrangements to speak at an organization, offer to also write a short "key points" piece for the organization's newsletter. Make sure your contact information is included in a brief paragraph at the end of the article.

16. **Hold a drawing.** Make sure to clear this with your hosts in advance. A drawing is one way to add a little excitement and fun. It's also a way to get the contact information of people who may be interested in your product or service and to whom you are now a known quantity. At the end of your speech, pass a plastic goldfish bowl around and have people place their business cards into it. Give away books, T-shirts, or other items related to your topic.

Chapter Bonus
Two Easy Ways to Distinguish Yourself with Media People

1. **Return calls from the media promptly.** Reporters are always rushing to meet deadlines. They have a constant stream of adrenaline in their systems. They expect and appreciate quick responses to their phone calls and E-mails. Oblige them accordingly.
2. **Send thank-you notes.** If you meet with a reporter face-to-face, send a handwritten note on professional-looking, personalized stationery or a note card thanking the media person for his or her time as follows:

COLE HANSON

Dear Hallie,

I've enclosed a Spa Industries Trends Report that I think you'll find of interest.

I appreciate your taking the time to meet with me Thursday. (Or, "I enjoyed meeting you at the PRSA luncheon," etc.)

If I can be of assistance with any future stories you plan on city-based health spas, please don't hesitate to call. I look forward to hearing from you.

Regards,
Cole

These courteous touches go far. We all live in a frazzled world. Nerve endings are often raw. The courtesy of a prompt response and the graciousness of a written word of sincere appreciation don't go unnoticed.

7 If It's Thursday, This Must Be . . .

TV, Radio, and Tours (on the Road and Online)

"The most important educational institution in the country is not Harvard or Yale or Cal Tech—it's television."

—Newton Minow, former FCC commissioner

Both TV and radio offer you powerful ways to reach huge audiences. Each of the nation's main television networks—ABC, CBS, and NBC—have affiliates in most cities. If you're in or near a sizable town, there are probably news programs carried by independent stations too. Then there's Fox News, PBS, UHF channels—and more. While national broadcast and cable TV networks and nationally syndicated TV and radio shows might be out of reach for you as a beginning publicist (for now), once articles about you and your business appear in local newspapers and magazines, TV and radio news coverage by local stations is a natural follow-up. Local talk shows (your city's versions of *Today* and *Good Morning, America*) may also be good opportunities to pursue. And if you choose to keep your business local, local broadcast media may be all you ever need to focus upon.

Why Broadcast Media Pack Such a Powerful Punch

Both TV and radio offer ways to reach audiences that print media can't duplicate. TV's power rests on the fact that it combines sight, sound, and movement. Because it involves multiple senses, it's powerfully persuasive. Not only can TV reach hundreds of thousands of people simultaneously across your city or state, but if you make it to the national shows, the numbers jump to the millions and even (on programs on CNN, for example) include international audiences. That's immense communication power.

A huge 95 percent of all homes in the United States have TV, and, on average, people spend more time with the television than with newspapers or the Internet. In fact, surveys show that they spend more time with TV than with any other activity except working or sleeping.

According to a recent study by the Annenberg Center, 93 percent of teenagers could name the characters of a popular animated TV show, but only 63 percent could identify the vice president of the United States. (Some work needs to be done on that issue, but the fact that it's true underscores the power of broadcast media's reach.)

Radio has the immediacy of TV, although it doesn't have TV's multidimensional punch. But radio also offers a terrific opportunity to reach your target audiences, especially on local morning talk shows and news radio programs. It seems everyone turns to radio to lessen the tedium of a morning commute.

TV Interviews: A (Publicity) "Star" Is Born—You!

First, of course, you'll need to decide whether the benefits of coverage by the broadcast media will be a comfortable fit for you as you pursue publicity for your business. If your business is featured on the local TV news, for example, it's more complicated than newspaper coverage would be. For a TV news story, you can expect to see a reporter, a camera operator, a sound specialist, and perhaps a producer show up to tape the segment.

If you're asked to be a guest on a local talk show, expect any of a wide variety of formats. Some TV talk shows feature one guest for an entire program. Others have several. Some will seat you across from your host-interviewer on a sofa in a "living room" atmosphere. Others seat you next to a desk behind which the

Bonus Points
How Do You Handle "Curveball" Questions?
With "Switchbacks"

One response that will buy you a few beats of time when an interviewer throws a buzz saw of a question your way is "That's an interesting question." And, you can use the time-honored technique perfected by politicians on programs like *Meet the Press* to avoid answering touchy questions—namely, build a short verbal "bridge" from an uncomfortable, hostile, or downright silly question back to your prepared remarks.

Example: you've been invited to talk about a new and improved shaving method you've invented. The interviewer asks, "How often do you cheat at cards?" You answer: "I guess, sad as it is, there are a few people who cheat at cards. What isn't sad is the fact that, with the Clean Sweep Razor, shaving takes only half as long." (Well, OK, you probably won't be as blatantly commercial as that in your "switchback," but you get the point.)

interviewer sits. Many shows allow people in the audience to participate in questioning you. You can anticipate spending a somewhat disorienting morning stepping over camera and sound cable cords (not all of which are taped securely to the floor) and trying to feel natural on a set that looks, to home viewers, like a living room or an office but is in reality a studio with bright lights glaring down at you while camera operators track you with the large beady eyes of cameras and the host and various people wearing earphones move around mysteriously and purposefully using a sign language all their own.

It can be fun, yes. It can also be disorienting and anxiety provoking to know your voice and image are being beamed to thousands or hundreds of thousands of homes across your town.

Can you think quickly when someone throws you a curveball question? Can you do so under the pressure of public scrutiny? As the old Greek maxim goes, "Know thyself." If the idea of a live interview that's beamed into countless living rooms simultaneously gives you pause, TV may not be your cup of tea and you may opt to stick with print media as a focus for your publicity efforts.

What They Get Is What They See

TV is a "hot" medium, unlike print, which is "cool" and allows distance from your audience. TV puts you "in their faces." And because it's a visually oriented medium, you may have to make an effort and devote a good chunk of time to creatively devising a story with strong visuals that you can pitch to TV media people. This can translate to a lot of time and energy on your part.

On the other hand, when viewers see you on the screen, it may be for only a few minutes—but it's a few minutes in which they see you and hear you "up close and personal." And it's a few minutes packed with the kind of intensity that makes a terrific impression. In short, TV allows you to connect with your target audience and spread your message like no other medium does.

Some personalities are "to the medium born"—they're charismatic TV naturals, and the medium shows them off to great effect. If you're one of these people—go for it!

So, Just How Do I Get on TV?

People get on TV talk shows in different ways. Their representatives send the station or program a pitch letter with a news release or press kit attached and then follow up with a call to "sell" their clients as guests. A reporter with a specialized beat (gardening, food, money, etc.) might respond to a pitch letter or news release that is sent to her or his attention. (See Chapters 3 and 4 for what reporters are looking for.)

Or, people are featured on TV news programs when they are part of a breaking news story or—more typical for a small-business owner—when they are part of an appealing (and very visual) special event.

Sometimes a TV assignment editor or talent coordinator will call you not quite out of the blue but because he or she has read about you in a newspaper or magazine. (Yes, your print media efforts can result in TV and radio coverage.) Assignment editors or planning editors for TV news programs (or talent coordinators for TV talk shows) are always looking for interesting guests to invite onto their shows. People are invited if they are seen as newsworthy or controversial, or if they have unique or specialized information that's valuable and timely in some way.

If you plan a special event and hope to get television coverage, here's how to get the attention of TV media people: about a week to ten days before your event, have your "representative" (see "But I Don't Have a Representative" sidebar) fax or mail a special events news release (see Figure 4.2 on page 63) to the assignment editor or the planning editor at your local TV news station. Have your "rep" follow up two to three days later with a phone call. You may have to jog the assignment editor's memory. He or she probably won't make a commitment, but if you are told "maybe," that's great. TV newspeople are pretty blunt. If it won't work for them, they will usually tell you no—and why not. If you didn't get a no, remember to refax the release the day before the event and to call again.

Note: always call TV news stations in the morning. In the afternoons the people you need to reach are scrambling to prepare for the day's news program. Also, don't call reporters directly. The protocol at most TV stations is that the assignment editor or planning editor should be your first point of contact to pitch any story idea. He or she decides whether a reporter should pursue a story.

If you have the budget for travel, consider approaching regional TV talk shows outside your hometown area (shows with names like *Good Morning, Chattanooga; Cleveland Live*; etc.). You should also consider syndicated cable TV programs that are a good fit with your business (*The Fishing Show* for a sports shop owner, *The House Jack Built* for a home building store owner, etc.).

National TV talk shows are very tough to book.

What About Radio?

There are hundreds of radio talk show programs across the United States. The top-tier markets—New York, Los Angeles, and Chicago—are very tough to crack. Smaller markets are less difficult to book.

Bonus Points
"But I Don't Have a Representative"

People in broadcast media expect potential guests to be represented by a third party. But don't worry if you don't have a representative to make calls on your behalf. Just have a business associate or a friend who can be trusted to represent you professionally call the producers of local radio or TV talk shows and offer you as a guest, or hire and train someone to call on your behalf. (Some people even invent an alter ego and call on their own behalf!)

Radio is a very effective medium for getting your message across and promoting your product or service. The beauty of radio interviews is that they can be done from your home via phone. And most radio talk shows will allow you to give out your contact information—a website or a toll-free phone number. (Always check beforehand to make sure it's OK to give out such information.)

Note: National Public Radio's "All Things Considered" airs editorials from people across the United States. To throw your hat into NPR's ring, send a minute-long commentary on audiotape (accompanied by a printed version of the same). Call NPR at 202-414-2000 for details on how to submit your editorial. (Cost to prepare and mail: less than two dollars. Potential return: nationwide publicity.)

How to Prepare for—and Ace—TV and Radio Interviews

- **Tape yourself.** One of the best ways to prepare for a TV or radio interview is to tape yourself answering questions you anticipate from an interviewer. Videotape and audiotape don't lie. You will be humbled in some areas ("Gosh, am I really that deadpan?"), and you may find your ego stroked in others ("I look great when I smile!"). Be an honest self-critic. Are you making your points clearly? Do you avoid technical terms and jargon? Does your voice project? Do you vary your tone to keep an audience's interest? Are you enthusiastic? Do you use short and interesting stories that illustrate your points? Do you use facts and statistics that strengthen your claims in concrete, specific ways? (Not, "Many men who use a razor to shave nick themselves," but, "A new survey shows four out of six razor users knick themselves twice a week.")
- **For news programs, practice talking in sound bites.** Learn to express key thoughts in fifteen seconds or less. If you make it easy for film and audio editors to cut and splice your responses, you increase the chances that excerpts from your interview will be used in news segments.
- **Remember to mention your company and how listeners can contact you.** Check with the station on how they wish to handle this. They may flash your contact information on the TV screen. Or they may allow you to mention a phone number or website. Websites are great in this regard. You can simply refer people to your website for more information, and stations may prefer this, as it sounds less like a commercial than giving out a phone number does.

Twenty-Four Tips That Guarantee a Smooth TV or Radio Interview Experience

1. **Call to reconfirm the details.** Nail down the time and date of broadcast, name of the interviewer, parking and transportation arrangements, and whom you should contact at the time of your arrival.

2. **Ask the station if they will broadcast your contact information during the show.** Also, tell them you would like a tape of your appearance, and ask them what you need to do to arrange for one. (TV stations may ask you to bring in a blank VHS tape or refer you to a company that can tape your appearance.)

3. **Prepare a list of ten questions the interviewer can ask you.** Send this in to the interviewer two or three days before your interview is scheduled. Bring another copy with you when you show up for the interview.

4. **Rehearse, rehearse, rehearse.** Be prepared. Know your stuff. Think through the key points you want to make. Practice saying them in short, effective, plain English sentences. Work up some great lines. Offer valuable insights. Practice making them with a friend playing the role of interviewer. If a friend is not available, practice into a tape recorder (for radio) or in front of a video recorder (for TV).

5. **Plan to arrive at the TV studio at least half an hour before airtime.** Unexpected things happen. Build in some hedge time.

6. **Be helpful if a TV news crew comes to your home or business to tape a segment.** When the crew calls to let you know they're coming, fax them directions. It's a nice touch to have coffee and donuts for them too.

7. **Bring visuals.** These can include your product and/or B-roll videotape of your product or service in action.

8. **Watch your step.** TV and radio stations are full of equipment, and, in some, it seems the wires snake over the floor everywhere. Watch your step and don't accidentally bump into anything or knock anything over.

9. **During the interview, talk slowly.** It will relax you and you will sound more confident. Speak in a normal, clear tone of voice. Media technicians are able to pick up and amplify sound as needed.

10. **Keep your objective in mind.** Your objective is connecting with your target audience and promoting your business. Respond to your interviewer's questions with answers that speak to your target audience's needs, hopes, and desires. This is especially important when you come

across the occasional unsympathetic interviewer. Don't respond to an interviewer who is giving you negative vibes with negativity. Visualize the people in your target audience and communicate to them. Stay upbeat. If an interviewer throws downbeat questions at you that could elicit negative answers, sidestep them. Stay positive.

For radio interviews done from your home:

11. **Keep a glass of water on hand.** This isn't the time to have a coughing spell or a suddenly dry throat.
12. **Before the interview, remove any jewelry that makes noise as you move.** These items create background distractions.
13. **If you have call waiting, switch it off.** This isn't the time to take a call from Aunt Peggy or from the Community Fund.
14. **Take the call in a room where you can close the door and be free of distractions.** Enlist your family's cooperation beforehand to ensure that there are no intrusions, no loud spats between your kids in the next room, and no pets announcing their presence. If there's construction or yard work going on outdoors, close your windows or move to an area of the building that is relatively noise-free.

For TV interviews:

15. **Wear clothes that show up well on camera.** A pastel blue shirt or blouse with a dark navy suit is a classic TV combination. Don't wear busy patterns or plaids—they don't show up well on TV. Avoid shiny jewelry, which can be blinding on the air. Make sure your socks stay up and are long enough so that the tops don't show under your pant legs.
16. **Plan for off-the-air activities.** Bring papers to work on or a book to read while you're waiting in the "green room"—the holding pen for news and talk show guests.
17. **Primp.** Call ahead to check if the show will have a makeup artist who will powder your face and fine-tune your hairdo. If it doesn't, go to the rest room, look yourself over, and fix what needs fixing.
18. **Stay alert.** If you're seated on an upholstered sofa or chair, sit perched on the edge, leaning forward attentively. Resist the temptation to settle into the cushions. You want to look interested and interesting. Be enthusiastic—even if your host isn't.

19. **Move gracefully.** The camera will pick up and exaggerate your movements. Avoid nodding your head nonstop or continuously frowning in concentration.

20. **Mind your manners.** Behave as if the camera is on you from the moment you take your place for the interview—even during commercial breaks. This is not the time or place to let a crude or thoughtless remark slip from your lips (to be accidentally broadcast to tens of thousands or hundreds of thousands of people).

21. **Be courteous.** Don't interrupt the interviewer. And remember his or her first name!

22. **Be humble.** Don't try to impress people with your intellect. It's more important to be your nicest, most likable self than to come across as a superbrain.

23. **Be understanding.** Don't be offended if the interviewer has little to say to you during commercial breaks. Many interviewers save their energy for on-camera moments.

24. **Be yourself.** But be your most engaging self.

On the Road: Publicity Tours

Going on tour is a traditional—and some believe the best—way to sell new products and services. Some Fortune 500 companies send their top executives, accompanied by PR representatives, on tour regularly, blanketing U.S. cities to get word out about new products. Tours can be extremely effective because all the elements of publicity can be put into play in a short period of time—speeches and TV, radio, and print appearances. With value-priced airlines like Southwest making air travel increasingly affordable, a multicity tour is doable, even for small-business owners operating with very modest budgets (although you may be limited to the cities where these airlines operate).

Here's a typical schedule for one day of a well-planned media tour:

Monday, May 7—Ivyton, TN

6:30 A.M.	Interview by a WKTY radio talk show host (via phone from hotel room)
7 A.M.	Speech at Ivyton Chamber of Commerce breakfast
8:30 A.M.	Guest on *Good Morning, Ivyton* TV talk show
10 A.M.	Interview with business reporter from the *Ivyton Times* (in hotel dining room)

10:30 A.M.	Interview with business reporter from the *Ivyton Herald* (in hotel dining room)
Noon	Luncheon address at Ivyton Rotary Club
2 P.M.	Speech to business students at University of Ivyton

As you can see, it's an action-packed day. A nonstop series of these can drain your energy. Some people try for one city per day, although most people intersperse "on" days with sanity pauses—a day or two devoted only to travel and rest. A nonstop week of being "on" every day touring can get quite hectic, and it's not very smart for another reason. Travel snafus can occur. If you schedule extra time, you help prevent the cardinal error of being a "no-show." (This is an unforgivable sin in broadcast media and speaking circles. They will not forgive or forget.)

Media tours are highly effective because one publicity event plays off the other on a tour. The fact that you are scheduled to address the chamber of commerce, the Rotary, and university students in a given town gives you credibility with the media people in that town. The fact that you are scheduled to be interviewed by the media gives you credibility with the town's service organizations and other institutions. So, as you line up your engagements, remember that once you get one interview scheduled, you can use it as leverage when you're pitching to other media outlets in a target city.

> "Hello, this is Candy Wheatman. I'm the owner of Organize Your Closet!, a Nashville company that helps people make the most of their closet space. I'm going to be in Chattanooga next week to talk to the Chattanooga Women Business Owners. My speech is titled, "What Your Closet Is Telling You About Your Future in Business." It's based on research I've done that shows, among other things, that women whose businesses are profitable are five times more likely to have well-organized closets. I wondered if the *Chattanooga Times* might be interested in learning more about . . ."

Note: if you are pitching to one of two rival organizations (the city's two major dailies, for instance), don't use the other paper as your credibility builder. Instead, mention the speech you'll be giving to the Rotary or your scheduled appearance on a local talk show.

No Travel Budget? Do a Virtual Media Tour

If budget or time constraints rule out an actual media tour, don't despair. Print interviews can be conducted by phone. So can radio interviews. Today major national TV networks and global corporations have top-quality video-teleconferencing equipment that works via satellite hookups. In the next few years, as high-quality versions of this technology filter their way down to the rest of us, video-teleconferenced tours and long-distance TV interviews will become increasingly common.

In the meantime, concentrate on print media, radio, and the Web. One plus of a virtual tour is that you aren't limited geographically in any way. You can schedule print, Web, and radio interviews in Anchorage, Sioux Falls, and Kansas City all in the same day. The one concern you will have is keeping it all organized. When you start mixing cities on the same day, it adds a layer of complexity. Write everything down!

Bonus Points
What Not to Do (Top Publicity Blunders and How to Avoid Making Them)

Following, courtesy of Talion.com "Red Dog" Publicity (talion.com), an online publicity firm, is a tongue-in-cheek look at the kinds of mind-sets that spell doom for would-be publicists:

Major Publicity Blunders (and How to Avoid Making Them)

These people can call their own shots with the media:

- Prince William, heir to the throne of England
- Basketball giant Shaquille O'Neal
- The artist formerly known as Prince who is again known as Prince

Now, for the rest of us: you need the press more than they need you. Witness the following blunders:

1. "Well! This is the second review product I sent to *USA Today*, at their request. If they lose this one, they'll just have to do without me."

    Reality check: *USA Today* can do without you.

2. "Radio talk show hosts need to know that I need three weeks' notice and I can't do any show between 7 A.M. and 6 P.M. Eastern time, because I work."

> OK. If you are satisfied with one-tenth of the results you would have gotten otherwise, go for it. For the best results, accept phone-in radio talk show bookings whenever you can get them and work your schedule around them.
>
> 3. "How much will magazines pay when they run my photograph?"
>
>   Most newspapers and magazines won't pay noncelebrities for their stories. They won't pay for photos either. And reputable journalists will never ask you to pay them for coverage. (Pay-per-placement deals occasionally pose as talk radio shows, but why pay? More than five thousand talk radio shows offer interview opportunities for free.)
>
> Source: Talion.com "Red Dog" Publicity (talion.com)

Media Tour Strategies That Work

Get hold of your planner. (If you don't have one, buy one. A planner is an indispensable tool in organizing your media tour.) It's important to write down appointments and important to-dos and things to remember as soon as possible. A media tour is an exercise in managing and nailing down hundreds of details. You need a written record of what's happening as it develops, grows, and—yes—changes. (Electronic planners are nice, but after losing months of contact info to an electronic glitch once, I prefer the old-fashioned paper-and-pen variety.)

Planner ready?

Good. Now here's a step-by-step method for scheduling a media tour:

• **Determine which cities you wish to target.** Do some research to find out which cities are most likely to contain a large number of people who fit your target audience profile. (Have you developed a new and improved walking cane? Retirement communities in Arizona and Florida are a good bet then. A better-tasting soy burger? California, where vegetarian eating has made solid inroads, might be the place to start. A mulch that grows better potatoes? Your target should be Boise, Idaho, and other major cities in the United States where potatoes are important to the state economy and where farmers and those who supply them and depend on them will be eager to hear your news.)

A second consideration in choosing which cities to target is population. Larger populations give you wider exposure and the possibility of generating more interest and sales. The downside is that larger markets are harder to break into. A good strategy for a beginning publicist is to target second- and third-tier publicity cities (first tier: New York, Los Angeles, and Chicago).

The third consideration in targeting cities for your tour is the number of cities you want to visit. Ten is a classic number for a full-fledged media tour. But after taking into account cities that make sense strategically, it's really up to you—and your budget. By staying in midpriced hotels, flying budget airlines, and carefully watching expenses, you might be able to do a ten-city tour for five thousand to ten thousand dollars. If that's out of your budget range or if you can't devote a week or two out of your schedule to travel and touring, you can still do a "virtual" tour (as discussed earlier).

The location of the cities you plan to visit—in relation to each other—will usually determine the sequence in which you visit them.

• **Book a speaking engagement.** Three to nine months before day one (the date you have decided you will start your media tour), call each target city and find an organization that will book you as a speaker. The further ahead you start making calls, the better. Local branches of national organizations (Rotary, Jaycees, etc.), chambers of commerce, and local universities or colleges are all good bets. (If you can't get a booking, don't worry. It's a plus, but not essential.)

• **Have your representative call the TV talk shows in your target city.** Ask to speak to the talent coordinator.

> "Hello, this is Tom Moore. I represent Oldies but Goodies, a car restoration business. Oldies but Goodies has won numerous awards for the restoration work it does. Rick Walters, the owner of Oldies but Goodies, will be in Morristown on May 7 to speak to the Rotary Club on 'Junker or Classic Car: How to Spot Treasure in the Trash Heap.' I wonder if *Good Morning, Morristown* might be interested in interviewing Rick, as our research shows that many of your readers may have a parent or grandparent who has an old car stored in a barn or garage. Some of those cars—even though they might look battered and worn—are worth tens, even hundreds, of thousands of dollars, and their owners don't even know it. Rick has developed six tips to help them spot 'a treasure in the trash heap.' Do you think you might have an opening?"

If you haven't managed to book a speaking engagement by this point, simply have your rep explain that you're on a publicity tour, that you'll be in (name of town) on the specified day, and that you'd like to schedule an interview.

- **Be prepared when a reporter or producer calls.** If a TV or radio assignment editor calls, make sure that in the course of the conversation you ask for the direct dial number of the person with whom you'll be working to coordinate the details. It will save you time and trouble later. If you miss a call from a TV or radio assignment editor or talent coordinator, make sure to call back as soon as possible. Broadcast media people move quickly and appreciate their contacts moving quickly too.

- **Call radio talk shows in your target city.** Use the same approach as for contacting TV talk shows. At this point, you'll have a schedule roughly blocked out. If you've successfully lined up some speaking engagements and TV interviews, pay attention to what times are no longer available to do radio interviews. If there's a conflict on a particular morning, try for the next day. I've done morning radio interviews from hotel pay phones just before departing for the town airport.

Bonus Points
What to Do When the TV or Radio Media Contact You

Once you start approaching the broadcast media, have this list of questions handy. This is what you need to note down when they call you:

- Which station do you represent?
- What's the name of the person who will interview me? How do you spell his or her name? What is his or her mailing address/phone number/E-mail?
- What's the direct dial number of the person with whom I'll be coordinating my interview? What's your direct dial number? The interviewer's?
- To whom should I fax (or mail) my bio, background information on my company, suggested questions, and so on? To what fax number?
- What's the specific subject matter of the interview? What's the focus?
- How long will the interview last?
- What questions will be asked?

And remember to close the conversation with a sincere "Thank you. I'm looking forward to the interview."

• **Call the major dailies in your target city.** Figure out to which section of the newspaper your story belongs (news, home styles, etc.). When you call the paper, ask which reporter covers that section, and ask for his or her phone number. Give the reporter your pitch. Schedule an interview. Make sure you schedule your interview so that it doesn't conflict with the timing of any speeches and talk show interviews you've already booked.

Note: you also can hold a press conference, an event to which you invite several media people simultaneously. However, these events are really designed for major news announcements. One-on-ones are better relationship-building opportunities, and they help you avoid the embarrassment of giving the "press conference to which no one came." (That does happen—even to professional publicists with large companies and long track records.) What's more, most media people prefer one-on-one meetings, as these enable them to develop unique stories and specific angles.

• **Make your travel arrangements.** This includes hotels, air travel, and rental cars (if needed). Remember to keep track of your expenses for tax purposes.

• **Fax a confirmation letter.** Each time you book an interview, ask the media person with whom you're dealing for a fax number to which you can fax a confirmation.

> To: [name of media contact who arranged the interview with you]
> From: [your representative's name, phone number, and E-mail address]
>
> This is to confirm that [name of host], host of *Good Morning, Morristown*, will interview [your name and title], between 8 and 9 A.M. on Monday, May 7.
>
> Thank you.

Include your contact information—address, phone, and E-mail. Fax the confirmation the same day the booking is finalized. Two weeks or so before you are scheduled to appear on the program, call to confirm the interview. Finally, a few days before the day scheduled for your interview, fax a reminder confirmation to the media person, and follow that up with a phone call. Be polite and friendly with each contact. All the faxing and phoning may seem like overkill, but it isn't. In the hectic pace at which most broadcast media people work, lots of things can—and do—fall through the cracks. (Yes, some of the media people you are dealing with

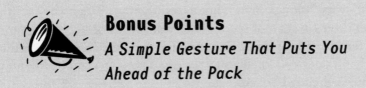

Bonus Points
A Simple Gesture That Puts You Ahead of the Pack

Send handwritten thank-you notes to reporters and TV and radio personalities who've interviewed you. Even—perhaps especially—in this E-mail age, a gracious touch is much appreciated. And it's appropriate to throw in an "I'd love to do it again sometime."

may think you are a control freak, but you won't show up for an interview someone has forgotten to plug into the day's schedule either.)

• **Create a one-page schedule per city.** List all the media events you book on your schedules. Update the schedules as plans change. (Those single sheets of paper can go far in keeping you sane on tour.)

• **Take a handful of press kits with you.** Yes, you can mail them ahead of time. But reporters and producers can lose materials. Having extra kits often comes in handy.

• **Stay connected.** Take along a cell phone that provides nationwide coverage and voice mail service. A pager is helpful too. Make sure both your phone and pager are off when you are being interviewed. A ringing cell phone or buzzing pager going off while you're on the air is an awkward gaffe (unless you're selling either item).

A laptop and an Internet service provider (ISP) that gives you access to the Net from anywhere in the United States are also musts. You can store press releases, fact sheets, and so on electronically and E-mail them to reporters as needed. Not all ISPs provide nationwide service. Check to see if yours does before you go on the road.

Chapter Bonus
Three Shortcuts to TV and Radio Publicity

Have your heart set on TV and radio publicity? Here are some tips that can increase the chances that you will get on the air and boost the frequency of your appearances:

- **Keep in mind that the best days to get on a TV news program are holidays, the day after holidays, and weekends.** These are all normally slow news days, and that means you have a greater chance of having your news covered.
- **Call TV and radio stations in your town and let them know your credentials.** Tell them you'd be happy to stand in for guests who are last-minute no-shows or cancellations. (This is particularly effective if you are able to set up a hot line number—pager or phone—and commit to responding within fifteen minutes or less if they call.)
- **Call your professional or trade associations to volunteer yourself for interviews.** Tell the contact person at each that if reporters call, you'll be happy to talk to them.

8 A Day (or Night) to Remember

Special Events

"A wise man will make more opportunities than he finds."

—Francis Bacon

As the owner of a small business, you may sometimes feel you're at a disadvantage compared to larger companies when it comes to "making news." Companies like Microsoft and General Motors, after all, have deep pockets for research, new product development, and all the other initiatives that can lead to news.

What you need to keep in mind, however, is that as a small-business owner you have one key advantage that the "big guys" don't have—you can be nimble. Small companies don't suffer from "bureaucratic drag." They can move quickly. What's more, who ever said big companies had a lock on creativity? They don't. And a small company with a creative approach is going to be way more appealing to a media outlet than a large company with stale and stodgy ways of doing things.

That's why special events can play a key role in your publicity planning. Even on a shoestring budget, with creativity and intelligence, a small company can create a special event that makes a news splash that draws positive attention and helps attract business.

Following are two key facts about special events:

- If you want the media to report on you or your business, you have to provide them with news.
- It's OK to "create" news.

One of the classic ways to create news is the special event. A special event can be as varied as announcing a contest; holding an awards ceremony, a groundbreaking, an open house, or a grand opening; or unveiling a new product. A special event is an event that has a focused, specific purpose.

You Don't Have to Break the Bank

What's important to remember—especially if you're concerned about expenses—is that your event doesn't have to be splashy and spectacular or require a circus-crew-size team to carry it out. It's fine to hold a carnival or to sponsor a walkathon if you can command the needed resources (time, money, and volunteers). But simpler (and much lower-cost) events can be quite effective in garnering media attention if you keep the eight principles that follow in mind:

1. **Be creative and novel and maybe even funny, and try to tie your event into current news events or trends.** When the Russian space station Mir was about to drop from the sky, Taco Bell floated a very large bull's-eye on the Pacific Ocean. They announced they would give everyone in America a free taco if Mir hit the bull's-eye. (Of course, the Taco Bell logo was in the center of the bull's-eye.) They sent a photo of the floating bull's-eye to the press, and the quirky—and timely—humor of this stunt resulted in coverage on network television and in newspapers across America.

When Xavier Roberts, the creator of the Cabbage Patch dolls, wanted to generate interest in his creations—dolls that looked like cuddly newborns—he dressed his art studio assistants in medical uniforms and called his studio a baby hospital. The Cabbage Patch dolls quickly caught on and within a few years became a national craze—without advertising.

While media people are generous about covering events that benefit charities in some way, they view commercial events with a skeptical eye. But like the rest of us, they aren't immune to charm, humor, and novelty. That's why creativity really makes a difference.

2. **Create a unique business concept, then hold a "grand opening" to launch your business.** See Chapter 3 for ideas on how to make your business unique in a newsworthy way.

3. **Support a worthy cause—and make sure there are visuals the media can capture to tell the story.** Back in the 1960s and 1970s, political activists knew the power of visuals. John Lennon and Yoko Ono's "sleep-in" to protest war was one of the decade's most publicized events. The nightly news was full of flags and draft card burnings and of hippies offering flowers to policemen. The media dutifully reported on each event because the photos and video helped tell the story of protest and change that earmarked those times. Whenever someone runs a documentary about the 1960s, the images of the Lennon and Ono's sleep-in and those of burning draft cards are trotted out. Images are amazingly potent—and lasting. And the media find good visuals impossible to resist.

Habitat for Humanity International, a Georgia-based charity, organizes volunteers to build homes for the poor. Habitat is so well known not only because it deserves to be but also because the work its volunteer home builders do is so visual. Media people like stories like this. (President George W. Bush recently worked as a Habitat volunteer. Yes, even presidents seek positive publicity. George W.'s advisers probably recognized that there was a win-win situation in the president lending his support to Habitat. A terrific organization got a great boost—and the president appeared on the nightly news across the nation—work tools in hand—building his image as a caring leader as well as encouraging participation in volunteerism.)

This works, on a smaller scale, for small-business owners too. Again, you don't have to be a huge business or an important politician to run an effective special event. One beauty salon held a daylong fund-raiser for a child with a life-threatening illness, in which a portion of the cost of each haircut was to be donated to help care for the child. The local TV news covered the event, showing video of customers in the salon getting their hair snipped and blown dry. Other examples of visual events that are naturals for TV news and photos include walkathons and marathons.

4. **Be intriguing and original.** When author and self-help guru Anthony Robbins was promoting *Unlimited Power*, his first bestseller, he invited the press to attend his "firewalk" event—a gathering where people walked barefoot across glowing coals without getting burned to demonstrate their newfound confidence and ability to overcome their fears learned from principles outlined in his book. The firewalk garnered quite a lot of press. Articles and photos of the fearless participants grinning as they braved the hot coals popped up in newspapers across the country—and sales of Robbins's book soared.

Now other motivational speakers hold firewalks—so many that "firewalk" has become a common expression for any difficult or traumatic experience. But Robbins was the first to claim media attention with firewalking, and he reaped a bonanza of publicity.

5. **Tap into feelings that have "come of age" and are ready for a symbolic outlet.** Nell Merlino, founder of Strategy Communication Action Ltd., a consulting firm she runs from her home, did just that in the 1990s when she launched and popularized the Ms. Foundation for Women's Take Our Daughters to Work Day. Many people felt that girls needed an extra boost when it came to encouraging them to pursue careers. Millions of Americans now participate in this event annually, and it has evolved into Take Our *Children* to Work Day.

6. **Create symbolism that ties into something larger or more important.** Members of the California legislature working for gun violence prevention released one hundred doves from the west steps of the Capitol a few years ago. The doves were meant to symbolize the number of people in California who were killed by accidental gun violence in the previous year.

Ecologist Michael Fay of the Wildlife Conservation Society trekked across Central Africa, a fifteen-month-long, two-thousand-mile walk, to draw attention to the fact that this part of Africa—one of the last truly wild places on Earth—may soon be lost to logging and desperately needs to be preserved. His feat was featured in *National Geographic* and also earned a full-page spread in *USA Today*—reaching hundreds of thousands of people with his message.

7. **Tie your event into an existing custom or celebration.** Do you run an organic egg farm? Why not hold an Easter egg hunt for kids in your town the Saturday before Easter, with a "Fun Week on the Farm" vacation prize going to the family of the child who collects the most eggs? Hold the event on your farm and you can take the media who attend on a tour, explaining how organic egg farming is more humane—and results in better-tasting eggs.

If you own a telescope shop, how about holding a Star Gazing Potluck Picnic on Astronomy Day (April 28)? Invite the public to look at features of the night sky (through a telescope you've set up) as they chow down on homemade treats with names like Stardust S'mores, Hot Plutos, and Moon Pies. Check *Chase's Calendar of Events* at your library to find an event that will be a good fit for your business.

8. **Play the celebrity card.** In the course of developing her business, Devita International, Inc., a spa-quality line of skin care products made with natural ingredients (devita.net), Cherylanne DeVita had gotten to know a few celebrity customers who lived in her home state of Arizona—including Alice Cooper's wife,

Sheryl. Sheryl Cooper regularly raises funds for the Solid Rock Foundation, an organization that provides financial assistance and help to inner-city teenagers and children. DeVita and a restaurant owner she knew teamed up to help the charity, with the restaurant owner offering the use of the restaurant at no charge and DeVita rounding up her celebrity friends to attend the event.

Sheryl and Alice Cooper attended, along with Kelly Stone (Sharon Stone's sister), local TV anchorpeople, and other Arizona celebrities. Funds were raised for the charity, DeVita says; in addition, for six months afterward, local magazines continued to run photos and mentions of the event, resulting in ongoing publicity for Solid Rock and also for DeVita and for the restaurant at which the event was held.

If your event is designed to benefit the community, the mayor and local TV or radio personalities might just be open to attending. People in jobs that keep them constantly in the public eye like to be visible to the public—and they are especially open to supporting a creative contributor to the community (you).

Stunts—and Why You Should Avoid Them

Publicist James S. Moran once sold a refrigerator to an Eskimo to draw media attention to refrigerators he was marketing for a client. He also called the press to attend and publicize the following events: walking a bull through a China shop, searching for a needle in a haystack, and drawing blood (for the Red Cross) from turnip-costumed actors. Although he made quite a stir for himself—and his escapades did get a lot of ink and airtime—there was one problem with them: they overpowered the products he was trying to sell. The stunts themselves became the focal point of the media coverage generated.

Today, Moran-type stunts would be considered "corny" and would produce little media coverage. But, even if the media did choose to cover stunts of this sort, what's the point if your business message is lost in the shuffle? Publicity should never be an end in itself but should always tie back to, and support, your overall marketing plan.

What about dangerous stunts—where the main draw is the fact that life and limb are in peril? Don't do them. You may succeed in attracting publicity, but the risk isn't worth it. People can get hurt, which is reason enough not to take chances. (People also sue, which is another good reason.) Dangerous stunts also can backfire and create negative publicity. Recently a man tried to parasail onto the Statue of Liberty's torch from which he intended to perform a bungee jump as a form of political protest. He acted independently, without even trying to clear his stunt with officials. When his chute got snagged on the torch's "flame," he had to cling to the statue for half an hour until he was rescued by police (who put their own lives at peril to pull him to safety). The police promptly arrested him, and he was fined ten thousand dollars. The story of his misadventure splashed across headlines throughout the world and hit most of the evening news programs, to be repeated the next morning on CNN and MSNBC. It was the kind of story that TV can't resist—a very visual event. If the coverage had been positive, it would have been a publicity coup. However, the only bonanza of this poorly conceived stunt was one of uniformly negative publicity.

Twenty-Three Tips to Ensure Great Publicity for Your Event

People love special events—any sort of get-together, really, that promises to be interesting, stimulating, funny, or just plain fun. Keep that in mind as you plan the publicity for your next special event. But, to make any event a success, lots of pre-planning is essential. Here's a list to help you with your event planning:

1. **Decide on your goal for the event.** Make the event tie back to the purpose you want it to serve. Make sure the event is designed with newsworthy elements. That means, make it original and interesting. Make sure the messages your event sends support your overall marketing plan.

2. **Start planning early.** Give yourself plenty of time to plan for your event—and for the publicity for the event. Start at least three months prior to the event date. Planning six months or a year ahead might be necessary if the event will require a large team effort. For complicated events, you'll need enough time to decide on a budget, appoint a planning committee, develop a master plan, invite speakers or presenters, and work on your publicity plan.

3. **Round up "the usual suspects."** Set up subcommittees for invitations, refreshments, programs, tickets, audiovisual support, giveaway items, traffic control and safety, setup and cleanup, and volunteers.

4. **Remember to budget for expenses such as refreshments, speakers, permits, insurance, security, and printing.** Do this early in the plan-

ning process. It can serve as a reality check against getting too ambitious.

5. **Make a checklist for executing the event.** It's easy for to-dos to slip through the cracks. A checklist prevents this.

6. **If you have a website, post the event information on your site.** It's one of the most convenient ways to provide people with information. If the event is big enough, you might think of setting up a website dedicated to the event alone. Register.com (register.com) allows you to register a catchy name and arrange for traffic to be redirected to one of your existing website pages for a modest fee.

7. **Decide how many people to invite; decide whom to invite.** Think through what benefits the event will provide to those who attend. The size of the crowd you draw and its makeup (who attends) will depend on the benefits your event offers. If you want to attract families, design a family event, with plenty of activities for kids. If you want to attract young career women, design an event that appeals to the interests of professional women on the early rungs of the career ladder.

8. **Decide where to hold the event.** Outdoors? In a building? On a cruise ship? Arrange for any needed tents, tables and chairs, signage, portable toilets, and parking. Be aware that it's easier to get publicity coverage in small towns than in big cities.

9. **Check with your town or city government to find out what permits or other requirements you need to fulfill to hold your event.** Also, check with them to make sure you don't schedule your event on a day another major and conflicting event will take place.

10. **Decide how you will invite people.** Will you use formal invitations, phone calls, E-mail, announcements in newspapers, flyers, posters, brochures? If needed, arrange to have invitations printed.

11. **Work up a mailing/calling list.** Decide how to mail any promotional materials (first-class, bulk mail, E-mail). Arrange for mailing services, if needed.

12. **Send out the invitations.** Put printed invitations in the mail. Send E-mail invitations if it's a very casual event.

13. **Fax a press release to the nearest regional office of the Associated Press.** Do this about two weeks ahead of the event. Include a note requesting that the event be listed in their Day Book of upcoming events. (AP sends its Day Book information to broadcast media

subscribers every morning.) Also, fax or E-mail the release to the photo editors of local papers, to assignment editors at TV and radio stations, and to the reporters most likely to cover the event at newspapers. For events, the special events news release format is "who, what, when, where, and why" (see Figure 4.2 on page 63). The AP's regional offices and fax numbers are listed on the AP website (ap.org). Follow up with a phone call requesting a listing in the Day Book. Call your local television stations. Most will announce bona fide upcoming events as part of their commitment to public service.

14. **Have programs printed.** Also, provide each committee member with a schedule for the day of the event, including information about who's responsible for what. This will help ensure coordination of efforts.

15. **Send confirmations and name tags.** A week to ten days before the event, send a confirmation letter to those attending. Your letter should include the date, time, and location and contain any needed name tags.

16. **Arrange for hosts for special guests.** You'll be very busy on the day of the special event. There are probably people key to your business you won't be able to spend much time with. A gracious way to make up for this is to let these key people know ahead of time that "Sally Walters" or "Jeff Stone" will be at the event and will provide any information and assistance they might need.

17. **Hold a dry run the day before the event.** Go over the details and distribute identification badges.

18. **Set up a welcoming/registration area.** This can include a table where volunteers distribute name badges and programs, assign tables, and so on.

19. **Do a final check just before the event begins.** Make sure all signage is posted, speakers are present, and equipment is working.

After the event:

20. **Hand out evaluation forms to participants.** Feedback is important. It will help you do even better at your next special event. And it might be an important source of testimonials. (See Chapter 5 for suggestions on how to elicit testimonials.)

21. **Send thank-you notes to volunteers and others who helped make the event a success.** These notes mean a lot to people. You can make

someone's day with a few well-chosen words expressing your appreciation for a job well done.

22. **Send out postevent publicity.** Send your target media a press release reporting on attendance (if it was good) and recapping highlights of the day or evening and their news value (raise money for charity, celebrate a record year or opening of a new facility, etc.).

23. **Debrief.** Meet with key participants and sort out what went right and what went wrong.

Yes, Events Can Take Place in Cyberspace Too

Today more than half the people in the United States have Internet access. That means events can take place in cyberspace as well as in an auditorium or on a playing field.

Even well-established companies hold online auctions to raise funds or to sell off equipment. Some companies host their own auctions. Many use the eBay website (ebay.com) for these events. Want some publicity? Find a newsworthy, one-of-a-kind object or objects to auction off. Few of us have one of Princess Diana's dresses, a moon rock, or an original Picasso to sell on eBay, but if you do have a unique item or items to sell, or if you can make your online auction tie into a trend, you can still make news.

Entrepreneur Charles Huggins garnered press attention by being one of the first people to auction homes online—and by tying the auctions to a trend. The *Los Angeles Times* reported on the growing trend of selling houses online. Huggins, president of Rbuy.com (rbuy.com), a Denver-based auction website, is quoted in the article as noting that an "auction revolution" is "out there quietly happening in the real estate industry."

Is there a "revolutionary" change the Internet or some other innovation is prompting in your industry, one the press hasn't caught onto yet? If you can make a case you can back up with figures and statistics, your information may make news.

Tie your online auction to a charitable endeavor and you will greatly strengthen your chances of coverage—at least in the area in which you or your company does business. Perhaps your company could auction off a collection of vintage Victorian-era Valentines on eBay a few weeks before Valentine's Day—and donate the proceeds to the Heart Association. What about auctioning off a set of golf clubs with a golf bag that's been signed by a major player and then donating the proceeds to provide sports equipment to disadvantaged inner-city children? Celebrities can be quite generous for good causes. Local celebrities are your best bet for local events. National celebrities are swamped by requests of this kind and so must be very choosy about what they elect to participate in.

If you host an online discussion group (see Chapter 4) that has a chat room feature, consider inviting an authority in your field or industry to join you in your virtual chat room to answer questions from discussion group members. Call it a "Virtual Q&A Session with [Name of Authority]" in the press release you create to publicize the event. Emphasize the fact that participants will be able to question your chat room guest one-on-one.

Chapter Bonus
The Secret to Successful Events? Dare to Be Different

The media have an aversion to "same-old-same-old" ideas. If there have been several spelling bees in your city in a short period of time, you will have to come up with a really creative spin to get the media to cover yet one more—maybe an underwater spelling bee (if the proceeds are supporting the local swim team) or one in which the contestants have to shout out the answers while steering bumper cars through an obstacle course (to promote the opening of a new amusement park for kids).

Stuck in a noncreative mode? Hold a brainstorming session with a couple of friends or business acquaintances you recognize as having flair and creativity. Or ask people you know about special events they've attended. Which ones stick in their memories as great? Why? Get the details and see if there are any elements you can use to create your own "magic moments."

As laughter therapist and author Loretta LaRoche says, "Nothing happens in the Vanilla Zone."

9

Cast Your Bread upon the Waters

Giveaways

"It is one of the beautiful compensations of this life that no one can sincerely try to help another without helping himself."

–Charles D. Warner

This book defines "publicity" as any communication that effectively reaches the people in your target market and convinces them to do business with you. "Giveaways"—newsletters, booklets, reports, posters, tip sheets, and so on—are time-tested, proven ways to do just that.

The dynamic that makes giveaways a powerful publicity tool is the old principle of "cast your bread upon the waters," or reciprocity. Do something nice for somebody and, sooner or later, it's quite likely to boomerang back at you.

With the growth of the Internet and the ability to distribute information through E-mail and by posting it on the Web, you can now create "E" versions of giveaways that are extremely cost-effective.

Newsletters

Trying to find a great way to keep in touch with your customers/clients and to spread the word about your business? Why not publish a newsletter?

A newsletter can be a one-pager of bullet points formatted in plain text and sent out on ordinary bond paper or via E-mail. Or it can be a stylishly designed multipage effort with several articles appealing to a specific interest group. It can be issued weekly, monthly, quarterly, semiannually, or "on an occasional basis."

Are you wondering what the content of your newsletter could be? Well, ask yourself these questions:

- Do I keep myself updated on news and trends affecting my field or industry? Is this information something my clients/customers would like to know about?
- Do I have a knowledge base I can dip into to present nuggets of information that my clients/customers would find of value?

If the answer to either of these questions is yes, you should definitely consider publishing a newsletter. Here's why:

- **Newsletters make a positive "blip" on your target market's radar screen.** Newsletters that regularly present useful information to your clients/customers keep you in the forefront of their thoughts in a positive way.
- **A newsletter reinforces and spreads the good word about your business.** If the information is of value, you are reinforcing your clients'/customers' good opinions of you and your business. In addition, if the information is useful, they will pass it along to associates—further spreading the word about you and your business.
- **When need for your product or service arises, they will remember you.** People like to do business with people they know and feel they have a relationship with. Regular contact through a newsletter helps build a relationship. In addition, with information barraging us from every which angle, it's sometimes difficult to remember a particular business and what it does. A regular reminder in the form of a newsletter ensures that your business is the one that comes to mind.
- **It's an unobtrusive way to maintain contact.** Customers/clients can read through a newsletter at their leisure. If you depend on phone calls

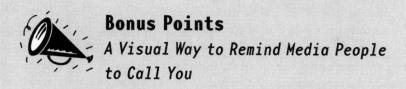

Bonus Points
A Visual Way to Remind Media People to Call You

Have a Rolodex card printed up to include with your mailings to the media, including press kits and news releases. Have the tab identified by your product or service or by your area of expertise. You want media people to think of you as a source. This is a visual way to remind them that you are ready and willing to provide input to their stories.

You can do this electronically, too. Microsoft Outlook enables you not only to organize and record your contact information on your computer but also to create an E–business card for yourself that you can attach to your outgoing E-mail. With a couple of keystrokes, your E-mail recipients can download your E–business card information and store it in their own Outlook files or in their PalmPilots.

to keep in touch, you may get them at a busy time, and they may not be eager to chat. A newsletter with a nugget or two of valuable information is a different matter. They can pick it up when they have a moment and when it is convenient for them. Your contact information is clearly printed on your newsletter—a great reminder of the availability of your products/services.

- **You can include a recent newsletter in your mailings to media people.** A well-done newsletter reinforces your image as someone committed to your field or industry and your status as a knowledgeable spokesperson for your field or industry.

Print or E-Mail?

Print newsletters require that you invest in paper and printer cartridges and pay postage fees. E-mail newsletters (if you don't count the cost of your PC and online service) are quite inexpensive to produce. E-mail newsletters can be created in plain-text (no frills) format. (This is the best option if your design skills are iffy.) Or, if you've mastered HTML (the coding language that controls how Web pages look), you can create attractive and even elaborate electronic newsletters that can be sent via E-mail. (See Chapter 4 for information on creating HTML mailings.) Or, you can post your newsletter online and send an E-mail message alerting your customers/clients that the new issue is out. Be sure to include a link in your message so they can access the website easily. The same pluses and caveats that apply to E-mail news releases apply to E-mail newsletters.

Note: according to the Microsoft Corporation, HTML newsletters generate a 35 percent higher response rate than plain-text E-mail.

If you choose to print hard copy (paper-and-ink) versions of your newsletter, a simple bullet point format in basic Times Roman or Courier font can be effective. It can even be a plus. If there's valuable content, it will read (and look) like a publication that provides the unvarnished, no-nonsense skinny.

If you don't have a handle on newsletter design, plain is better. It's better to go simple than to try and design a newsletter with a complicated layout—even with the help of programs like Microsoft Publisher (which provides preformatted newsletter designs).

Tip: if you opt to create a plain-text newsletter, whether you E-mail it or print it, don't make it a massive block of typing. Chunks of text need to be broken up. A large block of solid text with no indentations and no line breaks is guaranteed to put most people to sleep. Make the text more readable and appealing with white spaces.

Everything that comes out of your "shop" should reflect well on you and your business. If you have had no experience in layout and design, and you want a more ambitious look for your newsletter, go ahead and see if Microsoft Publisher is for you. Or consider taking a workshop. There are some excellent one- and two-day workshops that will give you an overview of the basics and improve your eye for good design. Check with the Public Relations Society of America (212-995-2230; prsa.org) or the International Association of Business Communicators (415-544-4700; iabc.com). Call and ask for a local chapter that you can contact to ask for workshop recommendations.

How to Sign 'Em Up

Microsoft offers a service called List Builder (listbuilder.com) for a small annual fee, through which you can create a sign-up form on your website that people can use to subscribe to your newsletter. List Builder allows you to send up to ten thousand newsletters a month.

Yahoo! Groups (groups.yahoo.com) provides listserv technology for free. (The catch is that they will add a line or two of their own advertising messages to the newsletters you mail out.)

Tips for Newsletters

- **Keep it simple.** Limit yourself to one to four typewritten pages max. When you first launch your newsletter, your enthusiasm may tempt you to go lengthy. Keep in mind, however, that this will be a sustained effort. If you are the chief cook, bottle washer, writer, and editor, aim to keep it manageable.

   With this in mind, you might want to limit your use of graphics (photos and art elements). Graphics complicate things. If your content is good, you don't need graphics. If your layout is simple and clean, it will work. Why keep it simple? Again because you will be more likely to stick with it over the long haul. If you're in business for yourself and your resources are limited, your time is precious.

- **Distribute quarterly or every two months.** Plan to distribute your newsletter quarterly, every two months, or on an occasional basis. Unless you have an assistant who will free up your time or you can hire someone, don't get carried away and commit to sending newsletters out monthly or weekly. Even the simplest newsletter—if it's to be of value to the people you send it to—requires several hours of thought, research, and writing. If you manage to send high-quality issues out quarterly, you'll keep yourself in your clients'/customers' thoughts in a positive way.

- **Use "Volume/Issue," not "Month/Year."** If you date each issue, your recipients may expect your newsletter to arrive at a preset time. Use the volume/issue system for tracking issues. (The first year's newsletters are all Volume I, with each consecutive issue being Issue 1, 2, 3, etc., so the first year you have Vol. I: Issue 1, Vol. I: Issue 2, etc. The second year, all issues are Volume II, with each consecutive issue being 1, 2, 3, etc.) This allows you a greater degree of freedom in your publishing schedule.

- **Give it a great title—or at least one that has a good ring.** Lonely Planet, a company that publishes travel guides, calls its newsletter *Comet*, a clever play on the "planet" in the company name—and the whimsy is in keeping with the breezy, upbeat writing style that earmarks the Lonely Planet guidebooks. Simple and straightforward titles work fine too. SitStay.com, a quality dog products supplier, has a Web-based newsletter simply called *SitStay.com Newsletter*.

- **Eliminate typos and poor grammar.** If you aren't confident that you can write well and without typos, hire someone to write for you or get an editing service to fine-tune your work. You can search the Yellow

Pages or online for proofreading and editing services. Send out *only* material that reflects well on you and your company.

- **Save time and money with E-mail.** Send your newsletters via E-mail and you save time and money, without losing the perception of value on the receiving end (if the content is good). If your mailing list remains manageable (one hundred people or fewer), you can use the Group feature of your E-mail mailing options to send out your newsletter. Send the newsletter "To" your own E-mail address, and "BCC" your group. This ensures that recipients don't see each other's E-mail addresses. (Many people want their E-mail addresses kept private and may not appreciate your broadcasting them to the world.) You can also look into signing up for Microsoft's List Builder or Yahoo! Groups, which are designed for E-mailing to large groups.

- **Provide value.** Make people look forward to your newsletter. Keep a file in which you tuck away news tidbits that you think might be of interest to your clients/customers: trends and developments in your field or industry, new books your readers would find of interest, a new insight you've developed on how to do things better, faster, or smarter in your field or industry, and so on.

- **Build your newsletter mailing list.** As you collect business cards of the people you meet professionally, put the people you think would benefit from your print newsletter on your mailing list. (A word of caution: many people loathe unsolicited E-mail. Even if your newsletter is the best thing since flying toasters, as a courtesy and a precaution include an opt-out line at the end. It should say something along the lines of: "This newsletter is sent to you compliments of YourCompany. To request removal from the YourCompany newsletter mailing list, simply reply to this E-mail with the word *delete* in the subject line," or describe whatever way you have set up to allow people to remove themselves from your mailing list. And—of course—send your newsletter only to people who might truly be interested in the information you present. That alone will greatly reduce the chances that you rub anyone the wrong way.)

If you go the E-newsletter route, you can set up a page on your website that invites visitors to your site to sign up for your newsletter by E-mailing you to request that you add them to your list. Or, you can automate the sign-up procedure on your website by using listserv technology (Microsoft List Builder or Yahoo! Groups).

Booklets and Reports

Do you want to pull customers/clients to you rather than try to push them to buy your products and services? One traditional way to get people in your target market to come to you has been to offer them a free booklet or "special report" that offers information they perceive to be of value. Your potential customers/clients benefit by tapping into your knowledge base. You benefit because you have contact information for people who are interested enough in your product or service to want to find out more about it.

Booklets and special reports are perceived as high-value items. The fact that your business has taken the time to prepare a booklet that addresses the common concerns of your target market also will be enough, in many cases, to differentiate you from your competitors as a quality provider.

Here's how to do it:

- **Decide on your subject matter.** What knowledge about your product or service do you have that your customers/clients may not have—and that they would find useful or valuable?

  Does your shop sell baby clothes? How about creating a booklet or report on "Ten Things You Need to Know *Before* You Buy Your Baby's Clothes: Facts About Safety, Comfort, and Style"? Do some research. Point out things parents should watch out for (like flame retardants in sleepwear), how natural fibers are more comfortable for babies, how to tell when a baby is ready to wear shoes, and how to select the right shoes. A paragraph or section at the end of the booklet can describe how your shop selects the baby items it offers for sale to meet the comfort and safety criteria and then invite readers to shop there.

  Or, suppose you run a paving company. How about a booklet on "Six Ways to Ensure Your Driveway Doesn't Crack"? You could provide home owners with tips that help them prevent costly repairs. After you've shared the tips, give information about the service your company renders (repairing cracked driveways), and include a few words about how your people will do a great job repairing whatever cracks may unfortunately already have developed in the reader's driveway.
- **Get it written.** Write it or hire someone to write it for you.
- **Print your booklets/reports.** Both booklets and reports can be produced inexpensively. Reports are the simplest. Print out a master copy, then

head to a local copy shop and reproduce the additional copies you need. Staple the pages together, and send them out.

If you choose to produce your own booklets, the process is only a little more complicated. You can format regular typing paper so that it prints out in two columns, landscape format (sideways), and front and back. Use a sheet of colored paper for the cover, and staple the cover and inner pages together at the center using a booklet (extra-long) stapler (available at most office supply stores). Most office supply chains have in-house print shops that can do this for you for a reasonable fee if you supply the master copy.

Electronic Versions of Booklets/Reports

Today, businesspeople also have the option of referring people to their websites to request an electronic version of a special report. In addition to reducing your costs, this method offers an advantage to customers/clients (which also translates into an advantage for you as a publicist)—namely it's much easier for people to jot down or remember a catchy website name (theknot.com, 123kosher.com) than it is to write down a phone number or a complete mailing address. Therefore, they are more likely to follow up on an inclination to request your information.

Note: make sure that you set up your website so that first-time visitors who want to read your newsletter or special report can sign on and provide their contact information. You will need a knowledge of HTML forms or Web software like FrontPage to create this sign-up feature.

Spreading the Word

How do you let your target market know that your booklets/reports are available? There are several methods:

- **Send out a press release.** Contact media outlets that people in your target market read, listen to, and watch. Announce that the booklet/report is available.
- **Run an ad in target publications.**
- **If you send out a newsletter, mention the booklet/report in the newsletter.**
- **Mention it whenever you are interviewed.** Let newspaper reporters know about the booklet/report. They are often glad to mention items

like this as a service to their readers. For radio and TV station interviews, make sure to get permission to mention your booklet/report beforehand.

Tip Sheets

You can find an example of a tip sheet in Chapter 5 (Figure 5.13 on page 132). The principle behind tip sheets is simple and it works. It's this: pack a sheet of paper chock-full of useful tips and valuable information, and people will likely hang onto it.

How does that help you and your business? Because your contact information and a few words about your business are also included on the tip sheet. When the need arises for your product or service, your name will be more likely to pop into people's minds. In addition, producing a tip sheet displays your expertise. This positions you and your business in a favorable light.

You can use tip sheets as giveaways at speeches you present, include them in press kits, distribute them at networking events, and offer them (in news release format) for publication in newsletters, newspapers, or magazines.

Posters

If you have the budget for a designer and for a professional print job, a poster can be an effective way to spread the word about your business. Why are a designer and printer essential? Because a poster needs to have visual appeal. People will hang up only posters that look good and that have great content.

You can use your tip sheet as the basis for your poster. Combine valuable information with attractive graphic elements related to your field or industry, and you'll produce something nice looking and useful. Inject a little humor, and the end result could be widely appealing. History can also provide a starting point. Recently, General Motors celebrated the hundredth anniversary of a historic division by issuing a poster featuring one vehicle from each of its past one hundred years. Is there a historical aspect to your business that you can feature in an engaging visual way? If so, you might come up with a keeper.

The poster should feature your business name and contact information, of course, but keep it discreet. Aim, first of all, to produce a terrific poster. If people keep it and display it, your contact information will be seen and remembered.

An inexpensive option is to create a small eleven-by-seventeen-inch poster that is simply a blown-up tip sheet. You can keep it plain—black text on white paper—or use colored inks or colored paper. Your local copy shop can help you to reproduce the quantity you need. If the tips are of the sort that it's handy to refer to regularly, utilitarian posters like this can get good results.

Tip: people are also inclined to hold onto and to post inspirational material. Creating an inspirational poster can be as simple as reproducing five to ten quotations that are in the public domain (i.e., there are no copyright issues). These should be on inspirational but business-related themes like "teamwork" and "persistence."

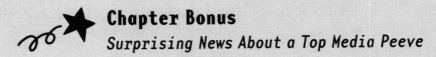

Chapter Bonus
Surprising News About a Top Media Peeve

What is one of the most surprising (and common) pet peeves media people have?

It's the fact that news releases and online press kits lack easy-to-find contact information. All too often the contact information is not only hard to find—it's missing! Why is this surprising? Because after going to the trouble and effort of creating a news release and trying to stir up interest, a publicist who does not provide easy-access contact information is shooting him- or herself in the foot.

Always remember to attach your contact information (name, mailing address, E-mail address, or phone number) with everything you mail out or post online. Your contact information should be on every page of your website. It should be at the top of the page in your news releases. It should be on each of your giveaways too.

## Part III

How to Get Continuous Great Publicity

10 Shoot for the Moon and You'll (at Least) Land in the Stars

Strategy Matters

"If you don't know where you are going, you might wind up someplace else."

—*Yogi Berra*

It's no accident that people who set goals move ahead farther and faster. A now-classic Harvard study published in 1985 found that only 3 percent of the university's 1953 MBA graduates had taken the time to write down clearly defined goals. In 1985, thirty-two years later, the 3 percent who'd written down their goals had four times the net worth of all their other classmates put together.

Setting goals for your publicity campaign and then planning out how to achieve them effectively requires concentration and time. But the results will be worth it. The scope of this chapter is to show how to plan your publicity efforts to achieve the ongoing results that will put your business on the map.

As the Song Says, "Go Where You Wanna Go"

Whether you're a seasoned businessperson or a newbie working from a spare bedroom in your home while your toddler naps nearby, you have to ask yourself where you want to be down the line.

Ten years from now, do you see your business leading the field? Or will you be happy to get neck-and-neck with one or two competitors? Or do you want to carve out a unique niche for yourself, one that others can't compete with because it's in a class of its own?

Ask yourself: Where am I going? What do I need to change to get there? What should I stop doing to get there? (Procrastinating, for example.) What should I do *today* to get there? Repeat these questions daily.

Whether your specialty is narrow (a hideaway hotel for people recovering from plastic surgery, a storage service for theatrical costumes, a bakery that creates birthday cakes that look like fairy tale characters) or something more general, you need to know where you want to be at your milestone anniversaries—one year, five years, and ten years from now. And you need to think about what you plan to earn this year, five years, and ten years from now. Is this the year you establish yourself? Will you be operating in the red? Or is this the year you pull in your first fifty thousand dollars? Your first hundred thousand dollars? Hit medium six figures? Earn your first million? If not, what milestones do you plan to achieve? When?

Draw a line down a piece of paper. Write down what you aim to achieve this year, in five years, and then in ten years in the left-hand column. Then jot down what you're doing or planning to do to achieve these goals in the right-hand column. There's something about looking at your goals side by side with your current and planned efforts that can jog you—like nothing else can—into an awareness of what you need to start doing that's new or different.

Expect Peaks and Valleys

Know that as you work toward your goals you can expect progress and setbacks. Don't be thrown by setbacks. The business world operates in cycles, and progress is rarely a steady upward climb. Expect peaks and valleys. Set goals and think long term.

Decide on a measurement system that will enable you to track how well you're doing. This can be as simple as putting dates next to the goals you plan to achieve, then breaking each goal down into smaller "to-dos," each with a target date.

Don't get rattled by the occasional publicity campaign that fizzles or the deal that doesn't go through. Maintain your confidence and your vision of the future. Stay energized by keeping your eyes on your long-term goals—and the benefits that achieving them will produce for you and for your family. Then, no matter how many setbacks you encounter as you strive to reach each goal along the way, you'll make steady progress over the long-term, and one day you'll look back and be amazed at how much you've achieved and how far you've come.

Down That Elephant

People who consistently achieve goals they set for themselves do so because they're persistent and because they don't allow themselves to be overwhelmed by what may, at first, appear to be overwhelming. When a friend of mine was getting stressed out about all the things that he felt he needed to accomplish on the job, his boss took him aside and asked, "If I told you that in order to succeed you had to devour an elephant, what would you say?"

He replied that it would be impossible.

"It wouldn't be," she said, "if you ate it one bite at a time."

She meant that he shouldn't let himself get rattled by thinking about everything he needed to do and letting it overwhelm him. He needed to take a methodical step-by-step approach to his goals.

As an old folk saying goes, "Yard by yard, a task is hard. Inch by inch, the work's a cinch." *Persistence* is another word for courage.

Get It Together

Achieving big goals is the result of achieving lots of little goals. To successfully achieve little goals, you need to get organized. If you don't have a day planner, go out and buy one.

Make sure your planner comes with (or that you can buy and add) a two-page foldout section that allows you to see the whole current year and jot down crucial dates. This is great for bird's-eye views of where you're going to be—and when—during the course of the year: media tours, vacations, key appointments, and travel days. You should also purchase the month-in-view sections (two side-by-side pages for each month), which give you a view of the month, and the week-in-view sections (two side-by-side pages for each week), which give you an overview of your week.

Buy some blank pages for your planner and use them to jot down your ten-year, five-year, three-year, and yearly goals. You can also use them to quickly note names of contacts and reporters, their phone numbers, their E-mails—and anything else you don't want to forget. Go through these notes regularly and extract the important info. File it, or record it—especially addresses and phone numbers—in your electronic organizer or your contact card file.

Your planner can keep you from getting lost in a maze as you begin to schedule and jot down dates for sending out news releases, making follow-up calls, participating in media interviews, any other must-dos that come along.

Decide on Your Targets

As you sketch out your long-term and short-term business goals, narrow down exactly who the people in your target market—the people who need your product or service—are. Then figure out the best publicity avenues that will connect you with them in a positive way.

Ask yourself these questions:

- Who are the people who need my products/services?
- Where are they, geographically?
- When and where can they be reached? What TV and radio programs do they like? What websites do they visit? What business publications/newspapers/magazines do they read? (Is your target market fashion-conscious teen girls? Then your media list should include teen magazines and radio and TV programs that cater to teen tastes. Are you a dentist or the owner of an independent garden supply store? Maybe the local newspaper and cable TV station will be all you need to focus on.)

Write News Releases That Sing

See Chapter 4 for information on writing news releases.

Be Alert to Opportunities—and Jump on 'Em

Piggybacking a small business story onto a larger breaking news story is an excellent way to get ink or airtime that might otherwise not come your way. When developing news ties into a story you're trying to pitch, act quickly. Say you sent a press release to try to interest your local paper in some new menu items you're offering in your restaurant that features Mediterranean food. There doesn't seem to be any interest. Then, that day, you watch a nationally syndicated health show in which a guest expounds on the many unique healthful properties of Mediterranean food prepared with the same ingredients you use in your new entrees (heart-friendly, loaded with health-promoting antioxidants, etc.). Call the reporter to whom you sent the release and let him or her know about the newly reported health properties—and that you'd be happy to help him or her work up a story on Mediterranean food and its healthful properties—"and, oh, by the way, we have two new dinner items on our menu. Both of them feature the ingredients that are considered most healthful."

A few weeks after the September 11 attack on New York and Washington, DC, National Public Radio broadcast a news segment in which a reporter interviewed the owner of a Boston bookstore who'd noticed how reading trends had changed after the attack. (As people tried to make sense of the attack, sales of the Koran soared, as did sales of books related to terrorists.) The bookstore owner's name and the name and location of her bookstore were mentioned twice during the segment.

The NPR reporter may have contacted the bookstore owner (say, if the reporter knew her from a previous contact). But the reporter would also have been open to doing this segment if the bookstore owner had sent in a news release or an E-mail noting these trends and presenting her credentials as someone qualified to comment on them.

Dance to the Beat of the Broadcast Media Boogie

Before you approach radio and TV media people to try to interest them in doing a story about you or your business, think through what your "not-gonna-happen" times and days are (the times you absolutely won't be available for interviews). Try to minimize these time slots.

Because of the supercharged pace at which they do their work, broadcast media people appreciate flexibility on your part. They like to book on the spot. It's a bit of a whirlwind experience. Use your organizer! Repeat the times and dates for any scheduled interviews to the person who books you—or make sure whoever books for you is careful to take down accurate information.

Be Totally (Yes, We Said Totally) Reliable

Whether you are doing a live TV interview or a phone-in with a radio program, honor each commitment as if your publicity life depended on it. It does. There is nothing TV and radio people fear more than dead airtime—which is what you produce if you're a no-show. Word gets around if you do this—and if it does, you can kiss future bookings good-bye.

Work Those Media Lists

There are two strategies you can follow to "work" your media lists:

1. Classic (best when you are somewhat established with the media)
2. "Work your way up" (best for publicity newbies)

Two Ways to Go: Classic Versus "Work Your Way Up"

The "classic" method of approaching the media is a methodical, "timed-release" broadcast of your news, in which you start the ball rolling by first contacting those media people who prepare their publications months in advance, then work your way across the media list, contacting additional media people based on how much advance notice each media outlet generally requires.

Once you start to integrate publicity opportunities into your day-to-day way of doing business, you will probably begin to think about creating a regular publicity "splash"—via an annual special event, regular significant involvement in charitable activities, a contest, regular new product introductions, and so on. The classic approach clearly works best for these sorts of preplanned events.

The "work-your-way-up" approach works best if you're new to the publicity arena, need to spread your wings slowly, and need to build credibility with the media.

Here's how to do it:

Compile Your Media List

Include all the local and national print and broadcast media outlets that make sense (that your target market watches, listens to, and reads or would deem creditworthy when you "recycle" your publicity successes in your marketing materials). That includes newspapers, magazines, radio, TV, and Web publications.

Note: national coverage for a story about a small business is a long shot—but not as uncommon as you might think. Don't entirely dismiss the idea of pursuing the "big (news) guns."

Always plan to address your releases to specific reporters, editors, and so on. If your target media list is local and/or small (thirty or fewer media outlets), it makes sense to research and compile your own media list. With the Internet, this isn't very difficult. If you don't have Internet access, get to a library or a Kinko's that offers Internet access on a per-hour basis and log on there. Or visit your local library's reference section. (See the Resources section for the media directories that most well-stocked libraries carry.)

Note: if you want to send your news release or press kit to very large groups (hundreds or thousands of trade reporters or hundreds or thousands of media people in a specific region), you need to consider using a news release service or purchasing a media distribution list. (See the Resources section for more information on these services.)

Decide on a "Launch Day," and Time Release the Distribution of the News Release to the People on Your Media List

The launch day is the date that one of the following happens:

- Your new product or service officially becomes available.
- Your book hits the bookshelves.
- Tickets to your for-profit event go on sale.
- Your nonprofit event takes place.
- Your company celebrates a milestone.
- You announce news tied in to a holiday or time of commemoration (Black History Month, St. Patrick's Day, Mother's Day, etc.).

The "classic" way to time release your news releases is as follows:

- **Twelve weeks prior to launch day, mail the release to long-lead publications.** Long-lead publications are magazines that prepare their editorials three to four months in advance. National talk shows also are long lead.

- **Eleven weeks prior to launch day, call the long-lead reporters and editors to whom you sent press releases the week before.** Ask if they got your news release, and launch into your pitch—a one- or two-sentence summary of what the news release was about. (Barraged as they are by news releases, it's likely they won't remember seeing your release.) After recapping the news story you're suggesting, ask if it's something they'd like to cover.

If you get a "maybe we'll cover it" or if they ask a lot of questions (signs of interest), make more follow-up calls. Remember to give them the nutshell version of your story each time you call. Reporters are as harried as the rest of us. They will and do forget.

Ask if they need additional information as you end your call, and tell them you would be happy to answer any questions they might have. If you've established a website for your business, let them know your information is available online.

Be prepared to explain the key benefits of your product or service in language that's factual but appeals to the emotions. If you mail media people additional materials (brochures, CDs, books, review products, news articles about your company already in print, etc.), make sure to mark the package or envelope "Materials You Requested Enclosed" or "Requested Materials."

If you get voice mail or if they aren't available when you call, call again. A second voice mail? Leave a message with a brief (and enticing) pitch.

• **Ten weeks prior to launch day, repeat the process already described.** Continue to send out press releases and follow up until you've mailed the info to all the long-lead reporters and editors on your list.

• **Ten days prior to launch day, send the release to short-lead publications.** Short-lead publications are those that print and broadcast daily, including local TV, radio, and newspapers.

Note: local media should be more open to you because a story about you has a built-in angle—you are a local. However, you'll still need that good and compelling additional "twist" to clinch your success.

Tip: remember that once you get in print, newspaper articles (clips) you generate locally can be "recycled"—reproduced and enclosed with the news releases you send to out-of-town media in the future. Clips, especially from major city papers, even if they're from your hometown, can add to the credibility of your future releases.

• **As launch day approaches, continue to follow up on press releases, line up interviews, and do interviews.** If your initial (long-lead) efforts have generated some interest, you will be busy providing reporters with information. If not, call any key reporters who may have seemed interested initially. They may need a memory jogger.

- On launch day, do interviews and line up interviews to follow up on the event.

A major benefit of the "work-your-way-up" approach is that it allows you to get early feedback on what's working and what isn't. This allows you to do valuable course corrections. In effect, you make your mistakes with smaller and less visible media outlets.

There are all sorts of variations to the "classic" and "work-your-way-up" approaches, and the two can play off each other, of course. For example, say you tried the classic approach to introduce a new product or service your company is putting on the market, and you got a poor response—only a short article in a suburban weekly. Your results may have fallen short of your expectations. However, that single article can be channeled into your future publicity efforts. You can reproduce a stack of neat copies and tuck them into your press kits and send them along with your future pitch letters on other stories (not to the same publication that ran the article, of course). Even that single article adds credibility—and will make other media people more receptive to your pitches.

Aiming for the A-List

If you are a completely unknown quantity to reporters and producers, you may not register high on their "credibility meters." To increase your credibility—and your chances of coverage—start developing a track record in the format that media people find most convincing—namely, copies of articles about you and your business.

Aim your first publicity efforts at easier-to-penetrate targets: association and trade organization newsletters or free weekly newspapers. Contact the editors and see if they would like you to write an article for them, or send them a news release to try to interest them in writing an article about you (see Chapter 6).

Once you get a credit in a newsletter or free weekly newspaper, include a clip (copy of the article) from the free newspaper or newsletter with the press release you then send to weekly newspapers that are sold on newsstands or delivered by subscription. Clips from these pay-for weeklies can then be sent with future press releases to dailies in cities that are lower-tier (easier to get into than, say, New York or Los Angeles) media outlets—cities like Fort Wayne, Indiana; Dayton, Ohio; and Lincoln, Nebraska.

If you get clips in one or more of these cities, try for clips in mid-tier media outlets such as San Francisco, Seattle, and Indianapolis. If you get clips in one or more of the mid-tier cities, you're ready to send those clips along with your news release to the A-list publications (*New York Times*, *Los Angeles Times*, *USA Today*, *Wall Street Journal*, and *Washington Post*). Does that guarantee they will write about you? Of course not. But it vastly strengthens your chances.

Why can clips sent along with a news release increase your chances of coverage? Because they make you more of a known quantity. And because they repre-

Bonus Points
"One-Shots" Miss the Mark—Think Long Term

With rare exceptions, one radio interview or a single article in a local newspaper or magazine won't bring you the kind of results you want for your business. You must be in it for the long haul. You must plan a series of publicity initiatives: regular bookings on the radio talk show circuit, regular appearances in newspapers or newsletters, and/or ongoing Web-based efforts.

How regular? That will be a function of how much time and energy you can invest. There has to be something new (and substantively new) about your business to create a blip in the publicity radar. You don't have to pour money into creating something new. But you will have to put on your thinking cap—and follow that with your "planning" and "executing" caps.

At a minimum, you should aim to create a blip at least once a year. The publicity you receive can then be recycled throughout the coming year in your marketing materials. Publicity does have a shelf life. Its worth diminishes over time. Fresher is better.

You may find you have a knack for publicity, or that for some reason reporters enjoy dealing with you, or that your business is one of those that the press takes to. And if, on top of that, you "understand" the news/publicity game and what it is media people are looking for, you may find yourself enjoying a steady stream of publicity.

sent a second, third, and fourth (and objective) voice—not just your own—singing your praises. Most of us, whether we admit it or not, are susceptible to "herd mentality." Media people are no exception. That's why your first few publicity successes may be hard won, but subsequent efforts may be much easier. And, of course, once you get to a position where you don't need publicity (Julia Roberts, Bill Gates, Oprah), it will be effortless.

The A-list publicity cities are New York, Los Angeles, and Chicago. An appearance in the *New York Times* or *Los Angeles Times* or on Chicago's *Oprah!* will grease your publicity skids like nothing else. Yes, publicity newbies can make it onto the A-list—but to do so generally requires a "work-your-way-up/pay-your-dues" strategic approach.

You Too Can Be a Media Darling!

A "hit" is publicity lingo for when a reporter responds to your pitch and decides to develop a story. When the magic happens, don't make it difficult or tricky to schedule you. If a reporter's in a hurry and wants to interview you right away, do it. If she or he wants a phone interview, and many time-pressed print interviewers prefer them, do the interview by phone. Most radio reporters and radio talk show hosts are happy to interview people by phone. TV talk shows and news programs obviously need you to be there or to be available for the cameras.

Keep Your Paparazzi Happy

Here are some don'ts. If a print publication sends a photographer to take a picture of you, don't pull other people into the photo out of a misguided sense of generosity about sharing the limelight. If the photographer wants a group photo, he or she will tell you so. Also, don't ask to see the photo proofs so that you can select the one you want to appear in print. (For a news photographer to consider allowing a subject to choose his or her own photo would be considered unprofessional and inappropriate.)

Let the Left Hand Know What the Right Hand Is Publicizing

When you send information or news releases to more than one department within the same media outlet, attach a Post-it Note that lists the other departments that you have contacted. That's the suggestion made by Jill Sabulis, *Atlanta Journal* home fashions editor, "so that we don't spin our wheels searching out duplication from department to department. When you have more than five hundred editorial employees, this gets difficult."

Post-it Notes don't work on E-mails, of course. But you can address the E-mail releases you send to several reporters at the same media outlet so that they can check the "To" list and see who else has received your material.

Note: be careful not to include all recipients in the "To" list when you send E-mails to reporters who work at different and (probably) competing media outlets. You have no obligation whatsoever to inform media people of your interactions with reporters and editors outside their particular "shop."

Tip: yes, reporters do like to get exclusive stories—but they know you have no obligation to provide only them with your material. However, if you develop a relationship with a particular reporter, you might sometime want to offer him or her an exclusive. That means you will funnel your information and assistance about a particular story to only that one reporter. Publicists do this when they feel the reporter will produce a substantive article.

Play the Waiting Game with Poise

How long will it take before the story about you sees print or airtime?

If the long-lead media you contact are interested, articles will appear ninety to one hundred twenty days after you first send a release or other information. It will take two to six weeks for you to be scheduled as a talk show interviewee (if your materials strike a responsive chord in the media people you sent them to at the station that hosts the show). Getting on national TV can take three to six months. Local TV news and radio programs often do same-day interviewing and airing. Newspaper reporter interviews can result in articles anywhere from the next day to several days or weeks later, depending on the news value of the story.

Be Honest—Always

Be honest with your customers and with the media. It's the right thing to do. It's also the smart thing (because the media will pay you back if you ever lie).

Note: it's OK to share your wildly enthusiastic feelings about what you're pitching. ("People tell me they've never tasted crepes as wonderful as the ones in my restaurant.") It's not OK to give wildly wrong information ("My chef won the Pillsbury Bake-off"—when he didn't).

And Now—Go Forth and Publicize!

Believe in your ability to achieve your publicity goals. Believe in success. As one wise man pointed out, if you don't believe in success, you believe in failure.

Don't make failure an option.

Persevere.

When you are starting out on your publicity journey, the process may seem overwhelming—preparing press kits, keeping organized, following up on initiatives, and all the many things you need to do to get the publicity ball rolling.

Plug away. Keep your long-term perspective. Work at the hour-to-hour and day-to-day tasks that inch you closer to your goal.

Do not take it personally if any particular publicity effort doesn't bear fruit. Keep your equanimity. Keep your eye on tomorrow. And keep on keeping on.

I'd like to close with a great quote from my friend Patrick Combs, a gifted speaker and the author of *Major in Success*. Although Combs was writing about careers in general, his words sum up both the setbacks and the magic of the publicity process:

> Nothing is more powerful than the devotion of time toward your desired outcome. Good Ol' Father Time works like this:
>
> Give time one year and time often doesn't come through for you.
> Give time two years and time shows you some promise.
> Give time three years and time does you good.
> Give time five years and time puts you on the map.
> Give time seven years and time makes you a star.
> Give time ten years and time works miracles on your behalf.

And now—go forth and publicize!

Resources

Where to Find Good Stuff

This section lists some of the many publicity resources available to you.

Note: there are many, many specialized lists and directories. Those included here are just a sampling. If you are a publicity newbie and are limited to a shoestring budget, you'll find that some of these resources are priced quite high—and probably don't make sense for a small business to purchase. All the same, it's a good idea to know what's available. As your publicity budget grows, you may find you want to invest in some of the higher-priced items. In the meantime, visit the local library. You'll find most of the media directories listed easily available on the reference shelves of well-stocked libraries.

Media Lists

Bacon's Newspaper Directory and *Bacon's Magazine Directory*, Bacon's Information, Inc. (bacons.com), 332 South Michigan Avenue, Chicago, IL 60604, 312-922-2400, directories@bacons.com

Updated annually, these volumes list all U.S., Canadian, Mexican, and Caribbean daily newspapers; all U.S. and Canadian community newspapers and national and regional supplements; thirteen thousand magazines and newsletters; news services and syndicates; and syndicated columnists. They provide contact information for staff editors, reporters, and columnists; editor pitching profiles;

magazine editorial profiles; types of press materials accepted; and editorial and advertising lead times. (Bacon's also offers Media Source, an Internet-based service that allows publicists to select a target market and broadcast their news releases via E-mail. Media Source also is available in a CD version that is updated quarterly.)

Bacon's Radio/TV/Cable Directory, Bacon's Information, Inc. (bacons.com), 332 South Michigan Avenue, Chicago, IL 60604, 312-922-2400, directories@bacons .com
   This lists all U.S. radio, television, cable, and network outlets.

The Broadcasting and Cable Yearbook, R. R. Bowker (bowker.com), 630 Central Avenue, New Providence, NJ 07974, 888-269-5372, info@bowker.com
   This gives up-to-date listings for all radio and TV stations in the United States and Canada; it's a great resource to help obtain local publicity in small communities.

Burrelle's Newspapers & Related Media Directory Set (two volumes), *Burrelle's Magazines & Newsletters Directory Set* (two volumes), *Burrelle's Newspaper & Magazine Directory Set* (four volumes), *Burrelle's Broadcast Media Directory Set* (two volumes), and regional printed directories (Midwest, New England, Southeast, Minnesota, Texas, etc.), Burrelle's Information Services (burrelles.com), 589 Eighth Avenue, 16th Floor, New York, NY 10018, 800-766-5114, ext. 3, directorysales@burrelles.com
   Burrelle's provides media contact information for daily newspapers, nondaily newspapers, radio, television, magazines, and newsletters. (Burrelle's also provides the Media Database Online CD, which allows publicists to create customized labels, lists, and files to distribute press releases. Media listings are updated daily, and subscribers can download the updates electronically.)

Editor and Publisher International Yearbook, Editor & Publisher Company Inc. (editorandpublisher.com), 11 West Nineteenth Street, New York, NY 10011, 212-675-4380
   Updated annually, this lists contact information for reporters and editors of newspapers in both the United States and foreign countries, with listings for all dailies worldwide and all community and special interest U.S. and Canadian weeklies.

Gale Directory of Publications and Broadcast Media, Gale Group (galegroup .com), 27500 Drake Road, Farmington Hills, MI 48331, 248-699-4253, galeord@galegroup.com

Updated regularly, this directory offers listings for radio, TV, cable, and print media. Contact information includes key personnel.

Gebbie Press: The All-in-One Media Directory, Gebbie Press (gebbieinc.com), P.O. Box 1000, New Paltz, NY 12561, 845-255-7560, gebbie@pipeline.com

This lists radio and TV stations, newspapers, and trade and consumer magazines. (Gebbie's media lists are also available on a CD that allows you to print out your mailing lists. Drawback: editors' and reporters' names are not included.)

National PR Pitch Book: The Insider's Placement Guide to the Most Influential Journalists in America, Infocom Group (infocomgroup.com), 5900 Hollis Street, Suite R2, Emeryville, CA 94608, 510-596-9300, webmgr@infocomgroup.com

This lists thirty thousand top journalists and provides their suggestions on how best to approach them—whether by mail, fax, or E-mail. It also gives the best times to call, quirks and peeves, and how, when, and what to pitch.

Newsletters in Print, Gale Group (galegroup.com), 27500 Drake Road, Farmington Hills, MI 48331, 248-699-4253, galeord@galegroup.com

This lists more than eleven thousand U.S. and Canadian newsletters in categories ranging from business and technology to general interest to science and industry. It includes information on target audiences and editorial policies and full contact information, including E-mail addresses and URLs. It is updated annually.

Oxbridge Directory of Newsletters, by Deborah Striplin, Oxbridge Communications, Inc., 150 Fifth Avenue, New York, NY 10011

This lists more than twenty thousand newsletters, loose-leaf publications, and bulletins. It is also available on CD-ROM.

LexisNexis PR Solutions, LexisNexis (lexisnexis.com/prsolutions), 120 Boylston Street, 10th Floor, Boston, MA 02116, 617-542-6670, info.prsolutions@lexis nexis.com

This profiles media people's working preferences, responsibilities, beats, editorial interests, and professional backgrounds and provides editorial calendars.

Standard Periodical Directory, Oxbridge Communications, Inc., 150 Fifth Avenue, New York, NY 10011

This lists more than seventy-five thousand North American periodicals including magazines, newsletters, newspapers, journals, and directories.

Working Press of the Nation, R. R. Bowker (bowker.com), 630 Central Avenue, New Providence, NJ 07974, 888-269-5372, info@bowker.com

This is a listing of radio, TV, magazines, in-house publications, newspapers, freelance photographers, and writers.

Ask your reference librarian for reference guides to local media (for example, *Doing Business in Phoenix*, *New York Publicity Outlets*, *Burrelle's Media Directory—Texas*).

Lists of Organizations, Groups, and Associations

Encyclopedia of Associations: National Organizations of the US, Gale Group (galegroup.com), 27500 Drake Road, Farmington Hills, MI 48331, 248-699-4253, galeord@galegroup.com

Updated annually, this is a directory of twenty-two thousand U.S. nonprofit, professional, trade, and cultural organizations, many of which publish newsletters or magazines.

Encyclopedia of Associations: Regional, State and Local Organizations, Gale Group (galegroup.com), 27500 Drake Road, Farmington Hills, MI 48331, 248-699-4253, galeord@galegroup.com

Updated annually, this is a guide to more than 115,000 U.S. nonprofit membership organizations with interstate, state, intrastate, city, or local scope and interest.

On the Net: Associations on the Internet (ipl.org/ref/aon)

This is a list of the websites of more than two thousand organizations and associations compiled by the Internet Public Library.

Publications That List Holidays, Anniversaries, and Special Days, Months, and Weeks

Chase's Calendar of Events, by Sandy Whiteley, McGraw-Hill (mcgraw-hill.com), 1221 Avenue of the Americas, New York, NY 10020, 877-833-5524, customer .service@mcgraw-hill.com

Updated annually, this lists twelve thousand one-day, weeklong, and month-long events (Take Our Daughters to Work Day, National Potato Lover's Month, etc.), anniversaries, special birthdays, and historical celebrations.

Gale Holidays and Anniversaries of the World, Gale Group (galegroup.com), 27500 Drake Road, Farmington Hills, MI 48331, 248-699-4253, galeord @galegroup.com

This lists twenty-three thousand holidays around the world, anniversaries of historical events, famous birthdays, and so on. It is updated annually.

Timetables of History, Touchstone Books (touchstonebooks.com), P.O. Box 2413, Carmichael, CA 95609, 916-348-7739, webmaster@touchstonebooks.com

This lists long-ago key historical events, which can be tied into present-day promotions.

Publications That List Expert Sources

The following publications list expert sources. Media people sometimes refer to directories like these to find experts to interview, quote, and so on. You can fill out an application to have yourself listed. (Most of these publications also will charge you an advertising fee to be listed.)

Radio-TV Interview Report, Bradley Communications (rtir.com), 135 East Plumstead Avenue, P.O. Box 1206, Lansdowne, PA 19050, 800-553-8002, contactus@rtir.com

This is billed as "the magazine producers use to find guests."

The Yearbook of Experts, Authorities and Spokespersons, by Mitchell P. Davis, Broadcast Interview Source, Inc. (yearbook.com), 2233 Wisconsin Avenue NW, Washington, DC 20007, 202-333-4904

This reference for the media lists expert sources for thousands of topics.

Publications That Provide Updates on the Media

The Bulldog Reporter newsletter, Infocom Group (infocomgroup.com), 5900 Hollis Street, Suite R2, Emeryville, CA 94608, 510-596-9300, webmgr @infocomgroup.com

Published two times a month, this provides information about key changes on the media scene (personnel and "beat" changes and media trends).

Contacts newsletter, MerComm/Contacts (mercommawards.com/contacts.htm), 500 Executive Boulevard, Ossining-on-Hudson, NY 10562, 914-923-9400, contacts@mercommawards.com

Published weekly, this newsletter offers information about "who in the media needs your info now."

Press Release Distribution Services

PR Newswire (prnewswire.com)
Internet Wire (internetwire.com)
Xpress Press (xpresspress.com)

Resources to Help You Place Articles for Publication

Writer's Market, Writer's Digest (writersdigest.com), 1507 Dana Avenue, Cincinnati, OH 45207, 513-531-2222, writersdig@fwpubs.com

Updated annually, this provides information on thousands of publications and what they're looking for (including trade publications), along with contact names and guidelines for submission. The print version is available at most bookstores and through online booksellers. Writer's Digest also posts guidelines for submission to publications on its website (writersdigest.com); at this writing, access remains free.

Gebbie Press List of Magazine Websites, Gebbie Press (gebbieinc.com/magurl .htm), P.O. Box 1000, New Paltz, NY 12561, 845-255-7560, gebbie@pipeline.com

This list provides the URLs of major magazines, trade publications, E-'zines, and so on, allowing you to visit and familiarize yourself with a given publication before submitting an article for publication.

Photos

ABC Pictures (abcpictures.com), 1867 East Florida Street, Springfield, MO 65803-4583, 888-526-5336, rodger@abcpictures.com

Offers value-priced reproduction of photos in large quantities for publicity purposes.

Media Monitoring Services

Media monitoring services keep track of media coverage of news about you and your company.

Note: Internet search engines and the proliferation of Web versions of print publications now enable small-business owners to monitor the results of their publicity campaigns to a degree. (Results won't be as thorough as those provided by a professional clipping service, and you need to schedule time to regularly search for coverage—as many websites post articles only for limited periods.)

When you have the budget for a professional media monitoring service, here are some to consider.

Bacon's Clipping Services, Bacon's Information, Inc. (bacons.com), 332 South Michigan Avenue, Chicago, IL 60604, 800-776-3342, info@bacons.com

This service monitors newspapers, magazines, TV news, and the Internet.

Burrelle's Media Monitoring, Burrelle's Information Services (burrelles.com), 75 East Northfield Road, Livingston, NJ 07039, 800-631-1160

This service monitors newspapers, magazines, newswires, the Internet, and broadcast media.

Video Monitoring Services (vidmon.com), 330 West Forty-Second Street, New York, NY 10036, 212-736-2010, nynewssales@vmsinfo.com

This company monitors TV and radio broadcast news in more than one hundred top U.S. and international markets. VMS has regional offices throughout the United States. Check its website to locate an office that serves your area.

To Order Additional Copies of This Book

To order additional copies of this book, contact McGraw-Hill customer service by phone at 877-833-5524 or by E-mail at customer.service@mcgraw-hill.com.

Note: McGraw-Hill books are available at special quantity discounts to use as premiums and sales promotions, or for use in corporate training programs. For more information, please write to the Director of Special Sales, Professional Publishing, McGraw-Hill, Two Penn Plaza, New York, NY 10121-2298. Or contact your local bookstore.

Index

About the Author

Jessica Hatchigan calls herself the Accidental Publicist. "My career as a publicist happened while I was on the way to somewhere else—but the sidetrack has turned out to be a fascinating whirlwind of a journey that I'm still enjoying."

Hatchigan never intended or even dreamed of a career in PR. She had, in fact, just published a humorous children's book, *Count Dracula, Me, and Norma D* (Avon Camelot), and was planning a career as a children's author when she was offered a job with a Fortune 10 company. "I loved writing for children," she says, "but the advance I earned on my first book wasn't stretching far enough to cover our family's needs. I thought, 'Well, I'll do this for one year.'" The one year turned into almost ten. She managed to write a second children's book, *Dinosaurs Aren't Forever* (Avon Camelot), while working for the corporation but then got caught up in "sixty-hour work weeks" and travel. By 1995, Hatchigan decided enough was enough. She quit her corporate job and launched her own business. "It was scary, quitting my corporate job," she says. "It had come to represent security for me. But when you start out on a journey of faith, things have a way of working out."

During her nine years as a corporate communicator, prior to starting her own company, Hatchigan was involved in every aspect of public relations communications and publicity. In writing this book, Hatchigan's goal was to make the insider knowhow she had accumulated available to small businesspeople. "I wrote this book," she says, "for people who are in business for themselves and who are marketing their products or services on a shoestring budget. Publicity is the best way to get the word out about what they have to offer. But many businesspeople don't know how to recognize what's newsworthy—and 'publicize-able'—about their businesses. Or the protocol for approaching the press. My book shares publicity how-tos in plain English—but not in plain vanilla. It is, I hope, a fun read."

In *How to Be Your Own Publicist: Everything You Need to Know to Act like a PR Pro*, Hatchigan explains PR concepts and techniques in plain English, making it easy for small businesspeople to learn how publicity works and how to put it to work for their businesses. Hatchigan believes her experience as a children's author may account for her ability to write business books that are easy to understand and fun to read.

How to Be Your Own Publicist has been endorsed by Jack Faris, Chairman and CEO of the National Federation of Independent Business, and Jim Rohn (mentor to Harvey Mackay, Tony Robbins, and Les Brown) has called it a "breakthrough."

The Accidental Publicist's work has won awards from the International Association of Business Communicators and the United Way. Speeches she's written for Fortune 10 executives have been published in *Vital Speeches of the Day* and have earned standing Os. She has been quoted in *USA Today* and featured in the *Speechwriter's Newsletter*. She also is the founder and owner of Greenbriar Communications (www.greenbriar.biz), a full-service public relations company she started after leaving her corporate job.

Hatchigan lives in Northville, Michigan, with her husband, Frank. They are the parents of two children, Jenny and James.

One of the principles Hatchigan teaches publicity newbies is the necessity of being alert to opportunities. "Opportunity surrounds us," she says. "Drop a spoon in a restaurant, and when you stoop to pick it up, you can meet someone who changes the whole course of your business—or personal—life. But you have to notice when they say, 'hello.' Publicity opportunities are the same."

Has there been a publicity opportunity you've recognized and tapped into? If the tips and techniques you learned in this book helped you get better at doing just that, send your story to Jessica Hatchigan at jessica@hatchigan.com, or mail it to P.O. Box 24, Northville, MI 48167. Your story may be featured in one of her upcoming articles or books.